ENGLISH
CHILDREN'S BOOKS
1600—1900

1 "Afternoon Tea." An illustration by Kate Greenaway to *The Girl's Own Paper*, c. 1886

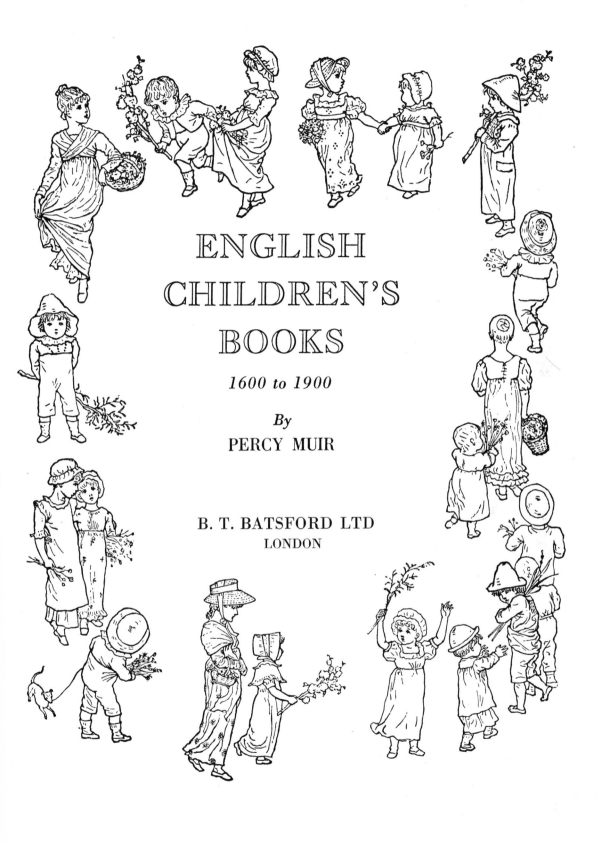

ENGLISH
CHILDREN'S
BOOKS

1600 to 1900

By

PERCY MUIR

B. T. BATSFORD LTD
LONDON

Second impression, 1969
Third impression, 1979
Fourth impression, 1985

First published 1954
© Percy Muir 1954
PRINTED AND BOUND IN GREAT BRITAIN BY
ANCHOR BRENDON LTD, TIPTREE, ESSEX
FOR THE PUBLISHERS
B. T. BATSFORD LTD
4 FITZHARDINGE STREET, LONDON W1H 0AH
ISBN 0 7134 07190

PREFACE TO THIRD IMPRESSION

When the present volume was first published in 1954, only a comparatively few collectors were interested in children's books. In 1951, when the first of the address books was published by the International League of Antiquarian Booksellers, 19 booksellers included children's books among their specialities. In 1977 the number had grown to 51. The number of books devoted entirely to the subject has grown proportionately.

In 1954 the Pierpont Morgan Library mounted an exhibition of children's books of great interest, consisting largely of loans, with a catalogue of modest proportions and a handful of illustrations. In 1975, under the direction of its specialist librarian, Mr. Gerald Gottlieb, they produced another catalogue, folio in format, with every item illustrated in collotype, 41 in colour, and almost all of them in the Morgan Library.

The catalogue also announced the creation by the Andrew Mellon Foundation of a fund to enable scholars to study the Morgan collection. Altogether a fabulous catalogue.

Other useful books and catalogues include:—Eric Quale, *The Collector's Book of Children's Books*, Studio Vista, (1971); J. I. Whalley, *Cobwebs to Catch Flies*, Elek, (1974); I. and P. Opie, *Three Centuries of Nursery Rhymes*, Oxford U.P., (1977). Judith St. John's catalogues of *The Osborne Catalogue of Early Children's Books, 1476–1910*, 2 volumes, Toronto Public Library, (1975), are virtually indispensable.

Several Sotheby Catalogues of children's books are useful, as are the lists of buyers and prices, if available. They include the sale of the English children's books from the collection of the late Edgar Oppenheimer to whom my book was originally dedicated. The wonderful German section was dispersed by Hauswedell & Nolte at their 200th auction sale in 1974, under the title *Alte Deutsche Kinderbücher*.

Fine collections of German books are also described in Adolf Seebass, *Alter Kinderbücher*, Basel, (1955) and in *Schöne alte Kinderbücher*, Frankfurt/Main, (1978).

Some Childish Things, Maggs Brothers Catalogue 993, lists a mouth-watering collection; and Justin Schiller specialises in the subject (address: P.O. Box 1667, FDR Station, New York, 10022).

Several important bibliographical studies call for additions and/or corrections in the books recommended for further reading.

Page 51—in 1956 the Pierpont Morgan Library in New York made a highly important and engaging contribution to the publishing history of the Perrault "Contes" by issuing a beautiful collotype facsimile of a seventeenth-century manuscript of five of the stories, which is in the library. The manuscript was made for presentation to 'Mademoiselle' (i.e. Elizabeth Charlotte d'Orléans, niece of

7

Louis XIV) and is dated 1695, two years before the publication of the book, which was also dedicated to her. It has a coloured frontispiece and six gouache vignettes, all of which were used in the published version. The dedication is signed with the initials P.P.—those of Perrault fils. A second volume accompanies the facsimile, giving a printed text of the manuscript and a scrupulous examination of the sources of the stories and their authorship, by Jacques Barchilon. He is convinced that the father Perrault was the author 'with the son as a contributor', while admitting that the evidence may be thought to indicate the contrary.

On page 72 Charles Welsh has now been almost completely superseded by S. Roscoe, *John Newbery*, The 5 Owl Press, Wormley, Broxbourne, Herts. This gives a complete record of the publications of the whole family; and is bibliographically accurate.

An excellent follow-up to this is Marjorie Moon's *John Harris's Books for Youth 1801 to 1843*, (1976), with the same publisher, which records in some detail more than a thousand books published by the successor to the Newbery business.

An important addition to the bibliography of an English Struwwelpeter (see page 81), if it can be confirmed, is a report that the late F. Algar's collection included *Funny Books. Boys and Girls Struwwelpeter*. Published by D. Bogue. Undated, but Algar believed, from a partly erased inscription, that the date was 1847. It contained the 10 stories altered by another hand. It is not in the *English Catalogue of Books*.

There were many imitations, among them *A Laughter Book for Little Folk*. From the German. Illustrated by T. Hosemann, Cundall and Addey (1851). The characters include Slovenly Kate, Envious Tom and Ned, the Toy-Breaker. It was adapted from Hosemann's *Lachende Kinder*, Frankfurt am Main, (1850). *Laugh and Grow Wise*, Griffith and Farran (1856) includes Cruel Jack, Meddlesome Mat and Greedy Bob. The lay-out is based directly on Hofmann's original.

P. H. M.
Blakeney, 1979

CONTENTS

LIST OF ILLUSTRATIONS

The tailpieces on pages 99 and 147 are from woodcuts by Thomas Bewick

ACKNOWLEDGMENT

FOR illustrations I am indebted to the British Museum for Nos. 3–12, 19, 20, 22, 27, 28, 30, 37–41, 43, 55, 60–64, 67, 71–73, 77–80, 82, 83, 95, and 98. From the Victoria and Albert Museum are Nos. 13, 29, 38, 45–49, 94, 96, and 102–105. From the Houghton Library at Harvard University, Nos. 57 and 58. From the collection of Dr. d'Alte A. Welch of Ohio, Nos. 14–17, 21, 23–25, 31–33, 52, 69, 70, 99–101. From the collection of Mr. Edgar S. Oppenheimer of New York, Nos. 26, 31, 32, 34–36, and 54. Messrs. Frederick Warne & Co. kindly permitted reproduction of No. 53.

Mr. L. E. Deval's careful reading of the proofs eliminated many faults and added many improvements.

INTRODUCTION

SOME temerity is needed to embark on a history of English children's books because F. J. H. Darton covered the ground so adequately in his *Children's Books in England*. Any later historian must pay ample tribute to this great work on the subject; and I should like it to be clear from the beginning that the present book makes no pretensions to supplanting him. On the contrary, I have leaned heavily on Darton throughout, and his book has been constantly at hand at all times. Had it not have been long out of print my book might not have been attempted.

My purpose has been more limited than his: I have not attempted the detail of his portrayal; but rather a broader sweep within a smaller compass. If I may venture to put it so, I have concentrated on a picture of the wood as a whole rather than the trees that compose it. And yet that is misleading: what I have rather tended to do is to select certain noble or outstanding specimens, grouping round them the separate parts of the forest.

This preference for a selective rather than an inclusive method was initially dictated by considerations of space; but in the sequel it has resulted in considerable changes of emphasis, so that, in fact, the picture that emerges differs in many essentials from Darton's.

There is, however, another fundamental difference in my approach to the subject as compared with Darton's, deriving from a firm conviction that all such matters as this should be approached from a bibliographical angle. Therefore, while I have confined check-lists and postscripts of a bibliographical order to places where they may be skipped by the reader, they are in fact the anatomy of this book, around which its body has been fashioned. In general the lists were compiled first, and the book takes its pattern from the indications given by them.

Darton, moreover, was writing more than twenty years ago, and in the interval interest in children's books of earlier days has greatly deepened and widened. New discoveries have been made: above all, the *Oxford Dictionary of Nursery Rhymes*, so eruditely edited by the Opies, has appeared. This book stands only second to Darton in my indebtedness. References both explicit and implicit will be found, especially in my early chapters; but it is in its general reorientation of the history that I have found it most valuable, especially in the evidence it provides of pre-Newbery activity.

The general background of this history has been the *Cambridge History of English Literature* in fifteen volumes, 1932, and the *Bibliography* thereto, four volumes, 1940. Details of the lives of some authors and publishers have been taken from the *Dictionary of National Biography* and from Allibone's *Critical Dictionary*. Indispensable to any study of the subject is the extensive catalogue issued in Paris in 1930 by

Gumuchian & Co., which, despite many errors inescapable in a pioneer effort on such a scale—there are over 6,000 entries and more than 1,000 reproductions —is really a mine of information, the exploration of which never ceases.

Other general works on the subject in England and in other countries which have been consulted are:

E. M. Field. *The Child and his Book*. Wells, Gardner, 1891.

Dyhrenfurth-Graebsch. *Gesch. d. deutschen Jugendbuches*. Hamburg: Stichnote, 1951.

A. Rümann. *Alte deutsche Kinderbücher*. Wien, etc.: Reichner, 1937.

J. de Trigon. *Histoire de la Littérature Enfantine*. Paris: Hachette, 1950.

A. W. Tuer. *Pages and Pictures from Forgotten Children's Books*. Leadenhall Press, 1898–9.

The following catalogues have also been useful:

Children's Books, Old and Rare. New York: Schatzki. N.D.

Early Books for Children. Ashmore Green: Edwards, 1945

An Exhibition of . . . early Children's books. St. Bride Institute, 1937

P. H. Muir. *Children's Books of Yesterday*. Cambridge University Press, 1946. (The Catalogue of the National Book League Exhibition.)

In order to save long and irritating footnotes, with continual hunting for the original references, I have compiled a list of books quoted in the text, with the key-word under which it is there mentioned.

Allibone. S. A. Allibone. *A Critical Dictionary of English Literature*. 5 vols. Philadelphia: Childs and Peterson, 1859–91. (Reprint. Lippincott, 1888–96.)

Armitage. S. A. Armitage. *The Taylors of Ongar*. Cambridge: Heffer, 1939.

Ashton. J. Ashton. *Chap-Books of the Eighteenth Century*. Chatto, 1882.

Carter. J. Carter and G. Pollard. *An Enquiry into the Nature of Certain Nineteenth Century Pamphlets*. Constable, 1934.

Cohn. A. M. Cohn. *George Cruikshank, A Catalogue Raisonée*, Bookman's Journal, 1924.

Collins. A. S. Collins. *The Profession of Authorship*. Routledge, 1928.

Darton. F. J. H. Darton. *Children's Books in England*. Cambridge University Press, 1932.

Edwards. *Early Books for Children*. Ashmore Green: Edwards, 1945.

Green. R. L. Green. *Tellers of Tales*. Leicester: Ward, 1946.

Greenhood. D. Greenhood and H. Gentry. *Chronology of Books and Printing*. New York: Macmillan, 1936.

Hambourg. D. Hambourg. *Richard Doyle*. Art and Technics, 1948.

Hugo. J. Hugo. *The Bewick Collector*. Reeve, 1866. *Supplement*, 1868.

Lennon. F. B. Lennon. *Lewis Carroll. A biography*. Cassell, 1947.

O.E.D. *A New Dictionary . . . Oxford University Press*. 10 vols. 1888–1928.

Opie. *Oxford Dictionary of Nursery Rhymes*. Edited by Iona and Peter Opie. Oxford University Press, 1952.

2 Kate Greenaway's title-page design for *The Girl's Own Annual*, 1887

Osborne. *Osborne Collection of Early Children's Books.* 2 vols. Toronto Public Library, 1975.

Rollington. R. Rollington. *The Old Boy's Books.* Leicester: Simpson, 1913.

Sadleir. M. Sadleir. *XIX Century Fiction.* 2 vols. Constable, 1953.

Scott. J. E. Scott. *A Bibliography of . . . Sir Henry Rider Haggard.* Mathews, 1947.

Sketchley. R. E. D. Sketchley. *English Book Illustration of To-day.* Kegan Paul, 1903.

Slade. B. C. Slade. *Maria Edgeworth, 1767–1849. A Bibliographical Tribute.* Constable, 1937.

Speaight. G. Speaight. *Juvenile Drama.* Macdonald, 1946.

Spielmann. M. H. Spielmann and G. S. Layard. *Kate Greenaway.* Black, 1905.

Storer. M. E. Storer. *La Mode des Contes de Fées.* Paris: Champion, 1928.

Welsh. C. Welsh. *A Bookseller of the Last Century.* Griffith, Farran, 1885.

3 A cut and verses from Bunyan's *Divine Emblems*, 1724 edition

XI.

Upon the Bee.

THE Bee goes out, and Honey home doth bring;
And some who seek that Honey find a Sting.
Now would'st thou have the Honey, and be free
From stinging; in the first place kill the Bee.

Comparison.

This Bee an Emblem truly is of Sin,
Whose Sweet unto a many, Death hath been.
Now would'st have sweet from Sin, and yet not die.
Do thou it in the first place mortify.

                                        XII.

4 (*right*) Portrait of Janeway: The frontispiece to his *Token for Children* [1671?]

St Iohn committs ye young Man to ye Bishops care

The young Man turns debauch't & a Robber

...n goes to ye Young Man and Reduceth him

5   An illustration to Crouch's *The Young Man's Calling*, 1678.
Compare with fig. 7

CHAPTER ONE

THE "PREHISTORIC AGE"

1. Mr. Bickerstaffe's Godson

IN 1709, in the ninety-fifth number of the *Tatler*, Mr. Bickerstaffe reported to his readers on a visit he had recently paid to his godson. The essay is well known, but passages from it are so immediately relevant to the present purpose that they will bear repetition.

> I perceived him a very great historian in Aesop's Fables; but he frankly declared to me his mind, "that he did not delight in that learning, because he did not believe that they were true"; for which reason I found that he had very much turned his studies for about a twelve-month past, into the lives and adventures of Don Bellianis of Greece, Guy of Warwick, the Seven Champions, and other historians of that age. . . .

Bevis of Southampton and St. George of England were among the boy's special favourites; whereas his sister preferred fairy-tales.

This passage is invaluable to the historian of children's leisure reading in England, for from it may be deduced a tolerably complete picture of the subject, not only in Steele's time but in almost any earlier period.

The first significant inference to be drawn from it is that at that time, and before it, there were few books written expressly for the entertainment of children, who were thus compelled to select from the reading of their elders anything that especially appealed to them, supposing that they could obtain or evade approval of their choice. The selection of Steele's young godson forms almost a complete epitome of their choice; it provides the basic constituents of nearly all the children's books that have been produced since that time; and it is also a warning not to presume that because many of the stories mentioned in the *Tatler* were afterwards edited or adapted for children's reading they were therefore originally published for that purpose.

Where did the children find them? Caxton himself translated the Fables of Aesop from the French and printed them in 1484. The popularity of this edition, and a proof that it was "read to pieces", is given by the survival of only one perfect and two imperfect copies at the present day. There is a text of the Fables in Brinsley's formidably titled *Pueriles Confabulatiunculae* (1617). The subtitle of this book is in

English—"Children's Dialogues, little conferences, or talkings together . . .", but it is in fact the grimmest kind of lesson-book, in which the text is entirely in Latin and Greek. Indeed Brinsley taught that English should be almost entirely excluded from the curriculum, all lessons being given and questions posed and answered in the dead languages.

Ogilby's translation, or paraphrase in verse, 1651, beautified though it was by elegant pictures by Hollar and Faithorne among others, was unhandy, being very large and unsuited for children. Sir Roger l'Estrange, the Tory campaigner, who died only five years before Steele's essay was printed, made the best and largest collection of fables in English, and he had children especially in mind when making his compilation. His book was expressly commissioned by a group of booksellers, and he was paid £300 for it.

He included many other fabulists besides Aesop, notably a selection from La Fontaine within twenty years of the first appearance of any of his fables in French. It is highly probable that this was their earliest appearance in English.

The date of l'Estrange's edition is 1692, two years after Locke had recommended Aesop as a first reading book for children. It was simple and racy in style, and it was almost certainly his version, which was continually reprinted, that was read by Steele's young godson.[1] The translation has hardly been surpassed for this purpose, and was used as recently as 1927, when the Golden Cockerel Press printed a selection from it.

Fables are ideal reading for small children, whose solemn anthropomorphism meets the talking animals half way—a point of view that is no less obvious in the modern child than it was in the eighteenth century, in Caxton's day, or, presumably, in the dim and uncertain pre-Christian era when the fables were first concocted. The Beast who terrified Beauty's father, Puss in Boots, the Lewis Carroll characters and Beatrix Potter's animal families are direct descendants of Aesop's fabular bestiary. Above all, fables have the indispensable feature of make-believe; and whether Mr. Bickerstaffe was recounting truth, or fabricating a piece to beguile his genteel readers, his choice of Aesop as first on his list has the unerring ring of conviction.

Finally, the intensely moral nature of these fables should not be overlooked. Whether the moral tale is repugnant to children or not it has been a persistent feature of books intended for their reading until well into our own day, and the stories of one of the most prolific and popular writers for children to-day exude morals in every line.

2. The Chapman

Mr. Bickerstaffe's godson read also the romances of chivalry and adventure, with knights in shining armour, battles with giants or against tremendous odds, the rescue of lovely princesses and other victims of oppression, with always the

[1] Croxall's edition, also designed for children, was not published until 1722. See also p. 73.

24

triumphant emergence of the immortal hero from the gravest of perils.[1] It would be superfluous to dwell on the essential likeness between these characters and the Space-ship Superman of some modern comics and television; and if the reader prefers Sir Bevis and Robin Hood to these latterday incarnations of mighty righteousness, that merely goes to show that, like the present writer, he is a curmudgeon whose own youth is too far behind him.

As with Aesop, and some other writings mentioned in this chapter, the child's first acquaintance with these heroes probably came from their stories being read aloud or recounted in the family circle. Victorian pre-occupation and success with "family reading"—the *Times* hand-list of periodicals gives some forty journals the first word of whose title is "Family"—represents an English tradition older than reading itself, for troubadours and minstrels sang their narrative verses to the families of rich patrons, and Caedmon's paraphrase of Bible stories was certainly fashioned for consumption in family and tribal groups.

Therefore it is reasonably certain that when, in 1485, Caxton produced the first printed edition of Malory's story of King Arthur and the Knights of the Round Table—quite possibly while the author was still alive—the book was destined for the family circle.[2] It is to be hoped that the reading was selective for, in 1568, Robert Ascham was among the first to denounce the book as immoral. He found its main concern almost equally divided between "open manslaughter and Bold bawdry"; and Tennyson, in refining the stories to the modest taste of his own readers, almost repeats Ascham in describing Malory as alternating between "war and wantonness".

The occasion of Ascham's denunciation makes it clear that the book was read to or by children, and Hugh Rhodes, in his *Book of Nurture* (1554), also warns their elders to "keep them from reading of feigned fables, vain fantasies, and wanton stories, and songs of love, which bring much mischief to youth". Chesterfield, two centuries later, exhorted his natural son to forswear the reading of frivolous romances and stories of enchantment and giants, and while he allowed his godson to read fables, so long as they were by La Fontaine, and in French, he could not stomach the reading of fairy-tales and romances.

If Malory may be taken as typical of the kind of medieval romance read by children in Steele's time we may well ask where they found a text; for, although there were many editions between Caxton's in 1485 and Stansby's in 1534, the book does not appear to have been reprinted again until 1816.

The answer, although conjectural, is not in much doubt. The "Ballads [and] foolish Books" denounced by Thomas White, and the "fingle-fangle" that Bunyan set out to displace were the wares of the chapmen, pedlars who hawked their

1 Montaigne, who was born in 1533, tells us that the favourite reading of his youthful companions was of Lancelot of the Lake, Amadis of Gaul, Huon of Bordeaux and their like.

2 Caxton's edition is even rarer than his Aesop. Only one perfect and one imperfect copy have survived. Neither is in the British Museum. A single leaf is in Lincoln Cathedral Library.

goods in towns and villages, and at country fairs. Their activity is older than most of their surviving wares.[1] In 1553 an Act of Edward VI ordered that they must be licensed; and Chettle, in *Kind Hart's Dreame* (1592), declares that "Chapmen are able to spred more pamphlets . . . then all the booksellers in town."

They sold other things besides books, of course. Their packs contained a variety of small articles useful or attractive to housewives; but they invariably contained a selection of cheap booklets, originally, perhaps, ballad sheets either in broadside form or folded to make a booklet of eight or twelve pages. Eventually chapbooks assumed the familiar form of a miniature booklet, with a paper cover usually with a picture. They cost from a farthing to a few pence.

The calling of the chapmen was old. Shakespeare, in *Henry IV*, refers to "these same Meeter Ballad-mongers", and Urquhart's Rabelais, 1653, describes "An old paultry book . . . sold by the hawking Pedlars & Ballad-mongers". After the abolition of Star Chamber in 1641, with the consequent increase in the number of small printers, the scope of the chapmen was greatly broadened; and it was not very long before miniature editions of old favourites were printed in editions especially prepared for, and with the imprint of, the Walking, Running, or Flying Stationers—strange contradictions in terms, the Stationer being originally one who had a fixed station for the sale of his goods.

The *Dictionary of the Canting Crew* (1700) defines Running Stationers as " . . . those that cry News and Books about the Streets"; and in 1796 Grose has Flying Stationers as "Ballad-singers and hawkers of penny histories". In 1751 Dr. Johnson has Cantilenus in *The Rambler* produce the ballad of "The Children in the Wood"[2]; and in the seventeen-sixties Tristram Shandy's Uncly Toby tells how he bought with his own school-boy pocket-money what must have been chapmen's editions of "Guy of Warwick", "Valentine and Orson", and "The Seven Champions of Christendom".

J. O. Halliwell, unwelcome son-in-law of the infamous Sir Thomas Phillips, was a disciple of Cantilenus in this matter. In 1849 he listed his collection of those printed at various "Churchyard" addresses in London. This mournfully unsuitable location had a great attraction for children's publishers. There were the Marshalls in Aldermary, the Diceys in Bow, and the Newberys and Harris in St. Paul's Churchyards.[3] In 1864 Halliwell catalogued his "Penny Merriments and Histories printed at Glasgow, 1695–8".

Among the titles in these collections of chapbooks are found many of the favourite medieval romances, several of which have already been mentioned; legendary tales like "Jack-the-Giant-killer"; romances with some factual foundation, like "Dick Whittington"—often without the diminutive form of his first name—and

---

[1] *Chapbook* is a more modern coinage than *chapman*. The earliest use of it in *O.E.D.* is by Dibdin in 1824.

[2] The original of "The Babes in the Wood", but in a popular doggerel version.

[3] In the fifteenth and sixteenth centuries an address for a printer or stationer near a church door was greatly sought after, customers for his service books being likely to congregate there.

"Friar Bacon", the story of "The Wandering Jew", "Tom Thumb", Fortunatus and his purse, "The Wise Men of Gotham", Wat Tyler, Jack Straw, Jack of Newbury, and other heroes of lowly birth. There were also Joe Miller, and other jest books; collections of dream-books in which the significance of the position of moles on the body was also interpreted; collections of riddles, and cooking recipes. Thus not all of them were for children, and even those with a superficial attraction for them were not always among the most suitable; indeed it is doubtful whether these were not also provided for their elders, and perhaps first overheard by the children in family or group readings by one of the few locals who was not an-alphabetic.

Humorous tales were especially likely to indulge in ribaldry and coarseness of a kind quite unsuited to juvenile reading in the most broadminded of families. "Little Jack Horner" was an offender in this respect, but was not so obscene in its humour as the story of "The Friar and the Boy"; whereas neither "The Fortunes and Misfortunes of Moll Flanders" nor "The French King's Wedding, or the Royal Frolick, being a plesant account of the Amorous Intrigues . . . and Surprizing Marriage of Lewis the XIVth with Madame de Maintenon, His late Hackney of State . . ." both favourite chapbook titles, were exactly suited to juvenile consumption. Yet all the chapbooks had a family likeness, so that the children, at any rate, would not find it easy to choose between one and another.

On the rare occasions when they did write directly for children the hacks who produced the texts often made a very poor job of it, as in *The Children's Example*, in which a little girl, on her way to school, encounters the Devil, who enquires:

> Where are you going, pretty Maid
> To School I am going Sir (said she)
> Pish, child, don't mind the same, (saith he)
> But haste to your Companions dear,
> And learn to lie, and curse and swear.

But the pretty dear knew exactly how to treat such a wanton, and really not very flattering, invitation:

> Satan avoid hence out of Hand
> In name of JESUS I command!
> At which the Devil instantly
> In flames of Fire away did fly.

Nevertheless there is abundant evidence of the buying and reading of these cheap little books by children; and when, later on, the adaptation of other adult stories in juvenile form comes to be considered, this will arise even more clearly.

A book that may very well have been found in a chapman's pack was Thomas Newbery's *A Booke in Englyssh Metre, of the great Marchante Man called Dives Pragmaticus, very preaty for Children to reade* . . . , which was printed by Alexander Lacy in 1563. It is a small quarto of eight pages, and the text is in rhymed couplets.

Its main purpose was to teach children to read; but the author, who has been surmised to be the bookseller of that name,[1] shows some appreciation of the need to beguile his young audience. The subjects of his rhymes are mostly traders or shopkeepers; and they are invited to purchase the considerably varied wares offered for sale by Dives Pragmaticus.

> Dripping pans, pot hooks, old cats and kits;
> And preaty fine dogs, without fleas or nits.
> Axes for butchers, and fine glass for wives:
> Medicines for rats to shorten their lives.

3. *The Calvinists*

The *Tatler* essay does not cover all the ground, however. In the seventeenth century there had been pathetic attempts to beguile children, albeit in a form and from a source that a godson of such a fine old English gentleman as Mr. Bickerstaffe would have been unlikely to encounter.

The *Cambridge Bibliography of English Literature* lists no children's books of a recreational kind before 1671, when Puritanism was already a dying creed. Yet the early authors were most frequently Calvinists of an unrelenting severity like James Janeway, Henry Jessey, Thomas White, and William Jole. Some of them went to prison for their faith in an age when horror at the excesses of the regicides had caused a reaction against the narrowness of the creed avowed by those ultra-Cromwellian partisans.

The Puritans were dedicated to a revolution founded on the deep conviction that religious beliefs form the basis for the whole of human life. Their outlook was as completely ideological as that of the most fervent of Marxists, whose programme is Puritanism standing on its head. Whereas the Puritans deduced political theory and practice from a code of religious belief, the Marxist sublimates his political and economic theories into a code of theological dogma, with a deity and his prophets needing only the sanctity of time for their creation.

The Puritans were fully aware of the importance of indoctrinating the young, and Marxist versions of classical fairy-tales, such as used to decorate the pages of the *Daily Worker*, have their exemplars in the catchpenny titles with which the Puritans hoped to amuse their infants.

Bunyan was the best of them by a very long way. The *Pilgrim's Progress*, while not expressly written for children, has long been annexed by them. It is, in outline, an adventure story, complete with giants and fabulous monsters, sword contests, ill fortune from which the hero is regularly delivered, and the happiest of all endings. Hallam called it the most perfect and complex of fairy-tales; and it shows an alarming familiarity with the writings of the damned.

[1] He has no known connection with the family of John Newbery; but the name is common in bookselling circles in the sixteenth and seventeenth centuries.

But when Bunyan addressed himself expressly to a juvenile audience he failed almost as miserably as any of his contemporaries. The title of his book is the best thing about it: *A Book for Boys and Girls: or, Country Rhymes for Children*. When it was originally published, in 1686, price sixpence, two years after the second part of the *Pilgrim's Progress*, it had no pictures[1]—although it is rather unexpected to find one verse with a few bars of music. The verses are about animals and the countryside, but they are so blatantly overlaid with moral precepts as to make them grotesquely inappropriate in modern eyes.

There is, in the preface to this book, a curious sidelight on the relations between adult and child readers, where Bunyan admits that the young have not been exclusively regarded in its writing, for "childish Motions" make children of some greybeards and "Girls big as old Women"; and it is clear that he thinks that those of all ages may profit by his moralising. To them, as to the children, he wishes:

" . . . to show them how each fingle-fangle,
    On which they doting are, their souls entangle . . ."

There is no nonsense or pretence about it, he is out to save their souls, and to rescue them from the insidious clutches of Satan. Meditating on a hen's egg he is inspired to remark

"The Egg's at first contained in the Shell,
    Men, afore Grace, in Sins and Darkness dwell."

or

"The Shell doth crack, the Chick doth chirp and peep,
    The Flesh decays, as Men do pray and weep."

Rotten eggs remind him of hypocrites:

"The rotten Egg, though underneath the Hen,
    If crack'd stinks, and is loathsome unto Men."

"The Hypocrite, sin has him in possession,
    He is a rotten Egg under Profession."

The busy bee inspires him less kindly than it did Isaac Watts. He warns his readers that honey may be had without a sting only if the bee be first killed; and draws the moral:

"This Bee an Emblem truly is of Sin,
    Whose Sweet unto many a Death hath been . . .", etc.

A boy chasing a butterfly reminds Bunyan only of the worthlessness of this

[1] A later publisher, who provided it with cuts, did it no great service in changing the title to *Divine Emblems, or Temporal Things Spiritualized*, although this was more representative of the contents of the work. The cut shows a page from an early illustrated edition, which is said to have "large additions" (3). In fact, the main work itself was severely cut down in all the reprints I have seen; but the edition illustrated has an addition in the shape of a reprint of a broadside by Bunyan (6).

29

world's treasures—"but painted Nothings and false Toys"; while "The awakened Child's Lamentation" must be read to be believed.

Besides the verses the book contains the Ten Commandments, the Creed and the Lord's Prayer in verse, an ABC, simple lessons in reading and arithmetic and a list of approved Christian names, the spelling of which is to be learned.

Bunyan was not the first of these preachers of the gospel to address himself to the young. It is not easy to distinguish the grimmest of the grisly band. James Janeway's title is sufficiently eloquent of the morbidness of his approach: *A Token for Children: being an Exact Account of the Conversion, Holy and Exemplary Lives, and Joyful Deaths of several young Children* (4). Death might indeed be a happy release from the regime enforced by the inexorable author. Toys are forbidden—whipping tops are especially only for the hell-bent—a rigid abstinence from all forms of secular enjoyment, courage to rebuke frivolity in others, especially those nearest and dearest, soberly to rejoice at the funerals of the blessed, constantly to remind oneself of the inherent tendency to sin, and to be on guard against the wiles of Satan, will uplift the heart.

The book opens with a brisk exhortation to parents. Do they wish their children to become Brands of Hell? Shall the Devil run away with them? Do they spend their time "in Play and Idleness and with wicked children?" There is also a foreword for the children. "You may now hear (my dear Lambs) what other good children have done. . . . May you not read how dutiful they were to their Parents? How diligent at their Books? How ready to learn the Scripture, and their Catechism? . . . how holy they lived; how dearly they were loved; how joyfully they died.

"Do you do as these children did? Did you ever see your miserable state by Nature? Did you ever get by yourself and weep for Sin, and pray for Grace and Pardon? . . . I would fain do what I can possibly to keep thee from falling into everlasting Fire."

It seems to have escaped the blind piety of the author that the only moral to be drawn from his dismal book is that reward for all this unswerving theopathy must be an early death, for that is the fate of all the young exemplars lauded in his pages.

This book appeared in about 1671; Janeway died in 1674.[1] In 1672–3 came the attractively titled *Looking Glass for Children*—a title too seductive to escape the attention of later writers, although their reflections were usually less depressing than those of Abraham Chear, Henry Jessey, and P. H., who combined to coin its phraseology and to compile its desolating contents. The tone is set by an initial warning of the latent snare for the unwary to be found in all looking-glasses. The young maid who is tempted to verify the flattery of those who tell how sweetly God did form her, should ponder the thought:

> "What pity such a pretty maid
> As I should go to Hell!"

[1] He was highly thought of by the pious, as witness the broadsides printed after his death.

6   A Bunyan broadside [1684] which was included in later editions of his *Book for Boys and Girls*. Only two copies have survived

RELATION V.

AFter this, Achas the Fifth Brother voluntarily
offer'd himself to the Slaughter, and spoke
to the King in this manner, ' Behold, O Tyrant,
' I am come to be tormented without being for-
' ced thereto ; do not therefore have a thought
' that I will alter my Mind, since thou seest how
' desirous I am to suffer thy barbarous Treat-
' ment ; the Blood of my Four innocent Brethren
' whom thou hast cruelly Murdered, have alrea-
' dy condemned thee to everlasting Destruction ;
' I shall make up the Number Five, and by tortu-
' ring me, thy own Torments shall be encreased.
' Tell me, thou bloody Wretch, for what Offence
' by us committed, dost thou punish us ? For

8   Cut and verses from Crouch's *Youth's Divine Pastime*, 1691

7   A cut from Crouch's *The Young Man's Calling*, 1695. Compare with fig. 5

III. *Upon Noah's Flood,* Gen. 6. 7.

WHen Men by Sin and Violence
Did stain the Earth with Blood,
God did resolve to wash them thence
By Waters of a Flood.

Yet did he warn before he struck,
Noah was sent to tell
They by their Sins would God provoke
To cast them down to Hell.

He also set an hundred years
Betwixt the threat and blow,
If haply they by Prayers and Tears
Might yet prevent their Woe.

He

Another of the chosen, who died at the age of ten, was constantly in tears at the thought that her fine clothes would condemn her to everlasting damnation, and when her mother remonstrated that a wicked heart was the more reprehensible, the precocious little beast replies, "Aye, mother, but fine Cloaths make our hearts proud."

Jessey was lamented in a broadside similar to the Janeway efforts.

Thomas White's *A Little Book for Little Children* warns them against ballads and foolish books, recommending in their stead Baxter's *Call to the Unconverted*, and Foxe's *Book of Martyrs*. Example being preferable to precept this holy man fills his pages with gruesome stories of religious martyrs. The book also contains an alphabet in rhyme, a fair sample of which is, under the letter "C":

> Children that make their Parents hearts to Bleed,
> May live t' have Children to revenge that deed.

These ghastly compilations, and others like them, were not books for the schoolroom, either on week-days or Sundays, but were intended as light literature to bring joy to the hearts of their young readers. In this the authors were unquestionably sincere, for they could conceive no greater joy than the certainty of saving a soul from perdition, a joy of which each of them was personally assured.

Their books are admissions, dreary and dismal though they be, that children were ill provided for, and that something ought to be done about the lack of suitable reading material, if only to spare simple minds from the damnable influence of such ballads as "The Babes in the Wood" and "The Seven Champions of Christendom". And from this same background a pupil of the same school would soon produce songs unexceptionable from the moral standpoint, yet so much sweeter and more truly childlike as hardly to bear comparison with the hell-fire doggerel of Bunyan and his followers.

But before we come to him there is one figure of the period who is something of a portent, who shows some inkling of what children really enjoyed reading.

4. Nat Crouch

His contributions are not remarkable by later standards; indeed most of his books are hackwork of a rather miserable order, and are as badly put together textually as they are typographically. Nevertheless he forms a landmark, however tawdry and disreputable, in the evolution of children's reading, and, without exaggerating his importance, his significance is evident.

Nathaniel Crouch was a bookseller contemporary with John Dunton, who gives the longest account of him that is known to me. One could bear to know more of him than is given in the tantalising glimpse given by the half-crazed "Athenian" and to wish that Crouch had written as much about himself as Dunton has.

Crouch, writes Dunton,[1] was the author of *The English Post*, and of that "useful

1 *Life and Errors*, II, pp. 435–6.

Journal intituled 'The Marrow of History'" first begun by George Larkin. Dunton suggests that there was something underhand in Crouch's acquisition of this journal and plainly hints at its deterioration in his hands.

His journalistic activities do not concern us, fortunately, for Dunton's references are difficult to verify. It is with his *alter ego*, as author, compiler, or adapter of other men's work under the pseudonyms of R. B., and Richard, or Robert, Burton that he comes into this history.

He belonged to a large family of booksellers-cum-scribblers, combining in his own person the functions of both, by publishing—as Crouch—what he wrote— as Burton. In this Dunton writes of him that "R. B. (alias *Nat Crouch*) is become a celebrated Author. But I think I have given you the very soul of his Character when I have told you that his talent lies at Collection. He has melted down the best of our English Histories into Twelve-penny Books, which are filled with wonders, rarities, and curiosities; for you must know, his Title-pages, are a little swelling". He is, says Dunton, a "Weekly (and Monthly) Author . . . a Phoenix Author (I mean the only man that gets an estate by the writing of Books)".

This just characterisation, especially of the "Phoenix author" rising from the ashes of another, is well seen in one example of his work.

In 1664 Samuel Crossman published his *Youth's Monitor*, a serious work of the regular Puritan kind, to rescue children from their almost inevitable fate. "Your natures are too easily disposed to receive evil impressions. Satan sees it; and watches betimes to forestall your tender minds therewithall", etc., etc. The tenor of the book is rather sweet and gentle, and its appearance is serious and dignified, laid out like a Bible with marginal glosses in Hebrew and Latin. In 1678 Crouch got hold of it, suppressed the author's name on the title—which he subtly altered to *The Young Man's Calling*—preceded Crossman's text, which consisted largely of the usual slaughter of innocents, by a miscellaneous collection of more or less exciting, semi-historical stories of youth, ranging from the adolescent Isaac, through Queen Elizabeth to Henry, Prince of Wales, illustrated by a series of rather crude but lively engravings. These included beheadings and burnings of martyrs, with a very jolly one illustrating an apocryphal story of St. John, showing a party of debauchees in seventeenth-century costume (5, 7).

The 1678 edition is quite a handsome book of some 450 pages, in clear type, on good paper, costing three shillings and sixpence. By 1695 Crouch has compressed the same text into 320 pages, on poor paper, the plates have become very worn, and the price is only one shilling. Advertisements at the end of the book list thirty-five other publications, mostly "Twelve-penny Books", and only seven of them under "Divinity".

In 1691 Crouch produced *Youth's Divine Pastime*, with "R. B." as author, consisting of thirty-six Bible stories in doggerel verse ranging from Adam and Eve to the shipwreck of St. Paul. The cut and verses on Noah's Ark are typical (8).

"R. B." was also responsible for *Winter Evening's Entertainments*, divided into two parts, the first comprising short stories slightly revamped from previous borrowings, the second of fifty riddles, each illustrated with cuts. Ingenuity of design enables the use of only twenty-seven different cuts to illustrate all the riddles. The same cut, of a man searching his clothing, serves for riddles on the louse and the flea; a miser watching an hour-glass does duty for two subjects; and a ship on the water also does a double stint. The use of cuts in this connection shows a poor grasp of the purpose of illustration, for the illustrations give away the answers.

The Apprentice's Companion (1681) is largely stolen from Wingate's *The Clerks Tutor* (1671), including the copper-plates of handwriting at the end by Cocker.

The English Hero; or Sir Francis Drake reviv'd; *The Kingdom of Darkness, or the History of Daemons*; and *Martyrs in Flames*, this last with some of the same incidents as *The Young Man's Calling*, although possibly not primarily intended for children, will almost invariably have been seized upon by them.

This enterprising and industrious hackney scribbler and bookseller seems to mark the first real effort to provide children with reading-matter—it is far from literature—to which they would look forward with pleasure and excitement in their leisure time.

It is permissible to doubt Darton's estimate of him as among the "good, godly writers". He is more likely to have been looked at askance, much as the exploits of Blueskin were in the eighteen-sixties, or as Sexton Blake, and Jack, Sam, and Pete were in the early nineteen-hundreds.

5. Fairy-tales

Returning now to Steele's Mr. Bickerstaffe, we recall that the sister of his godson was "a better scholar than he. Betty . . . deals chiefly in Fairies and Sprights; and sometimes in a winter night will terrify the maids with her accounts until they are afraid to go up to bed".

Where did Betty find her fairy-stories? The extreme antiquity of many of them is well known, and, for example, the great harvest gathered in a later century by the Grimm brothers shows that these were traditional and handed down by word of mouth.

Some English nursery favourites were popular with the chapmen. "Jack-the-Giant-Killer", "Dick Whittington", "Tom Thumb", and others have already been mentioned. But the introduction of fairy-tales to the nursery bookshelf was of continental origin; and although our concern is with English books, the translations and adaptations of the best French stories made such an early and important impact here, and have retained their position so unmistakably ever since, that some account of their curious origin is indispensable.

In France, as in England, fairy-tales had been for generations favourite bed-time

35

stories for children, and some of them had been printed in chapbook form.[1] But in the last quarter of the seventeenth century fairy-tales suddenly acquired a fantastic popularity with adults.

This was a peculiarly French development and arose from the opulence of the *grand siècle* under the magnificence of *Le Roi Soleil*. The personnel of the literary salon of the period would consist of the wits, writers, and philosophers of the day; and not only were women admitted to the circle, but they also formed circles of their own, in which women were the principal figures, with a few sympathetic males occasionally in attendance. Thus the circle formed by Mlle L'Heritier included the Marquise de Béthume, sister of the Queen of Poland, the Princesse de Neufchâtel, the Duchesse de Brissac-Béchamell, Mme de Bellegarde-Vertamont, the Duchesse de Bourgogne, and Mmes Deshouliers, d'Aulnoy, and de Murat, while she was on corresponding terms with H.R.H. Mademoiselle d'Orléans. Verton, historiographer to the King, the Abbé de Mauroy, de Saçy, and Charles Perrault were also among her intimates.

A feature of these salons, male and female alike, was the reading aloud of *pasquinades*, *vaudevilles*, *sonnets à bouts-rimés*, and similar short pieces; and the Comtesse d'Aulnoy seems to have introduced the telling of fairy-stories in the female salons. The idea caught on and became the rage. The fashion eventually extended to the male writers but, with one exception, they were less successful and less prolific than the women. The extent of this raging fashion may be gauged by the fact that when the stories were eventually collected together in the *Cabinet des Fées*[2] they extended to forty-one volumes.

The curious point to be taken is that the stories were devised, or adapted from ancient originals, for the amusement not of children but of adults. The consequence is that, although the characters and the background belong superficially to fairyland, most of them are much too sophisticated for children. The Comtesse d'Aulnoy, who started the whole thing, and was the first to print any of them,[3] was an exception in that three of her stories have been accepted by children, although they are more popular in France than in England.[4] She, like her rival authors, however, was under no illusion about the audience to which her tales were directed. Children were not among them, they consisted exclusively of adults, and they were usually tried out by being read aloud to the members of her circle, or distributed to them in manuscript form.

[1] One of the best-known series is the one usually described as the *Bibliothèque Bleue*, of which examples from the early seventeenth century have survived. They correspond very closely to our chapbooks and were similarly distributed by colporteurs.

[2] Amsterdam and Geneva, 1785.

[3] In a fairy-story introduced into her novel *Histoire d'Hypolite*, *Comte de Duglas* (Paris, 1690). The story, entitled *Conte du Dragon*, occupies pp. 143–81 of the second part.

[4] These are *The Blue Bird*, *The White Cat*, and *The Yellow Dwarf*. For a further account of her books of fairy-stories, with the dates of original publication, see Storer pp. 18-35. In *The Blue Bird* she introduced the original "Prince Charming".

THE
ORIENTAL MORALIST
OR
The Beauties
of the
ARABIAN NIGHTS ENTERTAINMENTS
Translated from the original &
accompanied with suitable reflections adapted
to each Story.
BY THE REVᴰ. Mʳ COOPER,
Author of the History of England &c. &c. &c.

LONDON.
Printed for E. Newbery the corner of
St Pauls Church Yard.

9 Title-page from an early
Arabian Nights for children,
published by E. Newbery about
1798

10 One of the illustrations from the same book

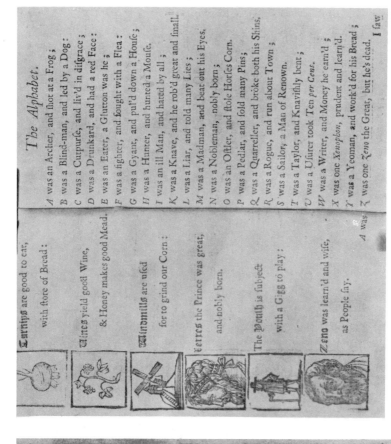

16 **The Child's Weeks work.**

Crags, Goats love beft ; And when
Young Kids and Lambs
Frisk round their Dams,
They do not fear Old Ren.

3.

The Buck and Doe,
The Hare and Roe,
Men Hunt with Horn and Hound :
The fly, bold Cat
Kills Moufe and Rat :
The Mole digs up the Ground.

4.

In Pond and Stream   III. Fifhes,
For Trout and Bream
With Hook and Net we Fifh :
If you be fharp,
Of Tench and Carp
You foon may catch a Difh.

Sa-tur-day's Lef-fons, Fore-noon.

WHO taught the *Ant*,   IV. Infects.
For fear of want,
To lay up Food in ftore ?
The *Bee* who tells
To give her Cells
Six Sides, not lefs, nor more ?

2.

Who moves this Frame?
Who rules the fame,

And

Turnips are good to eat,
with ftore of Bread:

Vines yield good Wine,
& Honey makes good Mead.

Windmills are ufed
for to grind our Corn :

Xerxes the Prince was great,
and nobly born.

The Youth is fubject
with a Gigg to play:

Zeno was learn'd and wife,
as People fay.

A was

The Alphabet.

A was an Archer, and fhot at a Frog ;
B was a Blind-man, and led by a Dog :
C was a Curpurfe, and liv'd in difgrace ;
D was a Drunkard, and had a red Face :
E was an Eater, a Glutton was he ;
F was a fighter, and fought with a Flea :
G was a Gyant, and pull'd down a Houfe ;
H was a Hunter, and hunted a Moufe.
I was an ill Man, and hated by all ;
K was a Knave, and he rob'd great and fmall
L was a Liar, and told many Lies ;
M was a Madman, and beat out his Eyes,
N was a Nobleman, nobly born ;
O was an Oftler, and ftole Horfes Corn.
P was a Pediar, and fold many Pins;
Q was a Quarreller, and broke both his Shins,
R was a Rogue, and run about Town ;
S was a Sailor, a Man of Renown.
T was a Taylor, and Knavifhly bent;
U was a Ufurer took Ten per Cent.
W was a Writer, and Money he earn'd ;
X was one Xenophon, prudent and learn'd.
Y was a Yeoman, and work'd for his Bread ;
Z was one Zeno the Great, but he's dead.
  I faw

11 The first printed appearance of "A was an Archer" in
A Little Book for Little Children, by T. W. [c. 1703].
Compare with figs. 19 and 20

12 (left) A page from William Ronksley
The Child's Weeks-work, 1712

Many of the stories were nevertheless adapted from nursery tales related by governesses[1]; others were taken directly from chapbooks[2]; but, as Mme Durand writes, in excusing her choice of audience, "the titles [of these stories] are now found only in the mouths of children, to whom their governesses recount them in a most imperfect form . . . ".[3]

She and her fellows endeavoured to rescue fairy-tales from that lamentable fate described by the Abbé de Bellegarde in a letter to the Duchesse du Maine, in which he described them as "invented by nurses to send children to sleep".

There was one person, however, who actually preferred the stories in their simple, unaffected, nursery form, and who wrote out a handful of them in almost the exact words that he had so recently heard them—for he was hardly more than eighteen years old at the time.

Pierre Perrault d'Armancour[4] was the eldest of the three children of Charles Perrault, a figure of some importance in the cultural life of Paris in the seventeenth century. When his collection of eight fairy-tales was published in Paris in 1697 the title-page bore no author's name. The tales were called simply "Stories or Tales of Past Times, with moralities". There was a frontispiece showing three children grouped round an old wife at the fireside, and on the wall behind them is a plaque reading *Contes de ma mère L'Oye*. The earliest English translations described them as "told by Mother Goose", a traditional figure in both countries on whom old wives' tales were mothered.

Whether it was the son or his father, as many people think, who took down the stories and published them, it was from the old woman depicted in the frontispiece, their governess, that they originally heard them; and countless children since, all over the world, have cause for gratitude that neither the contents of the stories nor their simple phraseology were seriously tampered with in publication.[5]

---

[1] Mlle L'Heritier, in addressing her story of *The Adroit Princess* to the Comtesse de Murat tells how, when she was a child, she had heard it hundreds of times from her governess. Other writers made similar admissions.

[2] Storer, p. 254, gives a curious instance of a lady borrowing a chapbook fairy-tale from her blushing maid.

[3] *Les Petits Soupers d'Été* (1699).

[4] For a discussion of his share in the responsibility for these tales and the early editions of them, see the Postscript to this chapter on pp. 45 ff.

[5] Storer gives many examples of the touches that betray the nursery origin of the tales. Simple jingles like "*tire le chevillette, la bobinette cherra*"; the grandmother in "Red Riding Hood" "*cuit et fait des galettes*"; in "Hop o'my Thumb" one is said to "*habiller* la viande" and the little hero "*emplit*" his pocket with stones. These provincialisms and slang expressions would have found no place in the vocabulary of elegant bluestockings, or of Perrault senior, the Academician and man of letters. The Sleeping Beauty, when awakened, is wearing a stiff collar (*collet monté*) fashionable at the end of the seventeenth century; and first attempts to revive her are made with Royal Hungarian Water, much affected by Mme de Sevigné. An ogress calls for Sauce Robert (an invention of Louis XIV's chef), to spice her ghastly meal; Cinderella offers to her sisters at the ball oranges and lemons, which would be interpreted by the children as a mark of great favour, for they were rare treats in the French nursery of those days.

Indeed, as a contemporary put it, "You tell me that the best stories we have are those that imitate best the style and the simplicity of children's nurses, and it is for this reason that you are so happy with those attributed to the son of a celebrated Academician". (Abbé de Villiers, *Entretiens sur les contes de Fées* (1699), p. 108.)

How soon the stories were translated into English is uncertain.[1] What is quite certain is their immediate and lasting success with English children. "Cinderella"[2] is still the prime nursery favourite among all fairy-tales, closely followed by "The Sleeping Beauty", "Red Riding Hood", "Puss in Boots", "Blue Beard", and "Hop-o'-my-thumb". Only "Riquet with the Tuft", and "Diamonds and Toads"[3] of the original group of eight have fallen by the wayside.

Perrault never repeated his success. Indeed, the son, to whose sponsorship I unhesitatingly cling, died in 1700, three years after the publication of his little book. He had no worthy successors until the Grimms began to publish their collections in 1812; unless it was in the first translation into any western language of the stories generally known as the "Arabian Nights", the work of a Frenchman, Antoine Galland (1646–1715), sometime French Ambassador at Constantinople, and a traveller in the Levant. His version of *Les Mille et une Nuits* was first published in Paris in twelve volumes (1704–17), and an English translation was begun almost immediately.[4] Like the stories of Perrault, and the medieval romances, these oriental tales became familiar to children first and principally in chapbooks, each containing one story.

From the *Thousand-and-one Nights* the selection was much narrower than from Perrault. "Ali Baba" seems to have been easily first in favour, with "Aladdin" (10) and "Sindbad" some distance behind, and the rest nowhere.

6. "Adopted" Books

The "Arabian Nights" brings us immediately to the last category of background books—those written for adults but firmly taken over by children. The *Pilgrim's Progress* is almost in this class, but the two outstanding examples in the early period are *Robinson Crusoe* and *Gulliver's Travels*. Both had to be heavily pruned for juvenile consumption, the former of its heavy moralising—although much of this was restored in nineteenth-century editions for young people—and the latter of its frequently obscene savagery.

"Crusoe" had seven years' start of "Gulliver", and has since developed a long lead in popularity, not only in English, but in almost every European language. The first part of the story was published on April 25, 1719, and was very soon pirated. By the first week in August an unauthorised abridged edition had been published as a pocket-sized volume, and with this publication Defoe's story may be said, in the very year of its birth, to have started its career as a book for children. The second part also appeared in 1719, and a third in 1720.

[1] See Postscript, pp. 45 ff.

[2] Evidence of the traditional origin of fairy-tales is clearly shown by the title of Marion Cox's *Three hundred and forty-five variants of Cinderella, Catskin, and Cap O' Rushes* (London, 1893).

A striking example of the persistence and recurrence of an idea is in *The Four Sons of Aymon* where a spell is cast by an enchanter on Charlemagne's soldiers by which they begin to dance and are unable to stop; which recalls the fate of the little dancer in Andersen's *Red Shoes*.

[3] "Diamonds and Toads", however, was the first published story with illustrations by Kate Greenaway (Warne, 1871).

[4] Marshall's list of chapbooks in 1708 includes the title *Arabian Nights Entertainments*.

In 1722 Edward Midwinter, a London printer, commissioned Thomas Gent, a bookseller in York, to compress the whole story into one volume—its 750 or more octavo pages being reduced to less than 200 in duodecimo—and this edition was continually reprinted during the eighteenth century. Its obstinate popularity may be gauged from the fact that the authorised publisher of the unabridged version was eventually driven to buy a share in this abridgement.

13 A beardless Crusoe from a chapbook of about 1810

The desert-island theme was a sure-fire winner. Its popularity is not yet exhausted, although in a world of such shrunken dimensions as ours, in which, nevertheless, everything must be always bigger and better than before, the modern castaway must be wrecked on a planet, his vessel a space-ship. But it is all basically Defoe, hotted up, if not necessarily improved. It is amusing to note, in passing, that a French translator, in 1721, added a section to the story in which Crusoe is given a

41

"vision du Monde Angélique", to which the illustrator, possibly Picart, responded with a frontispiece of the hero, his redingote and tricorne hat not in the least disturbed by his passage through the solar system, well on his way to Saturn.

Adaptations of the Crusoe story in every modern language are virtually countless. J. H. Campe, a German author, was the first to adapt the story, and his *Robinson der Jüngere* was published at Hamburg in two volumes in 1779–80. The author himself translated it into English and French; but the best English edition was Stockdale's in four volumes, 1788, with cuts by John Bewick, Thomas's less famous, but greatly gifted, younger brother.

The *Swiss Family Robinson* in its modern form is a composite work. Originally conceived by the Swiss Lutheran pastor, J. H. Wyss, and published in 1812–13, it was first translated into English in 1814, probably by William Godwin, who also published it. In 1814 and 1824–26 also, Madame de Montolieu, the translator of Jane Austen, produced a French version, in which she added further incidents and characters of her own devising, notably the donkey, with the rather contemptuous consent of Wyss himself. W. H. G. Kingston enlarged it still further.

There have been boy Crusoes, girl Crusoes, arctic Crusoes, and even a dog Crusoe. Indeed the *Robinsonade* became a world phenomenon, and the writer of a preface to one of them puts it very effectively when he says: "The word Robinson has for some time replaced for us Germans the French word *aventurier*. It describes for us a creature for whom the world holds an infinity of possibilities, fortunate and unfortunate."[1]

Gulliver was also a shipwrecked sailor. His appeal to children may possibly have been less immediate because of his persistent failure to learn by experience the penalty of going to sea. His shipmates may well have looked upon him as a Jonah. All the same his adventures had the added charm of being amongst the little people, giants, and talking animals. There was also the element of topsy-turveydom, popular with chapbook readers in many versions of *The World Turned Upside Down*, later to claim the attention of another genius in the Lewis Carroll stories.

It is strange, therefore, that Gulliver appears comparatively infrequently in chapbooks. Perhaps he was too difficult to abridge, or he may have suffered early from that almost inescapable curse of literary immortality, to be chosen as a school text-book.

The form that most abridgements for children would take was already indicated in the first abridged edition of all, which was published, without authorisation, by J. Stone and R. King in 1727. This contained "Lilliput" and "Brobdingnag" only. The first chapbook editions seem to have appeared in about the middle of the eighteenth century, and to have contained "Lilliput" only.

Such, in brief and rough outline, is the background against which a series of publishers, with one of them especially enterprising, had begun, by the middle of the eighteenth century, to exploit a practically virgin market and to provide, for the first time in English publishing history, a library suitable for the young.

[1] Translated from an anonymous quotation in Dyhrenfurth-Graebsch, *Gesch. d. deutschen Jugendbuches* (1951), p. 204.

All the basic elements were to hand—the magic and make-believe of fairy-tales and fables, with their anthropomorphic animals; chivalric heroism; and adventures on sea and land, with the profitable innovation of the desert island.

That is, in fact, a rather too promising picture for, with all this charming material available, there was yet a dead hand that cast its obstinate and depressing shadow across the scene, relenting little of its severity for more than another century. This was the influence of John Calvin with its insistence on the reality of original sin, and of the need before all others to pluck young brands from the burning of hell's immortal fires. This was hard indeed to shake off, and with it went the corollary that all forms of enjoyment were worse than frivolous. Time was too short in which to save the human soul from perdition and every moment spent otherwise was engaged in the devil's work.

Thus it was that while France was enjoying Perrault England was basking in the baleful light emitted by such as Janeway and Chear. The attempt was to be made repeatedly, even more than 150 years after the first appearance of fairy-tales on nursery shelves, to discountenance them for their moral leprosy—Cinderella being singled out for special condemnation.

Books Applicable to this Chapter

F. M. Harrison's *A Bibliography of the Works of John Bunyan* (Bibliographical Society, 1932) is the *locus classicus*. The Sotheby Sale Catalogue of Sir Leycester Harmsworth's Collection, 1947, is an informative supplement to it, containing dates and particulars of many later editions which are not in Harrison.

H. C. Hutchins's *Robinson Crusoe and its printing* (New York: Columbia University Press, 1925) is almost exhaustive on the early editions. Gumuchian's catalogue *Les Livres de L'Enfance*, 2 vols. (Paris [1930]), lists many sequels and imitations in various languages.

H. Teerink, *A Bibliography . . . of Jonathan Swift* (The Hague: Nijhoff, 1937), and H. Williams, *The Motte Editions of "Gulliver's Travels"* (Bibliographical Society, 1925–8), are authoritative on the early editions.

On Perrault the evidence is detailed at some length in M. E. Storer's *La Mode des Contes de Fées* (Paris: Champion, 1928). J. le Petit's *Bibliographie des Principales Éditions Originales d'Écrivains Français* (Paris: Jeanne, 1927), pp. 436–43, is also useful. He is convinced of the son's authorship.

For dates and contents of the original editions of Hans Andersen's books of fairy-tales and stories the standard work is B. F. Nielsen's *H. C. Andersen Bibliografi* (Copenhagen: Hagerup, 1942). Dates and titles of the early English translations are in E. Bredsdorff's *Danish Literature in English Translation* (Copenhagen: Munksgaard, 1950). No lists of contents are given and many of these early translations overlap one another. R. N. Bain's *Hans Christian Andersen* (Lawrence & Bullen, 1895) is an excellent biography with much useful information about the fairy-tales.

Of Grimm there is no bibliographical account known to me. The first English editions are in A. M. Cohn's *George Cruikshank, a Catalogue Raisonée* (Bookman's Journal, 1924.)

1563. Thomas Newbery. *A Booke in Englyssh Metre . . . very preaty for children to rede . . .* The only surviving copy is in the John Rylands Library in Manchester; but the text is printed in Huth, *Fugitive Tracts* (1875), and a facsimile of the original has been made.

1664. Samuel Crossman. *Youth's Monitor.* Afterwards taken over by Nathaniel Crouch, q.v.

[1671 ?] James Janeway. *A Token for Children.* The B.M. copy is undated, but there is apparently a copy dated 1671 in the E. A. Osborne Collection in Toronto.

[Before 1672.] Thomas White. *A Little Book for Little Children.* Note—The earliest edition extant is the "twelfth" dated 1702, but White died in 1672.

1672. Henry Jessey, Abraham Chear, and P. H. *A Looking Glass for Children.*

[After 1672.] *A Token for Youth.*

1686. John Bunyan. *A Book for Boys and Girls.* Later known as *Divine Emblems.*

[1684.] —— *A Caution to Stir Up to watch against Sin.*
The latter is a broadside in verse, which was certainly read by or forced upon children (6).

[c. 1688.] William Jole. *The Father's Blessing.*

1678 and 1695. Nathaniel Crouch (R. B.). *The Young Man's Calling.*

1681.   *The Apprentice's Companion.*

1691.   *Youth's Divine Pastime.*

1695.   *The English Hero; or Sir Francis Drake reviv'd* (4th ed.).

[169–.]   *Martyrs in Flames: or, the History of Popery.*

1728.   *The Kingdom of Darkness, or the History of daemons* (4th. ed.).

The above is a selection of the writings, compilations, or plain thefts by Crouch, several of them with his pseudonym "R. B.", or Richard or Robert Burton, attached as author. Some, although probably not all, were directly aimed at children. The chapbook form in which they were issued, however, and their general style makes it almost certain that they were read by children.

BOOKS "ADOPTED" BY CHILDREN

1678. John Bunyan. *Pilgrim's Progress.* Part II. 1684.

1692. L'Estrange's translation of Aesop, etc.

1719. Daniel Defoe. *Robinson Crusoe.* Parts I and II. Part III *Serious Reflections . . .* 1720.

1726. Jonathan Swift. *Gulliver's Travels.*

1727. Peter Longueville. *The Hermit: or the Adventures of Philip Quarll.*

Innumerable chapbook and other juvenile editions of all the above, several of which are discussed in the text.

It has been thought well to treat here all the important printed sources of fairy-tales—Perrault, Grimm, and Andersen—although the latter fall into a later period.

There can be little question that the Perrault tales are, in origin, traditional, and the frontispiece to the first and to many subsequent editions, as has been said, pays tribute to this in its depiction of children seated at the fireside listening to the stories told by an old wife, the original model for which was certainly the three children of Charles Perrault and their governess, and the use of which indicates the sponsor's desire to pay tribute to the origin of the stories. This seems rather more like the son than the father.

Nevertheless it is interesting and important to discover who sponsored their original appearance in print. Where, when, and how were they first printed? Some say that their first appearance was at The Hague over the imprint of Moetjens, in a periodical publication entitled *Recueil de pièces curieuses et nouvelles*, of which thirty parts were published between 1694 and 1701. It has also been stated, and is now generally accepted, that the periodical publication was a piracy from the book published in Paris in 1697 by Claude Barbin. The title of this is *Histoires ou Contes du temps passé. Avec des Moralitez*.[1] There is no author's name on the title-page, but there is a Privilege given at Fontainebleau on October 28, 1696. Such a Privilege was claimed by authors at this time, in England and other countries besides France, as the only form of protection of copyright. It was often largely ineffective, but it was all that was to be had; and it also served as an invaluable assurance of approval by the royal censorship.

Privileges were granted to authors and/or publishers; and an author had the power to assign his rights, which he normally did in favour of the printer or publisher of his book. The Privilege for the "Contes" was granted "au sieur P. Darmancour", and at the end of it are these words "ledit sieur P. Darmancour a cédé son Privilège à Claude Barbin, pour en jouir par luy, suivant l'accord fait entr'eux".

That seems perfectly clear. P. Darmancour, the author of the book, receives an official Privilege for the publication of his book and, having signed an agreement with Barbin to publish it for him, passes on the Privilege for their common protection.

"P. Darmancour" was, in fact, Pierre Perrault d'Armancour, the eldest child of Charles Perrault, a Parisian lawyer whose importance as an Academician is due less to his powers as a writer than to his considerable ability as a reformer and an organiser. He wrote a number of mediocre poems, in one of which he lauded the superiority of contemporary authors over Homer, Plato, Aristotle and Virgil, a popular opinion in the *grand siècle*. After quarrelling with Racine on the point, he followed up his poem with four large volumes of prose in which he extended his comparison to all branches of human activity, always coming down heavily in favour of his own times. Out of this grew his *Hommes illustres*, a folio, published in two volumes, 1696–1700, containing excellent short biographies of 102 of his contemporaries with an engraved portrait of each of them, an invaluable work showing considerable research. He persuaded his master, Colbert, to open the Tuileries Gardens to the public.

So far as one can ascertain he never himself made any claim to the authorship or sponsorship of the Mother Goose Tales; and before he died, in many editions of the book, some of them unauthorised despite the privilege, the authorship was attributed explicitly

---

[1] The first appearance of any of the stories, however, was the anonymous publication in the *Mercure Galant* (Feb. 1696) of "La Belle au Bois Dormant".

on the title-page to his son.[1] No edition during his lifetime attributed the stories to Perrault senior. The son was eighteen years old at the time, and it has been suggested that whereas the reduction to print was the work of Charles, the idea may have originated with Pierre, and it may have been to please him that the father allowed the book to bear an attribution to the son. If this were indeed the case it was most elaborately done, for not only was the Privilege granted to the son by name, but the dedication, headed "A Mademoiselle", says in so many words that the stories are the work of a child, and that, whereas it is not strange that he should have found pleasure in writing them, it may seem astonishing that he should have had the hardihood to present them to her.[2]

And there is more to come. In 1696, Mlle L'Heritier de Villandon published, through Guiguard in Paris, a volume entitled *Œuvres meslées*. It is a collection of essays, poems, and stories, one of which bears a longish dedication to Charles Perrault's daughter, the author's cousin, in the course of which reference is made both to the father and the son. The writer praises the father for the excellent education he has given to his children, and praises his acknowledged fairy-stories, *Griselidis* (published 1681), *Peau d'Asne*, and *Les Souhaits ridicules* (published 1694).[3]

All this formed part of a discussion at a party which she had recently attended, and they had gone on to talk of the naïve tales that one of the father's young pupils had recently committed to paper, which led them to the narration of some of them, and afterwards to the telling of other stories. When it came to her turn she told this story of *Marmoisan* which she is now dedicating to Mlle Perrault. The story was new to the company; and it was generally agreed to be worthy of submission to the young story-teller who had already proved so successful in this genre. In offering the story to her young girl friend she hopes that it will be passed on to her brother as possibly worthy to be granted a place in his own collection.

Certain conclusions seem to follow inescapably from this dedication. First that the authorship of the tales seems to have been generally accorded to Pierre before their publication; secondly that he was known to have written them down prior to publication; and thirdly that publication was being prepared. The Privilege in Mlle L'Heritier's book is dated June 19, and it was published on October 8, 1695, the latter date being more than a year before Perrault's Privilege.

Storer,[4] with no evidence whatever to support her supposition, says that L'Heritier, being in the family, was helping to sustain the supposed authorship of the son, at the father's wish, because he preferred to conceal his authorship. This seems extremely far-fetched, and certainly does not dispose of the anonymous author of the *Histoire de la Marquise Maquis de Banneville*, who, on the occasion of the reprinting of his story in the *Mercure Galant* in September 1696, makes the Marquise say that she has read *La Belle au Bois Dormant*, that she has never seen a story better told, but that she was not in the least surprised to learn the identity of the author, for he is the son of a Master.

---

[1] Brunet records a piracy with this attribution in the very year of original publication, and Gumuchian has one of 1700. By 1742, however, the author was being given as M. Perrault and even as M. Charles Perrault. The case for the father's authorship is fully stated by Storer.

[2] "Mademoiselle, on ne trouvera pas étrange qu'un enfant ait pris plaisir à composer les Contes de ce Recueil; mais on s'étonnera qu'il ait eu la hardiesse de vous les presenter."

[3] These are all in verse and rather feeble. Mlle de Villandon, indeed, quite properly characterises them as "les moindres productions 'de leur illustre auteur'".   [4] P. 94.

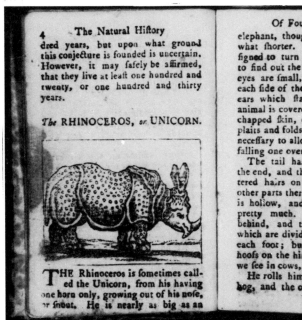

dred years, but upon what ground this conjecture is founded is uncertain. However, it may safely be affirmed, that they live at least one hundred and twenty, or one hundred and thirty years.

The RHINOCEROS, or UNICORN.

THE Rhinoceros is sometimes called the Unicorn, from his having one horn only, growing out of his nose, or snout. He is nearly as big as an

elephant, though his legs are somewhat shorter. The snout seems designed to turn up the earth, in order to find out the roots of plants. The eyes are small, and placed forward on each side of the head, and it has large ears which stand erect The whole animal is covered with a thick rough chapped skin, of an ash colour, with plaits and folds in all such parts as are necessary to allow the creature motion, falling one over another backwards.

The tail has a few black hairs at the end, and there are also a few scattered hairs on the ears; but on the other parts there are none. The back is hollow, and the belly sinks down pretty much. The feet are round behind, and the hoofs are forward, which are divided into three parts on each foot; but they have two little hoofs on the hinder part of the foot as we see in cows, deer, and sheep.

He rolls himself in the dirt like a hog, and the old ones are so strong,

B 3

they

14   A typical opening

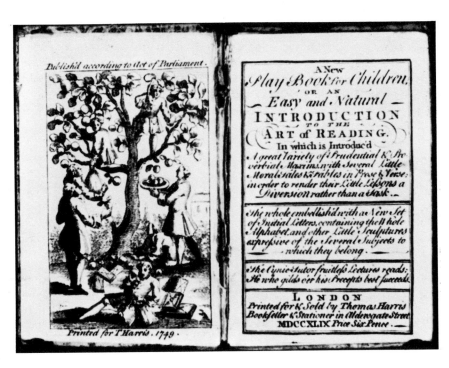

15   Title-page and frontispiece (1749)

CHILDREN'S BOOKS OF THE EARLY EIGHTEENTH CENTURY

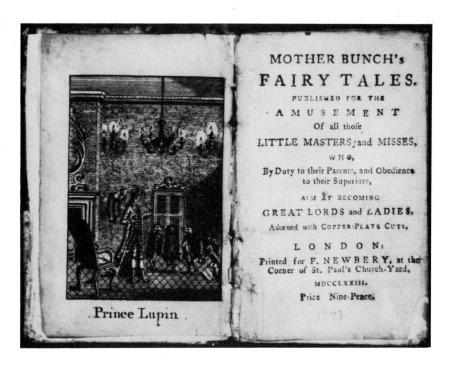

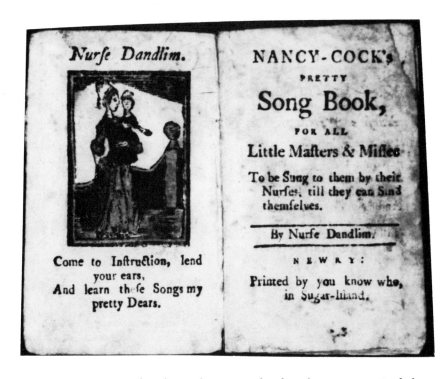

16, 17   Two typical eighteenth-century books: the top one, English;
the lower, Irish

All this leaves little doubt that at the time of original publication, and throughout the lifetime of Perrault senior, the son's authorship was generally accepted. To-day informed opinion in France also favours the son and we may very well leave it at that.

The earliest English translations of the stories have also been subject to doubts of authorship, and the dates are still uncertain. Until 1925 the statement in Lang's *Perrault* was accepted. This was that the earliest extant edition in English was a "third" edition dated 1741 of a text by R. Samber. The earliest known advertisement of this translation appeared over the name of J. Pole in the *Monthly Chronicle* on March 31, 1729, which was assumed to be the the the date of original publication.

In 1925 the Nonesuch Press issued a reprint of an illustrated edition dated 1719 and described on the title-page as the eleventh, accredited to G. M., who was presumed to be Guy Miege, a Swiss born in Lausanne in 1644. The text is almost identical with Samber's, and J. Saxon-Childers, who edited the Nonesuch edition, assumed that Samber had appropriated Miege's text, with the addition of a slight polish. The copy used was imperfect.

The Opies,[1] however, discovered in the great collection of children's books formed by Mr. Roland Knaster a perfect copy of the same edition also dated 1719 (i.e. MDCCXIX) with the imprint of B. C. Collins of Salisbury, an associate of Newbery's. Now Collins's twelfth edition of this text is dated 1802 and the gap between the two reprints seemed suspiciously long. Moreover the style and general appearance of the "eleventh edition" is much nearer to 1802 than to 1719. All doubts were set at rest by the discovery on the last page of Mr. Knaster's copy of a joint advertisement by Collins, E. Newbery, and others dated 1799. The title-page date, MDCCXIX is clearly a misprint for MDCCXCIX, or 1799. This disposes of two myths. First G. M. can hardly be Guy Miege and secondly the Collins text must probably be demoted and Samber's restored to priority.

Much further investigation remains to be made. First, who was "Mother Goose" on whom the tales were originally fostered? The Opies dispose irrefutably of the claim that she was of American origin. Much more ancient is the association with Bertha, wife of Robert II, King of France in the eleventh century. Her nicknames—*La Reine Pedauqe* and Bertha Goosefoot—arising from the Pope's denunciation of her marriage —suggest an already flourishing Mother Goose superstition, and the original old wife, on whom queer tales and superstitions were mothered, is probably even more remote than Queen Bertha.

Samber, the first translator, was responsible for the switch from *La Belle au Bois Dormant* to *The Sleeping Beauty in the Wood*, which is probably accountable to a faulty acquaintance with the French language; but I have been unable to locate the author or the period of the addition of the more merciful ending to "Red Riding Hood". Originally she, like her grandmother, was eaten by the wolf, and this was not changed until some time in the nineteenth century.

SUMMARY OF EARLY EDITIONS AND TRANSLATIONS

1. February 1696. "La Belle au Bois Dormant" appeared anonymously in the *Mercure Galant*.

[1] Opie, pp. 39–40, footnote.

2. 1697 *Histoires ou Contes du temps passé. Avec des Moralitez* (A Paris Chez Claude Barbin). This volume contained the following stories:

La Belle au Bois Dormant .	The Sleeping Beauty
La petite Chaperon Rouge .	Red Riding Hood
La Barbe Bleue . . .	Blue Beard
Le Maître chat, ou Le Chat Botté	Puss in Boots
Les Fées	("The Fairy" in Samber, but later "Diamonds and Toads".)
Cendrillon, ou la petite Pantoufle de Verre[1] . .	Cinderella, or the Glass Slipper.
Riquet à la Houpe . .	Riquet with the Tuft.
Le Petit Poucet . . .	("Little Thumb" in Samber, but later "Hop O' My Thumb".[2])

This is the first edition of the "Contes" and the first printing of all but the first of them.

3. 1697. *Histoires ou Contes du temps passé. Avec des Moralitez.* Par le Fils de Monsieur Perreault [sic] de l'Académie François [sic] (A la sphère). Suivant la copie à Paris, 1697. This edition follows the first edition closely both in time and style. It appears to have been set up from it. The publisher was Moetjens at the Hague (see next entry).

4. 1696–7. *Recueil de pièces curieuses et nouvelles . . . La Haye, Moetjens.* This periodical miscellany was begun in 1694 and continued until 1701, thirty parts in all being issued. Three parts were issued during 1696, in the second of which was included "La Belle au Bois Dormant", almost certainly reprinted from the text in the *Mercure*. In 1697 only one part was published, which contained the other seven "Contes", taken word for word from the Barbin edition (No. 2 above). Every peculiarity of punctuation and orthography is repeated by Moetjens, so as to preclude the possibility suggested by some that he had a separate manuscript, and might have anticipated Barbin. There was a third edition in 1697 and another in 1700.

No other edition is recorded until Paris 1707, said to be a page-for-page reprint of the first, with the cuts copied by another hand. In 1724 Gosselin published another edition with the original text. In 1742 another edition at The Hague incorporated *L'Adroite Princesse* by Mlle L'Heritier. Few of the subsequent editions before about 1860 conformed to the original. Most of them added other tales to the original set of eight, by Perrault senior, Mme de Beaumont, and/or others.

All the early editions are rare, those of 1697 extremely so. Of the first edition less than six copies are recorded, and not all are perfect. There are no recent auction records of it, but a copy is said to have changed hands since the war for the equivalent of £350. Two auction records of the Moetjens edition of 1697 are available, one, in 1946 of Fr. frs. 115,000 + 32%, and one in 1948 of Fr. frs. 103,000 + 17·5%. Those percentages are payable by the buyer additional to the purchase price. There is one record of the *Recueil* of 1694–1701 at Fr. frs. 30,000 + 17·5% in 1948.

1 No confirmation can be found for the ingenious suggestion that the slipper was originally of *vair*, or fur.
2 Not "Tom Thumb", which is English.

SAMBER

1. 1729. March 31. J. Pote of Charing Cross announces in the *Morning Chronicle* the immediate publication of a translation of the "Contes" "by R. Samber". No copy of any edition of this translation earlier than 1741 appears to be now extant (see No. 2).[1]

2. 1741. Third edition of Samber's translation. The earliest extant.

3. 1764. Sixth edition of the same.

G. M.

4. 1777. F. Newbery and B. Collins of Salisbury published the seventh edition of G. M.'s translation. This is recorded in Welsh, *A Bookseller of the Last Century*, but no copy of it, or any earlier edition of it, appears now to be extant. Opie plausibly reasons that as this consisted of 3,000 copies, and took three years to sell, the first printing may have been in about 1765.

5. 1799. Collins published the "eleventh edition" of this translation, a misprint on the title-page making it appear that it was issued in 1719.

6. 1802. Collins published the "twelfth edition".

Chapbook editions of the separate stories began to appear during the first decade of the nineteenth century and are innumerable.

Much work remains to be done on the bibliography of the English translations of the early French fairy-tales. It is distinctly possible that Perrault's collection was not the first to be translated. There were, for example, English translations of the tales of the Comtesse d'Aulnoy in 1707, 1716, and 1728, all of which precede any known English translations of Perrault.

One of the strongest influences on the spread of fairy-tales for children was the publication, between 1785 and 1789, of *Le Cabinet des Fées*, in forty-one volumes. Selections from this extensive collection, including "Beauty and the Beast", were soon translated and were frequently used by the growing number of chapbook publishers.

THE BROTHERS GRIMM

1812. *Kinder-und-Haus-Märchen.* [Vol. I] (Berlin: Realschulbuchhandlung).

1815. The same. Vol. II.

1818. The same. Vol. III.

1823. *German Popular Stories.* Translated from the *Kinder und Haus Märchen*, collected by M. M. Grimm [Vol. I] (C. Baldwin, Newgate Street). N.B.—The earliest copies omit the diaresis in "Märchen".

1826. Vol. II (James Robins & Co., London, and Joseph Robinson, Junr., & Co., Dublin). The first volume was reprinted in 1823 and again in 1824 and 1825. The second volume was reprinted in 1827 with no date on the title-page.

Both the original German and the first English translations are of extreme rarity in original binding and in pristine condition. No set of the first German edition has been sold by auction in this country during the last thirty years or more.

[1] A unique copy of the first edition of 1729 was included in the Pierpont Morgan Library Exhibition of Children's Books in 1954.

1829. March 17. In the daily newspaper *Kjøbenhavns-Posten*, appeared *Snee-Dronningen* [The Snow Queen], the first fairy-story by Andersen. It was not collected in book form until 1845.

1835. *Eventyr fortalte for Bjørn* (Copenhagen: C. A. Reitzel). This tiny paper-bound volume with sixty-one text-pages was the first collection of Andersen's fairy-tales to be published. It contained:

Fyrtøiet . . .	The Tinder-box.
Lille Claus og store Claus .	Little Claus and Big Claus.
Prindsessen paa Aerten .	The Princess and the Pea.
Den lille Idas Blomster .	Little Ida's Flowers.

Other collected volumes appeared at intervals.

1835. *Eventyr . . . Andet Hefte . . .* Ibidum.
The second collection, seventy-six text-pages, contained:

Tommelise . . .	Thumbelina
Den uartige Dreng .	The Naughty Boy
Reisekammeraten . .	The Travelling Companions.

1837. *Eventyr . . . Tredie Hefte . . .* Ibidum.
The third collection, sixty text-pages, contained:

Den, lille Havfrue . .	The Little Mermaid.
Keiserens nye Klaeder .	The Emperor's New Clothes.

Simultaneously with the issue of the third part, the three were issued together in one volume. Part publication and the subsequent issue of collections of parts in volume form continued until 1872.

ENGLISH TRANSLATIONS

1846. None of Andersen's fairy-tales appear to have been published in English before this date, although his two short novels, *Only a Fiddler* and *O.T.*, were issued together by Bentley in three volumes in 1845. The translator was Mary Howitt, who learned Danish for the express purpose of reading him in the original.

In 1846 she translated ten of the fairy-tales, which were published by Bohn with the title *Wonderful Stories for Children*. The same publisher, in the same year, published a translation by Beckwith of *En Digter's Bazar* (1842), with the title *A Poet's Bazaar*, which contains three of the tales. Bohn is also credited with *Danish Fairy Legends and Tales* (1846)— no translator's name is given, but Caroline Peachey was her name. Griffith and Farran issued two collections in 1846, translated by Charles Boner—*A Danish Story-Book*, and *The Nightingale and other Tales*.

A fairly full list of the early English translations is given by E. Bredsdorff, in *Danish Literature in English Translation* (Copenhagen: Munksgaard, 1950).

The earliest collections in Danish are of the utmost rarity; and the English translations in 1846 and 1847 are almost as rare.

18   A typical child's writing sheet (1762)

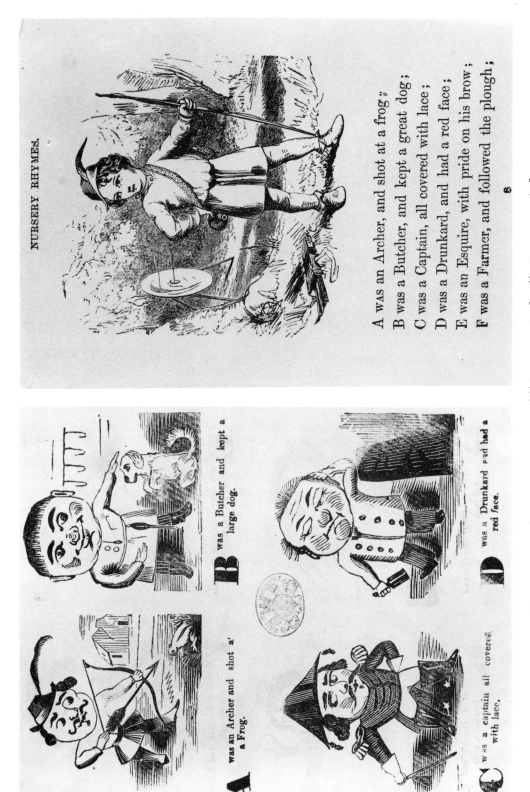

NURSERY RHYMES.

A was an Archer, and shot at a frog;
B was a Butcher, and kept a great dog;
C was a Captain, all covered with lace;
D was a Drunkard, and had a red face;
E was an Esquire, with pride on his brow;
F was a Farmer, and followed the plough;

8

A was an Archer and shot a' a Frog.

B was a Butcher and kept a large dog.

C was a captain all covered with lace.

D was a Drunkard and had a red face.

19, 20   Two nineteenth-century versions of ''A was an Archer''. *Compare with fig. 11*

CHAPTER TWO

GETTING UNDER WEIGH

1. "T. W." and Isaac Watts

FAIRY-TALES and adaptations have carried us well into the eighteenth century. Although we must now cast back a little to a slightly earlier date this overlap serves already to show that any notion that the provision of books for children began suddenly and spontaneously with the efforts of one publisher in about 1740 must be completely abandoned.

The Puritans may have made a poor start, but it was a start; and from then onwards only the paucity of survivals has disguised the fact that progress was fairly continuous.

In the British Museum are two tiny books bound together, each with the same title—*A Little Book for Little Children*. Despite the identity of title and of author's initials, the one by Thomas White[1] and the other by T. W., they could hardly be more different in content and outlook. White's book is dated 1703—it is the twelfth edition; T. W.'s book is undated, but it has a woodcut frontispiece of Queen Anne and may probably be dated as about 1712. It comprises only twelve pages, including the title and frontispiece, but although the contents are entirely instructional they strike an entirely new note. The first text-page is a letterpress representation of a horn-book, with the traditionally shaped frame containing an alphabet. Four pages of simple spelling instruction follow, and then an illustrated alphabet with jingles of which one page is shown in the cut. Also shown is the first appearance in print of the still familiar alphabetical rhyme beginning "A was an Archer . . ." (11). Then we get a lively object-lesson in faulty punctuation:

> I saw a Peacock with a fiery Tail,
> I saw a Blazing Star that dropt down Hail,
> I saw a Cloud . . .

On the last page is an advertisement of *The Child's Weeks-work, Containing, Godly Verses, Riddles, Tables, Jests and Stories . . . ,*[2] the reproduction of a page from which emphasises the exceptional nature of T. W.'s little book (12).

The "Little Book" was unmistakably educational rather than pure entertainment;

[1] Mentioned on p. 33.
[2] It is by William Ronksley and was published in 1712.

but the author, whose anonymity is distressing to the historian,[1] is the earliest on record in English to approach the problem from the point of view of the child rather than the adult, a landmark of no mean importance.

Isaac Watts was the son of a clothier, who was also a prominent figure in the Independent Meeting, and spent part of his life in prison, or as a fugitive from persecution by the orthodox. Isaac himself became the beloved pastor of an independent chapel in Mark Lane, under the patronage of the Abneys,[2] whose fame and piety are yet commemorated in the cemetery at Stoke Newington that bears their name. Watts, wrestling with himself in spiritual agony, latterly trembled on the brink of Unitarianism, although it remains uncertain whether he succumbed.

The harshness of parts of some nonconformist creeds repelled him, especially their antipathy to music as the work of the devil; and his contribution to relieving them of opprobrious references to "psalm-singing" took the form of a series of hymns many of which are still universally favoured in non-Roman communities. The best known of these are "When I survey the wondrous cross", "Jesus shall reign where'er the sun", and "O God, our help in ages past"[3]; but he wrote in all more than 450 hymns.

In 1715 he produced the first edition of *Divine Songs Attempted in Easy Language for the Use of Children*, which, like his books of hymns, took the nonconformist world by storm, so that eight editions of it were called for within fifteen years[4] and its fame persisted into our own time.

Here at last is the authentic note. Watts is not less concerned with morality and edification than the earlier Puritan writers for children; but he knew not only that what is cast in rhyme and metre is most quickly learned and most readily recalled, he knew also the limits of a child's powers of understanding and of its need for simple and beguiling verses which, although heavily provided with morals, should be persuasive rather than minatory. "'Tis the voice of the sluggard" may seem to us fair game for a Carroll parody; yet how many of us have succumbed to the temptation frequently to quote that "Satan finds some mischief still for idle hands to do"—even if we haven't always got the quotation right?

> Let Dogs delight to bark and bite
> For God has made them so;
> Let Bears and Lions growl and fight,
> For 'tis their Nature, too.
>
> But Children, you should never let
> Such angry Passions rise,
> etc., etc.

1 The B.M. Catalogue suggests that he was another Thomas White, but nothing is certainly known of him.

2 Watts went on a week's visit to the Abneys in 1712; and stayed for thirty-six years until his death in 1748. Lady Abney considered this "the shortest visit my family ever received".

3 The first of these appears in *Hymns and Spiritual Songs* (1707), the other two in *Psalms of David* (1719).

4 This takes no account of the innumerable chapbook and other unauthorised editions.

Prim? Priggish? Possibly! But what a long way we have come from Bunyan, and in less than thirty years! Watts is much nearer in both spirit and prosody to the Taylor sisters, who wrote a century later, than to Bunyan.[1] We may find slightly priggish also such lines as:

> Should I e'er be rich and great
>   Others shall partake my goodness
> I'll supply the poor with meat,
>   Never show scorning or rudeness.
>
> Where I see the blind or lame
>   Deaf or dumb, I'll kindly treat them . . .

In comparison with earlier writings for children, however, the compassionate and sympathetic note struck by such verses as these is astounding.

Or consider again the quite remarkable "Cradle Song" which beings:

> Hush! my dear, lie still and slumber;
>   Holy angels guard thy bed!
> Heav'nly blessings without number
>   Gently falling on thy head.

It is surely credible that Blake was not unaware of these lines when writing his own "Cradle Song" in *Songs of Innocence*.[2]

It was a contemporary of the Taylors, Mrs. Cockle, and not Watts himself, who, in 1829, provided his "Songs" with notes to explain to young people that, for example, the original cats and dogs in the Garden of Eden neither barked nor bit, they had fallen into evil ways because contact with humans had degraded them. How Watts would have loathed the wretched Cockle, not less for her sententious piety than for her undermining of the meaning of his verses.

Watts could hardly be expected to shake off the influence of the "good, godly books" entirely, and Davis points out that eight songs in this volume are of an unpleasantly minatory kind. One verse quoted by him will suffice to show what is meant:

> 'Tis dangerous to provoke a God;
>   His power and vengeance none can tell;
> One stroke of his almighty rod
>   Shall send young sinners quick to hell.

Janeway himself would have said amen to that!

[1] Nevertheless, Davis (pp. 76–7) instances very strikingly the influence that Bunyan's *Book for Boys and Girls* had upon Watts when he compiled *Divine Songs*. One poem after another has the same theme, often almost the same title as Bunyan's, and Watts sets them out in the same order. The contrast between the "tortured rhymes" and ruggedness of Bunyan and the gentleness and prosodic ability of Watts is clearly seen in Davis's quotations of a poem from each author on Ants (p. 77).

[2] Both poems are in the *Oxford Book of English Verse*.

The easy, jingling metre that Watts chose, and the simple innocence of his teaching, occasionally verging on the platitudinous, have combined to leave him underestimated in our sophisticated age. Whatever his merits as a poet may be, and I think them higher than many would allow, as a writer for children his importance is not easily exaggerated. He was the first to write for them in their own idiom; and a century was to elapse before another like him would arise; although every writer of children's verse in his century shows the influence of his work.[1]

The circulation and influence of Watts's little book are incalculable. Imitations, some of them slavish,[2] were frequent, and selections from Watts's own work were among the best selling lines in the chapman's pack. Stern Mrs. Trimmer could not resist their charm, and commended them to her Sunday-school readers as the most delightful religious work ever written for children.[3] Finally, when Anne and Jane Taylor published their *Hymns for Infant Minds* in 1808 they apologised for temerity in emulating Dr. Watts, explaining that as the "narrow limits to which he had confined himself exclude a number of useful subjects, the following Hymns, though with much diffidence, are presented to the public".

2. The New Art of Publishing

So far we have been concerned mainly with authors. We now approach a period when publishers began to pay attention to the fact that there was a section of the reading public which was not fully, or indeed at all regularly, catered for. It may seem remarkable that until well into the eighteenth century there was no publisher who catered especially for the children's market; but this would be to misconceive the position. The construction of the book trade in the seventeenth and eighteenth centuries was entirely different from what we know to-day. It has been said that Jacob Tonson, in the seventeenth century, was the first modern publisher, the first, that is, who commissioned books from authors and accepted them at his own risk. Tonson was not only an exceptional man in general, but especially in this particular.

Dr. Johnson has been called the first English writer to earn his living by his pen, but the circumstances under which most of his books were published are far more representative of publishing conditions throughout the seventeenth and eighteenth centuries than, for example, Tonson's relations with Dryden. It is rare to find a Johnson title-page with the imprint of only a single publisher, and the responsibility for his *Prefaces to the Works of the English Poets* (1779–81) was shared by

---

[1] His foreword to parents and guardians should be compared with those of the "good godly" writers.
[2] Davis quotes from *Moral Songs* by John Oakman (1802), the following verse:
> How craftily the spider weaves,
>   And draws her slender threads!
> Yet sudden chance her hope deceives
>   And spoils the net she spreads.
[3] *A comment on Dr. Watts's Divine Songs . . .* (1789).

no fewer than thirty-six different firms. It is doubtful whether the main livelihood of most of these was gained by publishing; all of them had retail shops in which most of them sold not only new but also secondhand books. They were not, in fact, generally called publishers,[1] but booksellers.

Specialisation was observable, but not very marked. Most of what specialisation there was consisted of the preparation of small books for self-sale, or for a special market like the chapmen. The facts are scanty, and much of the story must be built up by inference.[2]

Children's books are one of the most ephemeral of all forms of printed matter. The cheap methods of production and the rigorous treatment they are called upon to withstand shorten their existence. In earlier times, when children's books were scarce, they were passed even more frequently from hand to hand than they are now, and many titles have probably perished irrevocably. This robs the historian of much of the original material on which to base his survey; and may lead to the dangerous assumption that what no longer survives never existed at all.

"Few and far" indeed are the extant remnants of the period before John Newbery; and hence arose the unquestionably false impression that until he came on the scene no proper provision was made for children at all; and that with the publication, in 1744, of his *Little Pretty Pocket Book*, the scene was changed in the twinkling of an eye. This is a greatly oversimplified picture of the true situation; and without in the least denying the importance and significance of Newbery it is necessary to place him in truer proportion to the general picture.

One of the earliest signs that children must be catered for specially was in the devising of those extremely pretty educational objects, the Writing Sheets, or School Pieces. This is no place in which to enlarge on the influence of the English writing masters in the late seventeenth and early eighteenth centuries. A wide survey of their work is contained in Sir Ambrose Heal's attractive study of them.[3] But, picturesque though their efforts may appear to us, they were, in fact, intended to be sternly practical manuals for scholars of all ages.

James Cole, an engraver who flourished in about 1715, and who is referred to as "the late" on a publication of about 1749, is the earliest producer of special writing sheets for children that I have been able to trace, and he issued more than a hundred of them. They are gaily bordered sheets in folio size, with blank centres which were to be filled in by the child in its best handwriting for presentation to its parents, usually at Christmastide. They may be thought to be essentially educational rather than recreational. The point to be observed here is the provision

---

[1] The earliest use of the word "publisher" in the modern sense given in the *O.E.D.* is in 1740. The *Ency. Brit.* (3rd ed. 1797) refers to "Petty dealers or venders of smallware, like our publishers". In 1802, Montefiore, in the title of a work on Copyright, describes it as "A Compendium of Acts of Parliament and Adjudged Cases, relating to Authors, Publishers, Printers etc."

[2] But see Collins.

[3] *The English Writing-Masters and their Copy-Books* (Cambridge University Press).

of pretty pictures, often coloured, essentially as an attraction for children. Many of them were grouped to tell a story (18).

We have already considered the early appearance in English of the Perrault stories and the early adaptations for young readers of the works of Defoe, Swift, and other writers. There is also unmistakable evidence of the growing efforts of chapbook publishers to provide a regular supply of their booklets for juvenile reading.

But one of the earliest publishers who can be definitely stated to have laid himself out to cater for children is Thomas Boreman. Unlike Newbery, he seems to have had no traceable successors, neither have his records been preserved or set down. Reconstruction of his history is, therefore, extremely fragmentary, and must rely largely on his surviving publications. It seems that he was not a publisher on any large scale. It is stated in one of his books that he sold them himself on a stall within the Guildhall, although other addresses occur in some of his imprints, variously as "near the Gate", "at the Boot and Crown" or "at the Cock", all on Ludgate Hill. Possibly these were the addresses of warehouses where at different times he kept his stock, while his retail business was carried on at the Guildhall bookstall. He was not exclusively engaged in publishing children's books; his imprint appears on a book on the breeding and care of silkworms, on a survey of County Down in Ireland, and on a pamphlet of "Political Dialogues". But in 1736 he published *A Description of A Great Variety of Animals, and Vegetables . . . especially for the Entertainment of Youth*,[1] and in 1740 he issued the first of nine volumes of his "Gigantick Histories". These contained historical and descriptive accounts of famous London buildings, the Guildhall, the Tower, St. Paul's, and Westminster Abbey among them. All of these may be considered to be at least partially, if not wholly, educational. Nevertheless, they struck a new note. In 1742 he produced *The History of Cajanus, the Swedish Giant. From his Birth to the present Time. By the Author of the Gigantick Histories* (34). He is surmised to have written all these books himself. Whether that is so or not, the format, contents, and price all showed a keen sense of what was necessary to attract youngsters. The books were about $3\frac{1}{4} \times 2\frac{1}{4}$ inches in size, bound in the floral Dutch gilt boards associated with the name of Newbery, each of them contained a list of juvenile subscribers, usually about 130 in number, and the books were priced at fourpence each. The publisher's imprint is: "Thos. Boreman, Bookseller, near the Two Giants in Guildhall". Only ten or eleven volumes for children can be attributed to him, although he may have published others that have not come to light or survived.

The lists of subscribers in the volumes are informative (35). In the first volume of the earliest of them, *The Gigantick History of the two famous Giants, and other Curiosities in Guildhall*, the list contains eighty-five names, but at the end of the list each of the two giants—Corineus and Gogmagog—is credited with 100 copies.

[1] This is described as a supplement to a formerly published book of which the title and a note on the date are given on p. 74.

It may therefore be surmised that the first edition consisted of 300 copies. As these were to be sold retail at fourpence each the total return to the publisher on the sale of the whole edition cannot have exceeded £5. In the second volume the subscribers had risen to 123, and the number of copies printed to over 400.

His next venture was a history of the Tower of London, and the list of subscribers in the first volume includes "Master Anthony Chappelle", who took twenty-two copies. Now this was the son of Henry Chappelle (or Chapelle), a bookseller in Grosvenor Street, London, W. In the second volume "Master Dicky Caldwell" is down for fifty copies, clearly another bookseller, and Boreman's enterprise was proving successful. There were 649 subscribed copies to his three-volume miniature history of Westminster Abbey, the third volume of which carries the name of R. Ware as associated in the venture. For his final venture, however, *The History of Cajanus, the Swedish Giant*, only 106 subscribers entered their names, although the giant himself is credited with an extra 100 copies.

Meanwhile most of the earlier "Histories" had been reprinted, some of them more than once. Nevertheless the margin can never have been very great, and with no wide general list to support them such as Newbery had Boreman could hardly have hoped to make a success of his pioneer effort.

That he was a pioneer is attested not merely by his dates, but by the fact that Newbery issued a series of London books which was a complete imitation of Boreman's own series. These succeeded so well that, having been originally published in 1753, they were reissued in another form by F. Newbery in 1771, and continued in the firm's lists until at least 1793. Boreman's priority over Newbery is clearly established; and it is pleasant to pay him this belated tribute.

Charles Welsh's well-known volume spreads the known facts about Newbery very thinly over its 373 pages. Infinitely the most valuable part of the book is the register of his publications which it contains. This is by no means complete, but what does emerge from it very clearly is the fact that not more than half a dozen titles of a purely entertaining or recreational kind for children are credited to John Newbery in his own lifetime. This excludes such titles as *The Circle of the Sciences*, and the history and natural history books, for, although expressly prepared for children, and showing much of the new spirit, they are definitely instructional in nature.

How, then, has this disproportionate regard for Newbery's importance arisen among historians of children's books? Welsh is originally responsible. He was a partner in the firm of Griffith & Farran, which was in direct descent from Newbery, and the fact that John Newbery's successors were increasingly engaged in the production of books for children has been a further cause of confusion. Then there has been the rather fruitless discussion of Goldsmith's share in the writing of Newbery's children's books, most of which leaves us exactly where we stood before, and, for example, has contributed no new facts whatsoever to the probable authorship of *Goody Two-Shoes*. The good-natured, easy-going Goldsmith has himself been quoted *ad libidum* on the "philanthropic bookseller", in the passage in the

"Vicar" where Newbery is also credited with the authorship of the history of Thomas Trip. Dr. Johnson, like Goldsmith, frequently grateful for an advance of fees from Newbery on publications not yet written, is credibly said to have only slightly caricatured his publisher in the nineteenth *Idler*[1] essay. "Jack Whirler", the name of the character in the essay, is very like what we know of Newbery, a philosopher "in perpetual motion, and whose motion always eludes his business", "who is wanted in many places because he stays in none" but "is equally invisible to his friends and his customers". He is always cheerful, ambitious, and "once pined away many months with a lingering distemper for want of time to attend to his health". Johnson is in high good humour throughout the essay, which warrants reading in full.

Yet although Newbery was the publisher of Johnson, Goldsmith, and Smart, there can be no question that his considerable fortune resulted more largely from his proprietorship of Dr. James's Powder, and over thirty other nostrums, including Mordant Drops, Lozenges of Tolu, Arquebusade Water, Herb and Cephalic Snuffs, English Coffee (which must have been one of the nastiest of them), and a Carminative Mixture. It is significant that it was his son Francis—who inherited the patent-medicine business—and not his nephew of the same name, who was able to set up as a country gentleman by the purchase of Lord Heathfield's estate in Sussex, and who died as something approaching a millionaire.

The exact identity of name between the son and the nephew is very confusing, and Welsh does not clear it up very satisfactorily. It seems that the son entered into partnership with Thomas Carnan, a step-son, retaining the original premises at No. 65—formerly at the sign of the Bible and Sun—in St. Paul's Churchyard, whereas the nephew set up on his own at No. 20 Ludgate Street, the premises afterwards continued by Harris and eventually by Griffith and Farran. The partnership certainly continued until 1779, when Newbery went out of it, to devote himself entirely to the patent-medicine business in a building that he took over, and had entirely redecorated, at the north-east corner of the Churchyard. Carnan carried on alone until his death in 1788. He is best known to publishing history for his having overthrown the monopoly of the Stationers' Company in almanacks, which he accomplished in 1779.

That there was no love lost between the two succeeding Newberys is clear from some of their imprints in which one advertises that the other is entitled to no share in a particular publication. Newbery's nephew died on June 8, 1780, and his business was carried on by his widow, Elizabeth, who succeeded also to Carnan's property on his death. With the assistance of her husband's manager, John Harris, she carried on until 1821, when she died and was succeeded by Harris, whose son inherited the business and continued until he was in turn succeeded, in about 1835, by Grant and Griffith, later Griffith and Farran.

---

[1] There is no evidence in the various imprints on *The Universal Chronicle*—in which the essays contained in *The Idler* first appeared—for the statement made by Boswell, and copied by Chalmers, Forster, and Welsh, that Newbery was its publisher. He did, however, publish the first collected edition of these essays.

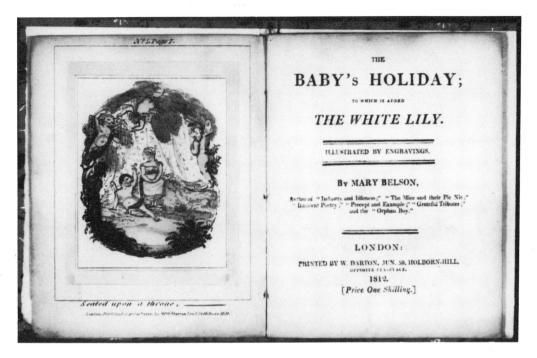

21   Frontispiece and title-page of Mary Belson's *The Baby's Holiday*, 1812. The author is
better known by her married name—Mary Elliott

Mrs. *Bountiful* taking *Goody Goosecap* from among the Charity Children.

22   Frontispiece to *The Orphan* by Toby Teachem. An early imitation of *Goody Two-Shoes*,
published by Marshall, *c.* 1780

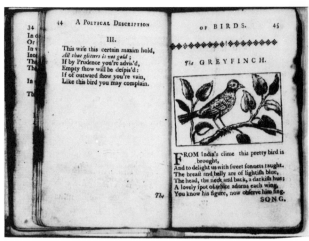

23, 24, 25 (*above, left, and bottom left*) Children's illustrated books from 1790 to 1819

26 (*below*) The earliest edition known of *Goody Two-Shoes*, 1766. *Compare figs. 30 and 67*

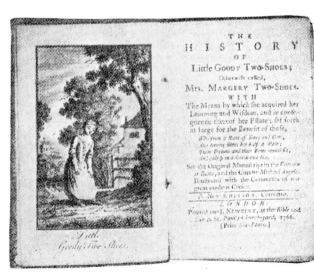

That, with a few additions, is the story as given by Welsh. It will not entirely hold water. For example, Harris's imprint, with the Churchyard address, is familiar at least as early as 1802; and nothing is explained as to Francis, the nephew, at an address in Paternoster Row, where he notably published *The Vicar of Wakefield*.

But to return to John Newbery, he certainly knew his business as a publisher, and his acumen did not desert him when he began to turn his activities to children's books. He paid great attention to every detail of their preparation; the titles, heroes, reputed authors, price, size, binding, and pictures were scrupulously attended to. As early as 1740, at the age of twenty-seven, when he had only recently acquired his master's business by the familar method of marrying his widow, he noted among a list of books that he intended to publish one to be priced at sixpence —"A collection of curious Mottos . . . for the use of Poets and Puppeys, by Lawrence Likelihood, Esq". The first book that he did actually publish for children was exemplary of most of the others. It was advertised in the *Penny Morning Post* on June 13, 1744, in the following terms:

> According to Act of Parliament (neatly bound and gilt).   .
> A Little Pretty Pocket-Book, intended for the Instruction and Amusement of Little Master Tommy and Pretty Miss Polly, with an agreeable Letter to read from Jack the Giant Killer, as also a Ball and Pincushion, the use of which will infallibly make Tommy a good Boy, and Polly a Good Girl. To the whole is prefixed a letter on education humbly addressed to all Parents, Guardians, Governesses, &c., wherein rules are laid down for making their children strong, healthy, virtuous, wise, and happy. . . .

> Printed by J. Newbery at the Bible and Crown, near Devereaux Court, without Temple Bar. Price of the Book alone, 6d., with a Ball or Pincushion, 8d.

The address was the first at which Newbery opened in business when he came to London from Reading in 1744, and he had also at that time a warehouse at the Golden Ball in Castle Alley, near the Royal Exchange. He moved to St. Paul's Churchyard towards the end of July or the beginning of August 1745, and, like many other tradesmen at the time, was hard hit by the distress consequent on the 'Forty-five rebellion. Rather than compound with his creditors, however, he offered them the security of his stock-in-trade, with a promise to pay twenty shillings in the pound when times should improve. His *Little Pretty Pocket-Book* occurs among the list of his assets at that time, and 1,000 copies of it were valued at £13 in the schedule. He survived this distress, and the "Pocket-Book" went on selling steadily, so that it was still in Carnan's list in 1783, only just short of forty years after its original publication.

His first advertisement shows Newbery not quite sure in his touch as yet. The description of the binding—I have not seen a copy of the original edition—suggests that it was in the charming Dutch gold floral boards which he used so extensively for his children's books, but the evident desire to cozen the parents and governesses shows a little uncertainty in the method of address, and the absence of Tommy

Trip, Woglog the Giant, Giles Gingerbread, and other felicitous inventions such as adorned most of his similar later title-pages, show that he was not yet into his stride.[1]

The offering of a ball or a pincushion was a good touch, but he was to do better than this, when, for example, he offered a publication free of charge, asking only payment of a penny for the binding.

Welsh gives several examples of Newbery's artful methods of puffing his books, notably by inserting references to other of his publications into his little tales. One character would excuse himself to step into Mr. Leake's shop in Bath to read one of Mr. Newbery's little books; another young prig, deservedly christenend Theophilus, bewailed to his father the ill fortune of those benighted youngsters whose parents could not afford to purchase them such a nice gilded library as that obtainable from the good friends of all children in St. Paul's Churchyard, and so on.[2]

Nurse Truelove's New Year's Gift (1760) was "designed as a present for every little boy who would become a great man, and ride upon a fine horse, and to every little girl who would become a great woman, and ride in a Lord Mayor's gilt coach", while her "Christmas Box" (1750) cost only one penny, and was subtitled "The Golden Plaything for Little Children". Tom Telescope's *Philosophy of Tops and Balls*, rather grimly subtitled "the Newtonian System of Philosophy" (29), was "collected and methodized for the Benefit of the Youth of these Kingdoms, by their old Friend, Mr. Newbery . . .". *Goody Two-Shoes* was printed from "the original manuscript in the Vatican at Rome, and the Cuts by Michael Angelo", and a New Testament, adapted to the use of children, with particularly nasty illustrations, was described as "Adorned with cuts by the celebrated Raphael and engraved by Mr. Walker" (26).

"Pretty" was a very favourite Newbery word for the beginning of a title. There was among others "Pretty Poems" for children "three foot high" and another for those "six feet high".

Newbery's astuteness is, indeed, unquestionable, and his success with children must have been considerable. This son of a country farmer; almost entirely self-educated,[3] who became the friend of Johnson and Goldsmith, and the step-father-in-law of poor Christopher Smart; who saw the commercial possibilities of children's books very early on; and who left a succession of descendants who carried on and improved his excellent work, is, perhaps, more a sign of the times than the lone pioneer that he has usually been depicted: but this honest, busy, ambitious, and successful man has earned an undoubted debt of gratitude from all children.

[1] Newbery authors and "heroes" include the following: S. Winlove; Mrs. Lovechild, Toby Ticklepitcher; R. Goodwill (reputed secretary of the Lilliputian Society, responsible for the production of *The Lilliputian Magazine*, 1752); Nurse Truelove; Tom Telescope; Peregrine Puzzlebrains; Peter Puzzlewell; Mr. Loveworth; Mr. Telltruth; T. Trapwit; Primrose Prettyface; and Margery Meanwell, otherwise Goody Two-Shoes.

[2] The puffs were not confined to books. The father of "Goody Two-Shoes" died because he was stricken down with fever in a place where Dr. James's Fever Powders, which would have saved him, were not to be had.

[3] Welsh prints a letter from his brother, Robert, who has succeeded to the paternal farm, ill-spelled and only semi-literate.

Were it not for the happy chance of Newbery's records and lists having been preserved, and for Charles Welsh's diligent research into newspaper files and other sources, we should probably know as little about Newbery's activities in the publishing of children's books as we do about his anticipators and contemporaries in the same line. If we knew as little about him as we know about Boreman and the others, if, that is to say, we had to gather our information from the imprints on the surviving books, the picture would be a very different one. Welsh records about thirty-five books published by Newbery for children, most of them more or less educational. But of these hardly a dozen have survived in the original editions with John Newbery's name in their imprints. All the rest are known only from copies with the imprints of his successors.

Stress has been placed on the tendency to exaggerate Newbery's importance in the history of children's books only for the reason that it distorts the picture. It is quite true that we know little enough of the others, but the Opies have provided yet further evidence that he was not the originator, either of the idea, or the general format or contents, of the familiar children's books of the eighteenth century. The titles they quote—*Tommy Thumb's Pretty Song Book* (probably 1744), *The Top Book of All, for Little Masters and Misters* (c. 1760), and *The Famous Tommy Thumb's Little Story-Book* (c. 1760)—could all have appeared in Newbery's list and would have found themselves perfectly well at home. The subtitle of the second book is also entirely in what has come to be known as the Newbery style—the choicest Stories, prettiest Poems and most diverting Riddles; all wrote by Nurse Lovechild, Mother Goose, Jacky Nory, Tommy Thumb, and other eminent Authors. Mary Cooper, S. Crowder, and R. Baldwin are the London publishers of these books, while Collins of Salisbury, partner in so many London ventures including many of Newbery's own, appears in the imprint of two of them.

It would be unwise, and perhaps unjust, to indulge in insinuations of copying by one from the other. The greater probability is that the thing was in the air, that several publishers decided to cash in on it about the same time, that they all took the chapbook as their model, and that Newbery was the most enterprising and the most successful of them.[1]

---

[1] The phenomenon was not peculiar to England; it was happening all over Europe. L. F. Gedike, a German schoolmaster, who visited the Leipzig Book Fairs every year, wrote of them in 1787: "No other form of literary manufactory is so active as book-making for young people of all grades and classes. Every Leipzig Summer and Winter Fair throws up a countless number of books of this kind like a flooding tide. And see how young and old rush to buy—there are few pearls and little amber, but much mud, and, at the best, painted snail-shells. They take all kinds of names and forms: almanacks for children, newspapers for children, journals for children, collections for children, stories for children, comedies for children, dramas for children, geography for children, history for children, physics for children, logic for children, catechisms for children, travels for children, morals for children, grammars for children, and reading books for children in all languages without number, poetry for children, sermons for children, letters for children, talks for children, and unlimited variations on the same theme, so that the literary doll-shops are crammed all the year round with them but especially at the time when loving parents and aunts and uncles may be attracted by the appositeness of the notice 'Christmas Gifts for good children'."

We have discussed the means by which the publishers lured the young purchasers into the net. What did they get when they had bought? The Opies give an extensive notion of the nursery rhymes that they read and learned by heart. What of the stories? They were of a rather inferior order, not very well constructed, and heavily overlaid with moral lessons. An excellent example is afforded by the most successful of them all—*Goody Two-Shoes*. The success of this little book is attested both by its being kept continually in print by Newbery and his successors until well

Good Lady KINDHEART.   25

who pitied even this wicked *Tinker*'s cafe, petiti-
oned the Judge to reprieve him, on condition he was
tranfported for life, which he gladly accepted of;
and there being a fhip ready to take fuch criminals
abroad, he was fent on board one bound for

Virginia, to fpend the remainder of his unhappy
life in flavery, a fentence too good for fuch an
abominable villain.

Before he departed from the *Englifh* fhore,
                                                    he

27 Page from a publication by Marshall, a great rival of the Newberys in about 1780

into the nineteenth century, and by the host of imitations that followed it, such as "Primrose Prettyface" and "Goody Goosecap" (22), both of which imitated the original in almost exact detail, with the exception of the changes in the names of the characters. They are, for the most part, a collection of insufferable little goody-goodies of whom Henry Sandford is the archtype, and the summary of his character and general behaviour and of a few others given later in this book suffices for the whole deplorable gang.[1]

[1] See pp. 91-93.

ANTONY AND AUGUSTUS; OR, A RATIONAL
EDUCATION PREFERABLE TO RICHES.

A VERY early friendship commenced between
Antony and Augustus, who were nearly of
an age, and as they were neighbours, they were
almost inseparable companions. The father of
Antony, whose name was Lenox, possessed a very
lucrative employment under government, and was
besides possessed of a considerable fortune; but

29   Illustration to an edition of *The
Newtonian System of Philosophy*, 1798.
The title stolen from Newbery by
Darton and Harvey

weeping sadly, she was met
by the kind old clergyman of the
parish; and he, taking pity on the
poor child, stopped to comfort
her and
ended
by
taking her to
the cobbler's and
buying her a pair of strong shoes
for her naked feet. Margery
ran off gleefully
to show the
gift to

30 A nineteenth-century *Goody Two-Shoes*.
Compare figs. 26 and 67

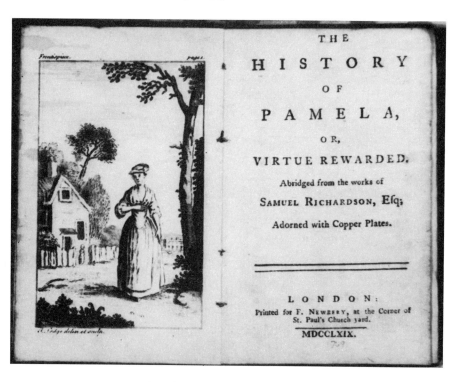

31 Francis Newbery's shilling abridgement of *Pamela* (1769)

3. Samuel Richardson

The first edition of Samuel Richardson's *Pamela* bore on its title-pages the words "Published In order to cultivate the Principles of Virtue and Religion in the Minds of the Youth of Both Sexes". That was in 1741, and although this novel can hardly be considered fit reading for small children it seems almost certain that they read it and that, in Darton's words, "the novel-reading habit reached the nursery almost before grown-ups had acquired it". *Grandison* (1753–5) was certainly widely read by young people—and not only in England, for when Beaumarchais was a young man his sister could think of no more acceptable tribute when writing to her father than to describe her brother as a veritable young Grandison. In 1756 Baldwin published, under the title of *The Paths of Virtue delineated*, abridged versions of *Pamela*, *Clarissa*, and *Grandison* in one pocket volume of 240 pages, priced at half a crown, and described as "Familiarised and Adapted To the Capacities of Youth".[1] Welsh records no Newbery editions of Richardson before 1789; but McKillop states that "by 1769 Francis Newbery had brought out shilling versions of *Pamela* [(31)], *Clarissa*, and *Grandison*, designed to afford moral reading for the young".

Prior to the writing of any of the novels, however, Richardson had produced, in 1740,[2] an edition of *Aesop's Fables*. *With Instructive Morals and Reflections, Abstracted from all Party Considerations, Adapted to All Capacities . . . .*". Richardson himself wrote in 1753[3] that the work had been commissioned by the publisher, John Osborn, junior, as a work suitable for children. He examined two earlier editions, those of L'Estrange, (1692) and Croxall (1722), finally deciding to use the former and to purge it of the Tory bias in its notes. It was advertised in 1739 as "a very proper New-Year's Gift to the Youth of both sexes", and later, after the publication of *Pamela*, as the edition quoted in that work.

Richardson's *Aesop* remained a popular edition for many years, and in records of its publishers in 1751 and 1762 it was accounted of higher value than any of the novels.

Apart from editorial labours on the papers of Sir Thomas Roe the *Aesop* was Richardson's first published book, but it would appear fairly certain that when Osborn suggested the *Aesop* Richardson was already at work on a kind of Complete Letter-writer, commissioned by Osborn and Rivington.[4] The author requested permission to introduce hints on conduct, and the resulting letters are almost a trial-run for *Pamela* and the later epistolary novels. The narratives in them are fragmentary, and are used purely as hints for conduct in difficult situations; but they are grouped round a young lady called Polly, and much of the advice is directed to young persons.

Richardson, indeed, is a not unimportant figure in the present history. From 1739 to 1741 at least he and his publishers were cultivating a juvenile audience, in

1 A Dublin abridgement of *Clarissa* dated 1751 is known.
2 Actually published Nov. 1739.
3 *London Mercury*, VII, 383.   4 *Familiar Letters*, 1741.

part at any rate; and the fact is significant of an awareness that such an audience was there to be catered for.[1]

There is indeed a child-like, not childish, atmosphere in Richardson's novels which, with due allowance for the difference of point of view between his century and ours, would have made it very easy to adapt them to the requirements of young readers.

Books Applicable to this Chapter

W. M. Stone's *The Gigantick Histories of Thomas Boreman* (Portland (Me.): The Southworth Press, 1933) contains a bibliographical list of those of his publications that were in the author's collection, with a chatty introduction and some useful facsimiles.

A. P. Davis's *Isaac Watts* (Independent Press, 1948) is an admirable short biography, with useful analytical studies of his books, dates of original editions, etc.

A. D. McKillop's *Samuel Richardson. Printer and Novelist* (University of North Carolina Press, 1936) may be supplemented by W. M. Sale's *Samuel Richardson, a bibliographical record* (New Haven: Yale University Press, 1936). McKillop's emphasis is mainly biographical and Sale's bibliographical; but each trespasses profitably on the other's territory.

On the evolution of the publishing trade and its position in the eighteenth century, two books by A. S. Collins, both published by Routledge, give a good general survey—*Authorship in the Days of Doctor Johnson* and *The Profession of Letters*. Mumby's *Publishing and Bookselling* (Cape) is also very useful.

Charles Welsh's study of John Newbery—*A Bookseller of the Last Century* (Griffith, Farran, 1885)—is in my opinion a much overrated book. It is largely scissors and paste, and its record of his publications is highly fallible. But it is the best we have on an important and enterprising publisher of children's books, who may, nevertheless, have been less of a pioneer in this respect than Welsh would have us believe.

Books for Children. 1700–67

[*c.* 1700.] *The Mad Pranks and Merry Conceits of Tom Tram* (Second Part). This is listed in Osborne. I have not seen the book, which is in Toronto, but from its imprint, "Bow Church-yard", I take it to be a Marshall chapbook.

[*c.* 1712.] T. W. *A Little Book for Little Children.* This appears to be the only edition known of this book and the only copy recorded is in the British Museum. Nothing is known of the author; and the surmise that his name is Thomas White seems to be based on no better ground than its being bound with an entirely different book with the same title which is by Thomas White [*d.* 1672 ?]. The dating of the British Museum

---

1 In both France and Germany Richardson's characters were taken as patterns for the behaviour of young people. *Clarissa* was translated into German very soon after publication, and was regarded as the embodiment of young ladylike perfection. All Richardson's novels were the subject of many imitations and sequels by other hands, most of them directed at a youthful audience. Mme de Genlis, in her *Veillées du Château*, permitted only three novels for children's reading. All were by Richardson.

copy is implausible, as the book advertises Ronksley, pub. 1712. It is a landmark, and the uncertainty of authorship, dating, and priority is deplorable.

1712. William Ronksley. *The Child's Weeks-work.*

1715. Isaac Watts. *Divine Songs Attempted in Easy Language for the Use of Children.* Later editions, including chapbooks, are innumerable. The first edition is an extremely rare book. As long ago as 1902, a copy was sold by auction for £155. True, it was a presentation copy from the author to Lady Abney, wife of his patron, but, since auction records have been published, beginning in 1886, only one other copy is noted. This was in 1907, when a stained and damaged copy sold for £55. It was then stated that not more than half-a-dozen perfect copies were known, which may well be true.

The original wording of the title should be noted. "The present title of the work: *Divine and Moral Songs*, was not used until 1785." (Davis, p. 253.)

Although outside the strict limits of our subject, Watts's pedagogical works should be mentioned. Dr. Johnson wrote of his *Improvement of the Mind* (1741–51), "Few books have been perused by me with greater pleasure . . ."; his *Art of Reading and Writing English* (1721), with its surprising snub to Latinists, "Let all the foreign tongues alone, Till you can spell and read your own"; his *Logic* (1724), from which Johnson borrowed hundreds of examples and definitions in his *Dictionary*; his *Knowledge of the Heavens* (1726); and other educational works are, in essence, popular versions of the teachings of Locke. The fact is that they did make Locke's ideas popular, and are thus a recognisable stepping-stone in the advance of modern ideas of education.

EMULATORS OF WATTS

1727. John Wright. *Spiritual Songs for Children.* 1728. Thomas Foxton. *Moral Songs composed for the Use of Children.* 1743. Philip Doddridge. *The Principles of the Christian Religion, Expressed in Plain and Easy Verse.* 1751. Nathaniel Cotton. *Visions in Verse* . . . 1751. John Marchant. *Puerilia; or, Amusements for the Young, consisting of a Collection of Songs.* 1781. Anna Laetitia Barbauld. *Hymns in Prose for Children.* 1789. Sarah Trimmer. *A Comment on Dr. Watts's Divine Songs* . . . 1802. John Oakman and others. *Moral Songs for the Instruction and Amusement of Children.* 1808. Mrs. Richardson. *Original Poems intended for the Use of Young Persons. On a Plan recommended by the Rev. Dr. Isaac Watts.*

SAMUEL RICHARDSON

1740 [1739.] *Aesop's Fables.*
1741 [1740.] *Pamela.*
            Familiar Letters.
1748 [1747–8]. *Clarissa.*
1751. Abridged edition of *Clarissa* published in Dublin.
1754 [1753–4.] *Grandison.*

1756. *The Path of Virtue.* Abridgements of *Pamela*, *Clarissa*, and *Grandison* in one volume.

c. 1769. Shilling editions of the three novels published by F. Newbery.

THOMAS BOREMAN

1736. *A Description of a Great Variety of Animals and Vegetables, especially for the Entertainment of Youth.*

1739(?). *A Description of Some curious and uncommon Creatures, Omitted in the Description of Three Hundred Animals* . . .

1740. *The Gigantick History of the two famous Giants* . . . *in Guildhall.* Two volumes.

1741. *Curiosities in the Tower of London.* Two volumes.

The History and Description of the famous Cathedral of St. Paul's. Two volumes.

1742–3. *Westminster Abbey.* Three volumes.

1742. *The History of Cajanus, the Swedish Giant.* One volume.

I am indebted for the compilation of the above list to Mr. Edgar Oppenheimer, who himself possesses all but the second title; and who also obtained for me a complete photostat of a small brochure on Boreman which had otherwise eluded me: W. M. Stone. *The Gigantick Histories of Thomas Boreman* (Portland, Maine: The Southworth Press, 1933).

Stone gives collations of all but the first two titles, which he did not possess. He mentions the second title from an advertisement; but the date should be regarded with caution. It is, moreover, by no means certain which of the first two titles is a sequel to the other, which may throw Boreman's date as a children's publisher back earlier than 1736. The date of the first title may be accepted. It is taken from Mr. Oppenheimer's copy.

OTHER PUBLISHERS

1743. *The Child's New Plaything* (2nd ed.).

Little Master's Miscellany (Birmingham).

[1744?] *Tommy Thumb's Pretty Song Book.* Only the second volume has survived. It is in the British Museum, and an account of it and its contents is in Opie.

1749. [Sarah Fielding.] *The Governess.* By the sister of Henry Fielding. Mrs. Trimmer reconstructed the book in 1820, retaining the title, but omitting what she regarded as undesirable—especially the fairy-tales, although she included one of them—and her edition was frequently reprinted.

1750. *Youth's Entertaining and Instructive Calendar.*

1755. *The Trifle, or Gilded Toy* (4th ed.).

[*c.* 1760.] *The Famous Tommy Thumb's Little Story-Book.* See Opie, facs. of title, etc.

[*c.* 1760.] *The Little Story-Book.*

[c. 1760.] *The Top Book of All.* See Opie, facs. of title, etc.

1761. *The Polite Instructor.*

1761. *A Present for Children* (Edinburgh, 2nd ed.).

1766. *Poetical Blossoms.*

Books Published by John Newbery
(Those marked * are principally recreational)

1744. **Little Pretty Pocket Book.*

1745–6. *Circle of the Seasons.* Ten volumes.

1750. *Alphabet Royal.*
    Nouveau Magazin François.
    New French Primer.
    Young Algebraist's Companion.

1753. **Lilliputian Magazine.* Probably issued first in threepenny parts in 1751.

1753. *Historical Description of the Tower of London.*
    Historical Description of Westminster Abbey.
    Historical Description of St. Paul's Cathedral.

    These three titles are largely based on Boreman's similar publications.

1755. *Spelling Dictionary.*
    New Testament Adapted to the Capacity of Children.

1757. *Letters on Common and Important occasions.*

c. 1757. *Young Man's Companion.*
    * Collection of Pretty Poems. Two series.

1758. *Wonders of Art and Nature.* Four volumes.
    *Fables in Verse . . . by Abraham Aesop.
    *Food for the Mind. A New Riddle-Book. (2nd ed.).
    Bible Abridged.
    *T. Trapwit. Be Merry and Wise. (C.B.E.L. gives 1761.)

c. 1758. **Sixpennyworth of Wit.*
    Museum for Young Gentlemen and Ladies.

1759. *Rollin's Philosophy for Children.*

1760. *The Polite Lady.*
    Atlas Minimus.
    *Nurse Truelove's Christmas Box.
    *Nurse Truelove's New Year's Gift.

1761. *New History of England.*

1762. **Millenium Hall.* Two volumes.
    *Pretty Book of Pictures.
    Pretty Plaything.
    Tom Telescope. *The Newtonian System.* (2nd ed.).
    ——   *Philosophy of Tops and Balls.*

Royal Primer. (This must be a reprint, as Collins of Salisbury valued his share of it at £20 in 1757.)

Goldsmith. *Plutarch's Lives Abridged*. Five vols.

Goldsmith and Newbery. *The Art of Poetry*. Two vols.

1763. **Pretty Book for Children*.

*Little Lottery Book.

Compendious History of the World. Two volumes.

Three Battledores—Royal, British, and Imperial. (The first appeared in Collins of Salisbury's list in 1750 as his "own invention".)

1764. Goldsmith. *History of England*. Two volumes.

[1765?] **Mother Goose's Tales*. (Welsh lists no edition of either this or *Melody* before 1777, when F. Newbery is credited with a seventh edition of the "Tales". Opie, pp. 40 onwards, surmises from this, rather implausibly, that an edition of *Mother Goose's Melody* may have been published by John Newbery in about 1765, and proceeds throughout to quote that as an approximate date.

Whereas the reasoning is fairly convincing as applied to the *Tales*—i.e. the Perrault volume—it remains a fact that no edition of the *Melody* can be attributed to any of the Newbery group earlier than the one entered by T. Carnan on December 28, 1780, for which the only extant evidence is the entry at Stationers' Hall.)

1766. **Goody Two-Shoes*. New edition. (No edition was known to Welsh earlier than the third. Recently, however, two copies of the second edition have come to light, also dated 1766. One is in the Opie collection, the other in the collection of Mr. Edgar Oppenheimer of New York.)

c. 1766. *Rival Pupils*.

1767. **Twelfth-Day Gift*.

*Whitsuntide Gift.

Note.—With the exception of *Mother Goose* the above register of titles is extracted from the ill-digested lists given by Welsh. It includes several books not originated by Newbery, in which he had only a part share. The dates should be regarded with some caution, and, even where no qualification is given, may not always be of the first printing. Welsh's details are frequently taken from newspaper advertisements or lists issued by Newbery; and in many cases no copy of the date listed is known to be extant.

A NOTE ON NURSERY RHYMES

The learned and fascinating *Oxford Dictionary of Nursery Rhymes*, edited by Iona and Peter Opie, is frequently referred to in these pages, and my debt to it is not easily expressed. Nevertheless, for the purpose of the present work, which is a short history of children's *books*, it has one great shortcoming. It has no index to the books quoted, which makes it very difficult to form a satisfactory picture of the place of the nursery rhyme in the history of publishing books for children. I therefore found it useful to my purpose to compile, from the *Dictionary*, a list of the earlier books in it, and to allocate to each the more familiar rhymes first printed therein.

The result has coloured these pages very considerably; and I have therefore though it useful to print the list here and to preface it by a few observations prompted by it.

The first striking fact that emerged from contemplating the list was that although only the second of the two volumes of *Tommy Thumb's Pretty Song Book*—the earliest recorded collection of nursery rhymes as such—has survived, this small book with its miniscule, extravagantly set pages, contains eleven rhymes still familiar to our own children.

Mother Goose's Melody, surmised by the Opies on rather inadequate grounds to have appeared first in about 1765 contains eleven more, and *Gammer Gurton's Garland* (1784) another seven.

The very earliest of nursery rhymes to be recorded in a book written for children is "A was an Archer" in T. W.'s *Little Book* published early in the reign of Queen Anne (i.e. certainly before 1714).

Boreman's "Gigantick Histories" published in the early seventeen-forties contain no nursery rhymes, but are books for children foreshadowing the new era which was to be finally established by the successes of John Newbery.

Without pressing assumption too far it is surely not unreasonable to assume that the gaps which yawn between T. W. and Newbery, one of which is filled in some sort by the writings of Isaac Watts, may be more apparent than real, and that traces will ultimately be found of children's books in that period that have not so far come to light.

It is, in fact, reasonable to assume that, within the eighteenth century at any rate, progress was more general and more dispersed than the few books that have survived would suggest. Neither the year 1744, when Newbery published the *Pretty Pocket Book*, nor 1736, when Boreman produced his first juvenile, can be regarded as a dead-line before which books suitable for children were unknown. The rivalry between the Puritans and the chapmen was fruitful. It was long to continue, with much overlapping and criss-crossing of the two points of view, until gradually something emerged that was fundamentally different from either in the shape of books intended purely for the beguilement of children. It is pleasant to note from the Opies' record that the ancestry of nursery rhymes also extends at least to 1744, if not beyond.

AN ALPHABETICAL LIST OF EARLY NURSERY RHYME COLLECTIONS WITH THE MORE IMPORTANT RHYMES FIRST RECORDED IN EACH

Child's New Play-thing (1743). A was an apple-pie. (This was a spelling-book.)

Christmas Box (1797). Hot cross Buns!

Cock Robin, a pretty gilded toy . . . (c. 1770). (First time in full. First four verses in T. Thumb, q.v.)

Famous Tommy Thumb's Little Song Book (c. 1760). Little Boy Blue. This little pig went to market.

Gammer Gurton's Garland (1784). There was an old woman, who lived in a shoe. Bye, baby bunting. Ride a cock-horse (in modern form; earlier form in *Tommy Thumb* . . . , q.v.). Hark, hark, The dogs do bark. Goosey, goosey gander. A diller, a dollar. Come let's to bed, says Sleepy-head.

Gammer Gurton's Garland (1810). Little Bo-peep. Old chairs to mend. Humpty Dumpty. I love sixpence, jolly little sixpence.

Mother Goose's Melody (c. 1765 (?)). Hush-a-bye baby, on the tree top. Cross-patch, Draw the latch. Two little dicky birds, Sitting on a wall. Ding, dong, bell. Three Wise Men of Gotham. Hey diddle diddle. Jack and Jill. See-saw, Margery Daw. One, two, three, four, five, Once I caught a fish alive. Pease pudding hot. Robin and Richard were two pretty men.

Mother Goose's Quarto (c. 1825). Peter, Peter, pumpkin eater.

Nancy Cock's Pretty Song Book (c. 1780). Taffy was a Welshman.

Newest Christmas Box (c. 1797). Diddle, diddle, dumpling.

Nurse Truelove's New-Year's Gift (1755). The House that Jack Built.

Original Ditties for the Nursery (c. 1805). Cobbler, cobbler, mend my shoe. Little Polly Flinders. Tweedledum and Tweedledee.

Songs for the Nursery (1805). How many miles to Babylon? Bobby Shafto. Little Miss Muffet. One, two, Buckle my shoe. Pussy cat, pussy cat, where have you been? The north wind doth blow.

Tommy Thumb's Pretty Song Book (c. 1744?) Great A, little a, Bouncing B. Ride a Cock-horse (not in its modern form, which is first in *Gammer Gurton's Garland*, q.v.). Baa, baa, black sheep. Cock Robin (first four verses only; entire rhyme see *Cock Robin . . .*) Hickory, dickory, dock. Ladybird, ladybird. There was a little man, and he had a little gun. Mary, Mary, quite contrary. Oranges and lemons. Little Tommy Tucker. Sing a Song of Sixpence.

Top Book of All (c. 1760). A gaping, wide-mouthed, waddling frog.

T. W. *A Little Book for Little Children* (c. 1712). A was an Archer.

STRUWWELPETER

This is a suitable point at which to add a note on this famous German nursery rhyme which, since its translation into English in 1848, has achieved a success in our nurseries rivalling its popularity in Germany.

Heinrich Hoffmann, the author and illustrator of the book, was a physician in Frankfort and he has himself told the story of how the book originated. He found that there were no books suitable for the entertainment of his young patients, and when they were brought to him for treatment he would frequently dispel their anxiety and tears by drawing a funny picture in his notebook. He added verses to some of these drawings and presented the album to his own children at Christmas time. It was a great success, and was often produced for the admiration of friends, among whom were Loening and Rütten, publishers who had recently founded the *Literarische Anstalt*. They suggested publication; and they found their new author as pernicketty as Macmillan were later to find Dodgson.

He insisted on seeing proofs of the coloured lithographs at every stage of their progress. "I visited the artist daily," he wrote, "to ensure that my amateurish style was not artistically improved and idealised. He was compelled to copy stroke by stroke exactly, and I checked every one of the stones."

The first edition was of 1,500 copies, and the price was 59 kreuzer, so that, as Hoffmann insisted, the buyer might think, "Why! it costs less than one guilder."

32   An early use (1775) of a subject that became very popular

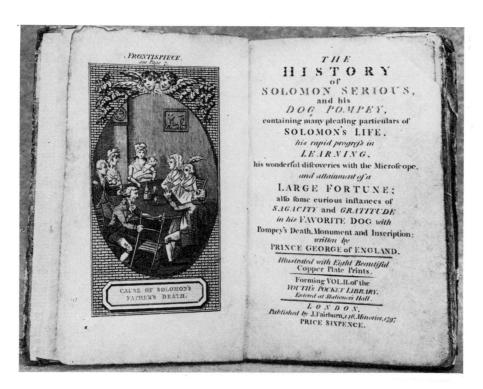

33   One of Fairburn's earliest publications (1797)

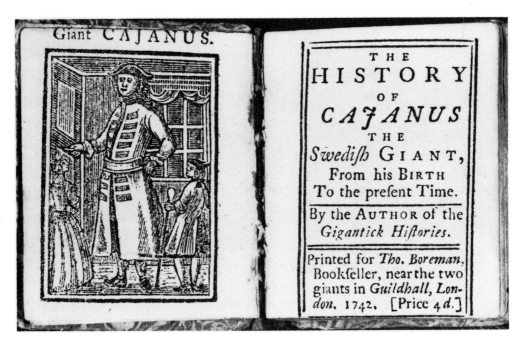

Giant CAJANUS.

THE HISTORY OF CAJANUS

THE Swedish GIANT,

From his BIRTH To the prefent Time.

By the AUTHOR of the *Gigantick Hiftories.*

Printed for *Tho. Boreman,* Bookfeller, near the two giants in *Guildhall, London,* 1742. [Price 4*d.*]

34   The last book known to have been published by Boreman (1742)

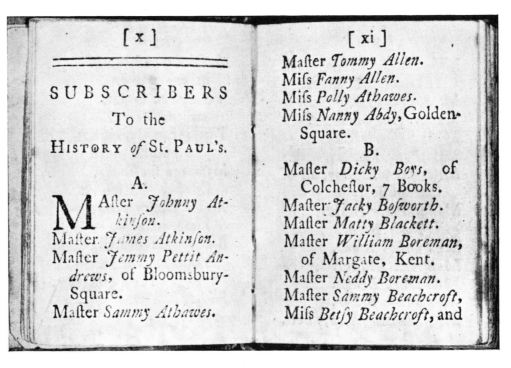

[x]

SUBSCRIBERS To the HISTORY *of* St. PAUL'S.

A.

Mafter *Johnny Atkinfon.*
Mafter *James Atkinfon.*
Mafter *Jemmy Pettit Andrews,* of Bloomsbury-Square.
Mafter *Sammy Athawes.*

[xi]

Mafter *Tommy Allen.*
Mifs *Fanny Allen.*
Mifs *Polly Athawes.*
Mifs *Nanny Abdy,* Golden-Square.

B.

Mafter *Dicky Boys,* of Colchefter, 7 Books.
Mafter *Jacky Bofworth.*
Mafter *Matty Blackett.*
Mafter *William Boreman,* of Margate, Kent.
Mafter *Neddy Boreman.*
Mafter *Sammy Beachcroft,*
Mifs *Betfy Beachcroft,* and

35   Part of the subscribers' list in Boreman's *History of St. Paul's*, 1741

Hoffmann also instructed the publisher to bind the book in boards so that copies should not last too long, and parents would be compelled to replace them.

The book was published in 1845, but undated, and was not called "Struwwelpeter" but *Lustige Geschichten und drollige Bilder*—"Jolly Tales and Funny Pictures" and Shock-headed Peter appeared only at the end of the book. The first edition was sold out in four weeks, and was constantly reprinted. It was translated into English—and several other languages—in 1848, the foreign editions being issued by a Leipzig publisher, who distributed them through his agents abroad.

[1845.] *Lustige Geschichten und drollige Bilder* . . . (Frankfurt A. M., *Literarische Anstalt*). Fifteen leaves, the pictures are printed by lithography and hand-coloured. Second edition has twenty leaves with the addition of "Zappelphilip" and "Die gar treurige Geschichte mit dem Feuerzeug". In the third edition the pictures were rearranged and the title was changed to: *Der Struwelpeter*. To the fourth edition three pages were added with "Hans Guck in der Luft". The fifth was the first complete edition to which yet another story was added "Der fliegende Robert". This was the first edition in which the pictures were printed from wood-blocks, also hand-coloured. (Additional information gratefully acknowledged to Mr. Walter Schatzki.'

1848. *The English Struwwelpeter; or Pretty Stories and Funny Pictures for Little Children. After the Sixth Edition of the Celebrated German Work of Dr. Heinrich Hoffmann*. Leipsic [sic], *Friedrich Volckmar. 1848*. The first English edition, which was marketed here by Williams & Norgate.

1868 The illustrations were redrawn and printed from wood blocks, coloured by stencils. In this form "Peter" first assumed the aspect now familiar to us, with hair on end; but the first use of the English version of the title "Shockheaded Peter", has not been discovered.

R. E. RASPE

1786. Baron Munchausen's Narrative of his Marvellous Travels and Campaigns in Russia . . . Oxford : Printed for the Editor . . .

This would be most suitably included among the "adopted" books. It was not originally intended for children, but soon became exceedingly popular with them.

The best discussion of the authorship and history of the book is by John Carswell, in the introduction and appendix to the text edited by him for the Cresset Press in 1948.

CHAPTER THREE

A MONSTROUS REGIMENT

THE seed sown by the Puritans was not set in stony ground; it was just a particularly unfruitful kind of seed. By rather haphazard experiment and selection a more graceful type of plant was gradually emerging. There were still no real experts at work, and experiments were very much of the hit-or-miss variety. Authors had made their contribution; and then it had been the turn of the publishers; but it was not until after Newbery's death that anything like an organised onslaught on the youthful market was attempted. Once convinced that juvenile literature could be made to pay more ambitious methods of catering for the young readers were soon in evidence. Hitherto the writing or compiling of the books had been either a leisure-hour occupation of the publisher himself, or had been commissioned from hack writers, at least one of them an inspired hack, regularly employed by these publishers, and ready to turn their hands to whatever might be required.

Before the end of the eighteenth century, however, there began to emerge writers with a special turn for producing stories for children, and it is not surprising that most of them were women. Mrs. Barbauld, Mrs. Trimmer, the Kilner sisters-in-law, Lady Eleanor Fenn, and, later, the Taylors, Mary Elliot, Miss Edgeworth, and Mrs. Sherwood were in the forefront of this new batch of writers. Mostly gentlewomen, satisfied with a modest return for their equally modest labours—from 10,000 to 15,000 words would amply fill an average-sized volume—they were indefatigable.

Like the original moves in the production of children's books, this change of front in the direction of commissioned authors seems to have been spontaneous and general, and to date, almost rigidly, from the year 1780. Joseph Johnson[1] published Mrs. Barbauld, Marshall the Kilners and Lady Eleanor Fenn, Longman sponsored Mrs. Trimmer—although Marshall was the publisher of her famous ''Descriptions'', which were very early attempts to teach children from pictures.

Elizabeth Newbery had also begun to engage special writers, but they contain no notable names unless Samuel Richardson authorised her abridgements of his

[1] He was William Cowper's publisher, but the ballad-sheet on which *The History of John Gilpin* was probably first published in about 1782 was not originally intended for children, although they very soon adopted it. It became very early on a favourite subject for jig-saw puzzle makers, and the chase was an obvious subject for the devisers of board games.

novels, which is doubtful.[1] But the Newbery family had lost their former supremacy in children's book publishing, which had now definitely passed to the Marshalls, in Aldermary Churchyard, and later in Queen Street, Cheapside.

There is a mystery about the publishing family of Marshall for the solution of which insufficient evidence is available. From 1695 to 1726 there was a bookseller-publisher of that name at the Bible in Gracechurch Street, and one Joseph Marshall was at the Bible in Newgate Street between 1707 and 1734. The first John Marshall was known as a publisher of chapbooks[2]; but Ashton gives reproductions of the title-pages of many chapbooks of this period, and the great majority of the London ones have the imprint: "Printed and Sold in Aldermary Churchyard". It seems impossible to doubt that there is a distinct connection between the two John Marshalls. Unfortunately, the most important point for the present purpose, the question of when Marshall began to turn his attention from chapbooks, as such, which included some for children, to actual children's books in the Newbery style, cannot be settled with any degree of certainty.

The children's writers were not exclusively females. Thomas Day is one very notable exception to the general rule. Stockdale was the original publisher of *Sandford and Merton*, first as a long-short story in 1783, extended to a further volume in 1786, and to a third in 1789.

A cut from a Dublin edition of Mrs. Pilkington's *Historical Beauties for Young Ladies, intended to lead the female mind to the love and practice of Moral Goodness . . .* published in 1800 illustrates a fair specimen of the lower order of books turned out by women at the time. Entitled "Ingratitude" and depicting an early version of "never darken my doors again", it more or less illustrates the hardy old favourite story "Incle and Yarico" a popular version of Rousseau's noble savage.

There is a certain family likeness about most of this group of women writers. They had obviously studied the previous output of children's publishers, and had made up their minds that they could do exactly the same sort of thing, only very much better than it had been done before. Therefore all their books are strongly flavoured with morals.

Dorothy Kilner, who usually wrote over the pseudonym "M. P."—the initials of the Essex village of Maryland Point in which she and her sister lived—was less offensively addicted to moralising than some of the others; and yet her *Village School*—one of her most obstinate successes—reads very thinly and nauseatingly to-day.

Young Jacob Steadfast is the central character—a kind of peg on whom the little histories are hung. His father tells him of the sad fate of Ralph Breakclod, who told stories, and played truant from school. Sent to take a pie to his aged grandmother,

---

[1] Three of Richardson's novels had been "familiarised and adapted to the capacity of youth" already in 1756. This volume bears the imprint of R. Baldwin, who was also one of the sponsor's of *The Top Book of All* (c. 1760). (See p. 94.)

[2] See Darton, p. 71, for a transcription of his advertisement.

he ate it all himself; wishing to play truant to join children from another school, who had a day's holiday, he feigned an injured leg, but was caught running races with the others. At last this consistent little liar was run over by a chaise, but, incredibly enough, his parents preferred to think that his tale was just another of his lies, although he was really mortally injured. "The violent pain of his back brought on a fever, and he died in about a week. . . ."

On the other hand, when Mr. Right, the squire, finds Jacob Steadfast absent from school and is wont to punish him, it turns out that Jacob had been engaged in tenderly restoring to its owner a little lamb with a broken leg. His father, of course, not only approves of this benevolent cause of his truancy, but reads him a short lecture on kindness to dumb creatures. "When children are tormenting flies, or any other insects, and pulling off their legs and wings,[1] they should consider how *they* would like to have *their* arms and legs pulled off: and they may be assured, that the poor fly is hurt to the full as much, though it cannot scream as they would."

Jacob tells how Mrs. Peatlove, the owner of the lamb, rewarded him with a nice large piece of plum-cake and an orange. "I would have brought them home for you and my mother," he says, "only Mrs. Bell [the schoolmistress] says, that it does not look civil to put cake or fruit into one's pocket. . . ." Mr. Right's only cavil, when told the story, is that Jacob should have run home first to ask leave to miss school in order to take the lambkin back. Incidentally, he presents him with a reward in the shape of "a most entertaining book called, *The Memoirs of a Peg-Top*". This was another of Miss Kilner's own works, and it seems that Mr. Right always obtained his school-prizes from among the "pretty new books from Mr. Marshall, the printer in London". Girls mostly received housewives and pincushions. Mr. Right reproves Roger Riot who read books only for the sake of the pretty stories. This is very wrong, for books are intended to improve our minds and morals.

There is a nauseating fascination about these arch and insipid anecdotes that tempts one to continue to quote them. But they are all very much of a piece, and whether the pivot of the story is a child, a mouse, a peg-top, or a pincushion, they are all variations on similar themes.

The Kilners, Lady Eleanor Fenn, Priscilla Wakefield, and others like them, had no preconceptions beyond turning out persuasive didacticisms of the sort that publishers could sell—the demand was possibly more from parents than from the children themselves.

Sarah Trimmer was a very different kind of person. She was a campaigner, she had principles, theories, strong views on what was bad for children, even more than on what was good for them. She was terrifyingly familiar with all that had been written for them in the past, and she disapproved of most of it. She belied her name, for opinions more forthright, or more forcibly expressed, than hers it would be difficult to imagine. She was an almost complete throwback to the predestinarians of the Calvinistic period. Like them, she believed that

1 Most of these writers reprehend this revolting habit, which suggests its prevalence.

THE ELEGANT GIRL,

OR

Virtuous Principles the true Source

OF

Elegant Manners,

Illustrated by Twelve Drawings with Lines to each,

and a Poem called

THE MOTHER.

Entered at Stationers Hall & Published for the Proprietor, by S. Inman, Nº 7, Lambs Conduit Street, London.

36   An elaborate imitation of Ann Taylor's *My Mother*, c. 1807

37 An illustrated edition of
Miss Edgeworth, 1854

What is so hateful to the sight.
What can so soon deform
Features intended to delight.
As passion's angry storm?

see Page 10.

38 Frontispiece to *Flowers of Instruction*
by Mary Elliott, 1820

children were naturally sinful creatures to be rescued from their own satanic impulses.[1]

This preposterous woman did produce one book that achieved an obstinate success. It was originally called *Fabulous Histories*, and was published by Longman in 1786. In a later edition the title was changed to the more familiar *History of the Robins*. It must have been written with more than one eye on the parents, the preface betrays the fact completely. The parent robins, she says, represent a loving father and mother of a human family, and although it is necessary that the little birds should be made to talk to one another, her aim is not to suggest the real subject or method of bird conversation, but "to convey moral instruction" applicable to the children who read her book, while also inclining them against wanton cruelty to the animal creation. The constant preoccupation with cruelty to animals undoubtedly suggests a certain depravity in the children of the time.

Principally, however, she was a writer about children, rather than for them. Her main concern was to instil into parents a knowledge of what she conceived to be the true principles of moral upbringing. She furthered this purpose not only by writing several books of guidance, and by the undoubtedly ingenious series of educational prints already referred to, but by founding, in 1802, a periodical called *The Guardian of Education*, which she continued until 1806. In its pages she made her notorous attack on fairy-stories, which she thought it positively sinful to allow children to read. *Cinderella*, for example, she thought to be one of the worst stories ever written for children, depicting the vilest of human passions, "envy, jealousy, a dislike for mothers-in-law [she probably means step-mothers] and half-sisters, vanity, a love of dress, etc., etc."[2] Janeway and Thomas White must have been comforted in their Puritan heaven that this holy woman should arise to rekindle their rather smoky torch a century or more after their death. She was, however, a pioneer in the education of small children by the use of pictures.[3]

Mrs. Trimmer was ably seconded by Mrs. Sherwood, the originator of the mission-field story for children, a prolific writer, whose message is typified in the title of her most successful book, *The History of the Fairchild Family, or the Child's Manual, being a collection of Stories calculated to show the importance and effects of a religious education*. This truly appalling book was based on an explicit belief in original sin and the tendency of children to prefer evil courses to good. Mrs. Sherwood could not leave ill alone for, having published the first part of the "History" in 1818, she continued it in 1842, and her married daughter helped in the production of a final instalment in 1847. Nearly one hundred books and tracts of an evangelical nature are credited to her, among them a bowdlerised edition of Miss Fielding's *The Governess*, in which she was very severe on the fairy-stories contained in it.

Mrs. Sherwood's books have to be seen to be believed. Some hint of her

---

[1] Berquin, whose *L'Ami des Enfants* is a treasure-house of moral tales almost as greatly favoured in England as in France, admired Mrs. Trimmer's works intensely.

[2] Quoted by Darton, pp. 96–7.   [3] See p. 94.

approach may be gathered from her seven extensive and tedious volumes entitled *The Lady of the Manor*, uncompromisingly subtitled *A Series of conversations on the Subject of Confirmation. Intended for the Use of the Middle and Higher Ranks of Young Females*. But she is at her very best, or worst, in *The History of the Fairchild Family*. Guardians and parents must surely bear the ignominy of the continual reprinting of this dreadful compilation throughout the nineteenth century. One wonders how many children, under their own steam, would get beyond the introduction, in which, after Papa has introduced the children to the globe of the world which has just arrived from town, and has given them a lesson in geography, one of his unnatural children begs to be shown where the Garden of Eden was, the response to which closes the lesson.

Thereupon, Lucy, little beast, pipes up, "Papa, may we say some verses about mankind having evil hearts?" Permission being given, each of the three little monsters quotes a gloomy passage from Scripture. This leads to a homily from Papa on the complete and utter corruption of the human heart, whereupon little Henry caps all by exclaiming, "Oh! I wish I could love the Lord Jesus Christ more than I do; but my wicked heart will not let me." This sort of thing continues for more than 540 closely printed pages, each of them crammed with the sternest sort of piety.

The point of view inherited by Mesdames Trimmer and Sherwood from the Elders of Puritanism is by no means extinct. Mr. Geoffrey Handley-Taylor is the active spirit of a movement calling itself "True Aim", which is attempting to lead a campaign for "Nursery Rhyme Reform". Deploring the low moral tone, the sadism, and violence of roughly one-half of the well-known ditties, he has compiled a statistical analysis of unsavoury elements found in approximately one hundred rhymes. There are, he tells us, and alas a careful study of Opie bears him out, twenty-six instances of violent death by choking, squeezing, shrivelling, boiling, and so on. Self-inflicted injuries, kidnappings, whippings, maimings, lunacy, drunkenness, house-burning, and racial discrimination are common features, while "Expressions of fear, moans of anguish, biting, pain and evidence of supreme selfishness may be found in almost every other page".

He or his lieutenants have suggested or completed the rewriting of various popular nursery ditties, with new titles such as "Who'll Wed Cock Robin?", "Taffy was a Welshman, Taffy was a Chief", and other such shaggy doggerel. Among noted aversions of True-Blue Aimers are "Pussy's in the Well", "There was a Little Man", "Three Blind Mice", and "The Jolly Miller".

Miss Edgeworth and the Taylors

It is pleasant to record that the first revulsion from monstrosities of this kind was also shown by women writers. Maria Edgeworth was among the first and the most important of those who, while retaining the unmistakable flavour of moral powder, were at least possessed of a sufficient narrative gift to improve the quality of the jam and to provide it in more generous proportion. Her father thought

Thomas Day the most virtuous creature he had ever met, and poor Maria, who worshipped her father, submitted willingly to being experimented upon in accordance with the notions of that wild theorist. Day originally wrote *Sandford and Merton* as a short story for inclusion in a projected serial work of Maria's father, called *Practical Education* (1780), in which, however, Day's story was not printed. The mixture of British manliness and French noble savagery exemplified by the two principal characters in Day's curious book is too familiar to need summarising here.[1] But the disciplinary theories of contemporary educationalists are seen in all their incredible crudity in the story of Maria's being regularly hung by the neck at school in order to increase her stature.

In 1796 Joseph Johnson published the first part of Miss Edgeworth's *The Parent's Assistant*[2] (37), which consisted of the usual preface "Addressed to Parents" and ten stories for children. The series was eventually enlarged to six volumes, and was later rearranged so that the stories for younger children were transferred to another series, *Early Lessons*. But the original series was already typical of Miss Edgeworth's contribution, and contained one story which she greatly liked herself, and which remained a prime favourite. This was *The Purple Jar*. It belongs to the same family as the stories of other, earlier writers, and it is difficult to explain just why it is so immensely superior. Rosamond, who became the eponymous heroine of a further series of stories, appears for the first time in this one. She covets the purple jar in an apothecary's window, and insists on preferring it to the new pair of shoes that is offered her instead. Her folly is brought home to her when her shoes wear out, and there is no money to buy her another pair. She admits then that she would have been wiser to choose the shoes, and she hopes, although she is not certain, that she will be more sensible another time.

Her father's matrimonial adventures had largely entailed upon Maria the upbringing of his nineteen children, by his four wives, and she remembered the waywardness of her own childhood, when, despite the harshness of discipline, she had wrecked her father's greenhouses for the sheer pleasure of hearing the sound of broken glass.

Ann (b. 1782) and Jane (b. 1783) Taylor may well have read Miss Edgeworth's stories when they were children,[3] although they were probably rather too late for them; but they were not far behind Miss Edgeworth in beginning a brilliant career as writers for young children themselves. There is some confusion as to the fate of their literary début. It seems certainly to have taken place in a children's annual called *The Minor's Pocket Book*. Stewart definitely states that Ann began to contribute to its

---

[1] A note on it, with a summary, will be found on pp. 91 ff.

[2] As with her father's *Practical Education* (1780), no copy of the first edition of this book appears to be extant. No copy of any edition of the first volume of Part II has survived. It almost certainly contained the first printing of *The Purple Jar*.

[3] Ann reviewed one of the volumes of Miss Edgeworth's "Tales" in the *Eclectic*, and Miss Edgeworth wrote to her of the poem *The Chatterbox*, in *Original Poems* (1804), "Perhaps, Madam, it may be written by you [it was]; and it will give you pleasure to hear that it is a favourite with four good talkers of nine, six, five and four years old."

pages in 1799, using the pseudonym of "Juvenilia". The date of first publication of the 'Pocket Book' is uncertain. It is very rare and no surviving copies have been located. Armitage prints the following letter:

"Isaac Taylor.   London, 1st. 6 mo. 1803.
    Respected Friend,
        We have received some pieces of poetry from some branches of thy family for the *Minor's Pocket Book*, and we beg that the enclosed trifles may be divided among such as are most likely to be pleased with them. My principal reason for writing now is to request that when any of their harps be tuned and their muse in good humour; if they could give me some specimens of easy poetry for young children, I would endeavour to make a suitable return in cash, or in books. . . ."

The date and the use of the second person singular in the letter betray its Quaker origin, and it was indeed from the firm of Darton and Harvey, the senior partner of which had set up in business as a publisher of juveniles in Gracechurch Street in about 1785. Both this firm, and a junior branch, started by a younger William Darton in Holborn Hill in about 1801, were extremely active in this sphere, and several of their authors were great favourites, like Mary Elliott. But none achieved the deserved popularity of the Taylor sisters.

The letter just quoted resulted in the two volumes of *Original Poems for Infant Minds*[1] (1804–5), not all the contents of which were by the two sisters, however. Others were added by Adelaide O'Keefe, the daughter of an Irish dramatist and song-writer, who was otherwise responsible for three or four rather undistinguished books for children.

"Twinkle, twinkle, little star", the best-known poem that either of them ever wrote, is not contained in these volumes. It came first in *Rhymes for the Nursery* (1806). But the first book includes at least two poems that rivalled it in popularity at the time. "My Mother" was reprinted in as many varied forms (36), and imitated as widely as *Robinson Crusoe*, and "Meddlesome Matty" is a delightful jingle, in which the very mild moral is only lightly stressed and is really more amusing than minatory. One short poem, from the 1806 volume, will suffice to show what a mastery of their subject the sisters possessed. The "Star" poem was by Jane; "The Field Daisy" is by Ann:

> I'm a pretty little thing,
> Always coming with the spring;
> In the meadows green I'm found,
> Peeping just above the ground,
> And my stalk is covered flat,
> With a white and yellow hat.

[1] Armitage quotes Ann as authority for the payment the sisters received for this tenacious success. For the first volume they were paid £5, but a second £5 was paid later. For the second volume the payment was £15, and for *Rhymes for the Nursery* (1806) they received £20. This may be contrasted with their profits on *Hymns for Infant Minds* (1810) which they published at their own risk, and received £150 profit in the first year of publication.

Little lady, when you pass
Lightly o'er the tender grass,
Skip about, but do not tread
On my meek and healthy head,
For I always seem to say,
"Surely winter's gone away".

Throughout the whole of their work there is never a trace of smugness or priggishness, or hardly ever, and when there is, as in Jane's "Mischief", or "Idleness", or "The Folly of Finery", it is carried off with such a light touch that it is quite inoffensive. By far the best version of "The World Turned Upside Down" is that of the two sisters, published by Tabart in 1810, and illustrated by their brother Isaac. Both showed an occasional taste for the macabre, as in Jane's rather horrid "Little Fisherman"; but Ann reserved it for her few poems for adults, of which "The Maniac's Song" is a powerful specimen.

Here, at last, were books that children surely chose for themselves, albeit with the undoubted approval of their elders.

There is little need to enlarge on the other writers of the period. The Taylors far surpassed them all, and most of the rest were much of a muchness.

A NOTE ON "SANDFORD AND MERTON"

Originally written for inclusion in R. L. Edgeworth's *Practical Education* (1780), the first version, complete in itself, was, however, first printed in 1783. The second and third parts, published in 1787 and 1789, were sequels to the first part. The work was frequently reprinted, both in full and abridged.

The title is now more familiar than its contents, for it is doubtful whether many modern readers will find the persistence needed to plough through it. The book is important, not only for its exceedingly wide and persistent reprinting, but also because it is the best and most complete example of the moral "stories" which were the most generally provided reading for children at the time.

The History of Sandford and Merton is a feast of nausea. It is so ludicrously serious in its preposterous moralisings that, in small doses, it makes hilarious reading, especially aloud. The first volume is the longest of the three, and also the worst. Darton calls it "a great work", describes it as "a vivacious attempt to present *Émile* in the guise of fiction for English boys", and adds that "Day could tell a story". It is true that a certain degree of narrative power is evident, the trouble is that there is an almost complete lack of narrative. There is, in fact, no narrative whatsoever in the main thread of the book; and although several stories are interspersed—the best being in the third volume—Day constantly interrupts himself. He is so overwhelmingly conscious of his moral and instructional purpose that he hamstrings nearly all the stories to indulge it.

Harry Sandford is a sturdy little farmer's son, he is also the world's prize prig.

He had only once ever ill-treated a dumb creature, when he twirled a cockchafer fastened to a thread by a crooked pin. When his father told him that this was equivalent to the thrusting of a knife through his own hand he burst into tears, took the poor insect home, restored it to life by feeding it with fresh leaves, and then liberated it in the fresh air. Thereafter he would step out of his way to avoid hurting a worm, and would often go supperless to bed that he might feed the poor, starving robin-redbreasts during periods of frost and snow. He preferred dry bread for his dinner to any kind of sweetmeat or fruit, and he knew that "we must only eat when we are hungry, and drink when we are thirsty . . . this was the way the Apostles did, who were all very good men".

Tommy Merton is a poor little rich boy, with servants to wait on him, fine clothes to wear, and doting parents. Harry saves him from the attack of a poisonous snake, and, as a result, Tommy is placed under the same preceptor as Harry—the sententious Mr. Barlow, who is the local clergyman. Thereafter, by Socratic methods, the whole of the first volume is devoted to teaching Tommy—Harry has already absorbed the teaching—that "the rich do nothing and produce nothing, and the poor do everything that is really useful", while the most admirable thing in the whole creation is "the savage grandeur of man in his most simple state".

All the stories introduced into the early part of the book show this same antithesis between the natural virtue of the poor and the viciousness of the rich, as such; and, lest the point should escape a youthful reader, the aforesaid interruptions are constantly indulged. These may be instructional, as when Harry makes some casual reference to the Spartans, whereupon Tommy, who shows the most abysmal ignorance about everything, asks who they were. "Why, you must know," says the ever-resourceful Harry, "they were a very brave set of people . . ." and we are off on a side-track again. Should Mr. Barlow mention a camel, a crocodile, or an elephant in the course of one of his stories, the little ignoramus will inevitably pipe up his question in his thirst for knowledge, and he will invariably find Mr. Barlow ready to go off at a tangent to oblige him. The information is by no means unexceptionable, as when it is stated that crocodiles, if humanely treated, are quite docile, and will give little children rides on their backs; or, again, when Mr. Barlow rescues the two boys from an escaped performing bear, he pooh-poohs their adulation of his bravery by telling them that most animals are easily awed by the appearance of intrepidity.

Simple savages, like "the Black" befriended by good little Harry, tell their personal story in most elegant language. When "the Black" is expounding on the housing methods of his African tribe and their simple requirements, he says, "with us a few reeds twisted together, and perhaps daubed over with slime or mud, compose the whole of our dwellings. Yet the innocent Negro would sleep as happy and contented as you do in your palaces, were you not to drag him by fraud and violence away, and force him to endure all the excesses of your cruelty". Or, describing the feasts which follow a successful hunt, "These are intended at once to reward those who have performed so gallant an achievement, and to encourage a spirit of enterprise in the rest of the nation".

But then all the characters talk like that, there is not the slightest differentiation between them, except for stupid and thoughtless Tommy and the intolerable know-it-all Harry, and there is an absolute and complete lack of any sense of humour.

Tommy's education is completed in the first volume, and he becomes a model citizen. In the second volume Harry stays with him in the Merton household, and soon shows that he is not only a prig, but also a bore. At a house-party he yawns and stretches, and finally falls asleep in the middle of a pianoforte recital, with no rebuke from the author. Tommy, on the other hand, falls back into his old sins, but is plucked once more, and finally, from the burning in the third volume, which, however, is a great improvement on the other two. Whereas the first volume is nothing but a vehicle of instruction, absolutely all powder and no jam—and Mr. Day is an adept at keeping his powder dry!—there are two quite acceptable narratives in the last volume, the reminiscences of the old Highlander who fought in the American wars being really thrilling at times.

One cannot help wondering why this masterpiece of sentimentality and bathos had such a long run.[1] It must be presumed that on the one hand it was a greater success with parents than with children, and on the other hand that children lapped it up in the absence of anything better.

But the book runs true to form to the very end. In the final paragraph Tommy is taking leave of Harry to return home, and does so thus:"'To your example I owe most of the little good that I can boast; you have taught me how much better it is to be useful than rich or fine—how much more amiable to be good than to be great. Should I be ever tempted to relapse . . . I will return hither for instruction, and I hope you will receive me.' Saying this, he shook his friend Harry affectionately by the hand, and, with watery eyes, accompanied his father home."

Kingsley must have profited by *Sandford and Merton* when he wrote "Be good, sweet maid, and let who will be clever"; although he needed no encouragement; and it seems a fitting commentary on both writers that J. H. Campe seized on Day's book for German translation immediately it appeared.

Day wrote one other story which acquired great popularity in the nineteenth century, partly because it was exactly the right length for chapbook publication. This was *The History of Little Jack*, which appeared in Stockdale's *Children's Miscellany* in 1787, with illustrations by John Bewick. The *Miscellany* was frequently reprinted as a whole, and *Little Jack* seems to have started as a separate publication in 1788.

Books Applicable to this Chapter

There is woefully little on the women writers for children who were active at the turn of the eighteenth–nineteenth centuries. Mrs. Slade's *Maria Edgeworth* (1767–1849;

[1] One of my copies is a Sunday-school prize of 1883, just one hundred years after the original appearance of the first instalment.

Constable, 1937) is a model of what such a work should be. Basically a bibliography, and a very good one, it is compiled in the modern manner with extensive notes concerning her life, the conditions of publication, and the like.

C. D. Stewart, *The Taylors of Ongar*. Two volumes, Garland Publishing, Inc., is now the standard work. It is exhaustive and exhausting; a warning to collectors of the virtual impossibility of building a complete collection of their first editions. D. M. Armitage, *The Taylors of Ongar*. Cambridge; Heffer, 1939 is a labour of love by a descendant. Badly arranged and inadequately indexed, it makes pleasant reading and contains information not available elsewhere.

The most informative sources for the other authors in this chapter are the *Dictionary of National Biography* and Allibone's *Critical Dictionary of English Literature*.

BOOKS BY THE "MONSTROUS REGIMENT"

A selection only of the more important writers is given. Further titles may be sought as follows: For Maria Edgeworth, in the excellent bibliography by Mrs. Slade, published by Constable in 1937; for the Taylors, see Armitage, *The Taylors of Ongar* (Heffer, 1939; not bibliographical, but the best reference available); for other writers, see the lists in *D.N.B.* and *C.B.E.L.*, vol. II.

1762. [Sarah Scott and Lady Barbara Montagu]. *A Description of Millenium Hall*. Goldsmith may have revised the text before publication.

HANNAH MORE

1762 or 1766. *A Search after Happiness: a pastoral By a Young Lady*.

1782. *Sacred Dramas*. These were intended to be learned by heart, and/or performed by young people instead of less edifying dramas. Between 1795 and 1798 she and her sister produced the well-known series of Cheap Repository Tracts, which were partly aimed at children. A complete list of titles is in *Notes and Queries*, September 24, October 8 and 29, 1864. The circulation of the tracts is said to have reached two million copies in the first year. This worthy effort led to the foundation of the Religious Tract Society.

SARAH TRIMMER

1782–4. *Sacred History* . . . Six volumes. This was the first of Mrs. Trimmer's series of prints, with explanations. She also covered English History and Roman History. Each series consisted of an extensive number of engravings to be displayed on the walls of the nursery or school-room, with accompanying volumes of explanatory text. All the collections were frequently reprinted.

Her attack on fairy-tales is in her periodical *The Guardian of Education* (1802–4), most of the contents of which she wrote herself.

1786. *Fabulous Histories*. The title was later changed to *The History of the Robins*.

ANNA LAETITIA BARBAULD AND JOHN AIKIN

1782–6. *Evenings at Home*. Six volumes.

39   (*above*) Tabart & Co. (from about 1800 onwards)

40   (*left*) From a book published by Newman in 1829

41   (*right*) Stall at a fair, *c.* 1878

42   (*below*) Harris's premises, formerly
Newbery (from about 1770 onwards)

WHERE CHILDREN'S BOOKS WERE SOLD

44 "Dicky" Doyle's frontispiece to Ruskin's *The King*

43 Newbery's successors at their worst

LADY ELEANOR FENN

[1783.] *Cobwebs to Catch Flies.* Two volumes.
    Rational Sports.
    Fables, by Mrs. Teachwell. Marshall c. 1794.
    Fables in Monosyllables, by Mrs. Teachwell . . . Children from Four to Six.
    Morals to a set of Fables.

DOROTHY AND MARY ANN KILNER

    Life and Perambulations of a Mouse. Two volumes.
    The Village School. Two volumes.
    Memoirs of a Peg-Top.
    Jemima Placid.
    Adventures of a Pincushion

    There is a considerable uncertainty as to the dating and authorship of books by these two sisters. The books are rarely dated, but were probably published—originally by Marshall—between 1783 and 1790. Dorothy used the pseudonym "M. P.", variously accounted for as the initials of the village of Maryland Point, where she lived, or of Mary Pelham: Mary Ann used the initials "S. S.".

LUCY PEACOCK

1785. *Adventures of the Six Princesses of Babylon.*
1802. *The Little Emigrant.*

MARY WOLLSTONECRAFT

    Original Stories from Real Life. (1788. New ed. with plates by William Blake.)

MRS. PINCHARD

1791. *The Blind Child . . . by a Lady*
1792. *Dramatic Dialogues.* Two volumes.

CHARLOTTE SMITH

1795. *Rural Walks.*

MARIA EDGEWORTH

1796. *The Parent's Assistant.* Two volumes in three parts. By "E. M." on the title-page.
    No set, or part of a set, of the first edition is known, but F. Algar had one of the parts.
1796. *The Parent's Assistant; or, Stories for Children* (Second edition). Three volumes.
    Of this edition only two volumes are extant, apparently the first and the third. (See Slade for the complicated details.)
1800. The third edition, in six volumes. With extra stories.

1801. *Early Lessons*. Ten volumes. The first two volumes of this series contain the story of "Harry and Lucy", which was the work of Maria's father and had already been printed in *Practical Education*, Vol. II (1780). (No copy of Vol. I is known.) The remainder of the volumes contain similar stories by Maria, some of them reprinted and others continued from *Early Lessons*. (On the rarity of the early editions, see Slade.)

PRISCILLA WAKEFIELD

1795–8. *Juvenile Anecdotes*. Two volumes.
1801(?). *The Juvenile Travellers*.

MRS. PILKINGTON

1797. *Edward Barnard, or merit exacted.*
   Obedience Rewarded.

ELIZABETH HELME

1798. *Instructive Rambles in London, and the adjacent villages*. Two volumes.

MARY PILKINGTON

1798. *Tales of the Hermitage.*
   A Mirror for the Female Sex.
1802. *Marvellous Adventures; or, The Vicissitudes of a Cat.*

ELIZABETH SANDHAM

1799. *The Happy Family at Sandham House.*
1822. *The History of Elizabeth Woodville.*

ANN AND JANE TAYLOR

1804–5. *Original Poems for Infant Minds*. Two volumes (Adelaide O'Keefe contributed a few poems, but was unknown to the Taylors. Other poems were by her father and brother and Bernard Barton.) Contains "My Mother", "The Pin", and "Meddlesome Matty" by Ann; "The Gleaner", "Mischief", and "The Cow and The Ass" by Jane.
1806. *Rhymes for the Nursery*. Contains "Twinkle, twinkle, little star" by Jane and "The Field Daisy" by Ann.
1808. *Hymns for Infant Minds*. The sisters were less successful with their hymns than with their secular verses. Although Ann's are usually better than Jane's the latter is responsible for the only hymn of theirs that is at all familiar to-day—"There is a path that leads to God." In 1844 Ann added to the "35th edition", a further twenty-three hymns of her own composition. In 1886 Ann's son, Josiah, edited a "definitive" edition in which the authorship of each hymn is indicated.

1810. *Signor Topsy Turvey's Wonderful Magic Lantern, or the World turned Upside Down.* Cuts by Isaac Taylor. Possibly the best treatment of this ancient theme of the Horse turned Driver, etc., which may have helped to inspire Swift, and which in turn was revived and extended by the appearance of "Gulliver".

ELIZABETH TURNER

1806. *The Daisy.* (1840, 25th ed.)
1811. *The Cowslip.* (1842, 22nd ed.)
     The Pink. (1842, 22nd ed.)

MARY MARTHA SHERWOOD

1818. *The History of the Fairchild Family.* A second part appeared in 1842 and a third in 1847. Innumerable later editions.
1820. *The Governess.* A rewritten version of Sarah Fielding's collection of stories—1749— removing features that were thought obnoxious.
1822.-37. *The History of Henry Milner.* 4 parts.
1835. *Caroline Mordaunt,* which may well be the first juvenile illustrated by the Baxter process, i.e. the first to have an illustration printed in colours.

CHAPTER FOUR

FROM HARRIS TO "ALICE"

1. *John Harris*

ONE of the most significant events in the early nineteenth century was the taking-over of the Newbery business by John Harris, Elizabeth Newbery's manager for many years. He was bursting with new ideas, in most of which she seems to have restrained him, but he was now to bring the firm back to its proper place among the leaders in juvenile publications. He gave his little books a new, gay, up-to-date appearance, was among the first to make extensive and effective use of metal engravings as opposed to woodcuts for the illustrations, and to make strikingly good use of colour.

Two of his most outstanding successes display very well the leading features of his methods. The first of these concerns the most famous and long-lived of all the dames in nursery literature—Old Mother Hubbard. Whether or not the character was invented by Sarah Catherine Martin, whose initials appear on the title-page of the first edition, does not really matter very much.[1] The important thing is that the Adventures, with an admirable series of engravings after Miss Martin's drawings, were first published by Harris on June 1, 1805. The book sold in thousands immediately, was reprinted over and over again from 1806 onwards, and was pirated and copied by many of Harris's rivals.

In 1807 Harris did it again. In 1806, in the November number of the *Gentleman's Magazine* appeared a pretty rhyme entitled *The Butterfly's Ball and the Grasshopper's Feast* (52). It has been generally presumed that Harris first saw it there; but there is reason to suppose that he knew about it beforehand. An original manuscript, which was included in the National Book League Exhibition (No. 345 in the catalogue)[2] is endorsed, presumably in Harris's hand, "The Butterfly's Ball from Mr. Roscoe". It may be, of course, that Harris did spot it in the magazine and was handed the manuscript by Roscoe's permission, so that the endorsement may be that of the editor; but the fact that a large edition of the poem, with six engravings after Mul-

---

[1] Opie, pp. 319–21, gives an admirable summary of the known facts, and a significant reference to likenesses to *Old Dame Trot*, who appeared two years before *Mother Hubbard*. The failure of Miss Martin's "Continuation", and of the "Sequel", "by another hand", both published by Harris in 1806, may suggest that the first set did not originate with Miss Martin.

[2] Now, with the bulk of the books of the Russell Collection, owned by Mr. Edgar Oppenheimer of New York.

ready, and with the text engraved below the pictures, was ready in plain or coloured form on January 1, 1807, suggests that it must have been put in hand more than two months before publication.

The author, William Roscoe, was a Member of Parliament, aged fifty-three, a

THE

RENOWNED HISTORY

OF

DAME TROT

AND

HER CAT.

————000————

BANBURY:

PRINTED BY J. G. RUSHER.

45 A chapbook by a famous publisher of them

retired attorney and banker in the city of Liverpool,[1] who had written the verses for his little son, Robert. Of this book, and a sequel, The Peacock ''At Home'', by A Lady,[2] also commissioned by Harris, and published soon after the original,

[1] He was also a serious historian, an authority on Italian literature, and a great book-collector. His library was sold by auction in Liverpool in 1816 for over £5,000, part of it being bought by friends and presented to the Liverpool Athenaeum, where the books are still exhibited. Some were bought by the first Earl of Leicester—Coke of Norfolk—whose manuscripts Roscoe began to catalogue for him in 1842.

[2] Mrs. Dorset.

40,000 copies were sold before the year was out. They were the parents of a host of sequels,[1] mostly unauthorised; pocket handkerchiefs were made of the pictures, which also appeared as card games and jig-saw puzzles. In fact the whole thing was an absolutely roaring success, even more so than *Mother Hubbard*.

Harris, wittingly or otherwise, had catered for the vast majority of children who just wanted to be amused, without having to pay the penalty of continual reminders to keep their faces clean, their hair tidy, and everything else up to scratch, including their morals.

There was nothing particularly new about this "discovery"; it was simply a belated realisation of the fact that the most persistent favourites with children have always been the old nursery rhymes and tales, in which there was no bothersome preoccupation with anything but the sheer delight of the jingles and stories.

The moralists kept their powder dry all right, but it never kindled very well. The return to full jam was a success no less with the parents than with the children, for the idea that enjoyment is sinful in itself, although by no means dead even to-day, was already less potent than it had been under the Puritans.

2. *William Godwin, Charles Lamb, etc.*

There was no novelty, either, in Harris's realisation that a return to simple amusement must succeed. William Godwin had a theory about everything in life, and always did his best to put his theories into practice. Most of his theories got him into trouble, some of it serious, but his theory about children's books was perfectly sound. It was, roughly, that there are no theories suited to children, they should be allowed to read works of pure imagination. He set himself to provide new ones, but as his name on a title-page would be anathematised as strongly by parents as it would be welcomed by his creditors, this radical, heretical, looseliving scapegrace disguised his identity as an author under the name Edward Baldwin, and as a publisher he sheltered under the name of his manager, Thomas Hodgkins. His first wife had written a rather forbidding collection of stories addressed to "infant minds", which had the distinction of being illustrated by Blake.[2] His second wife joined him in the publishing venture, and the *Fables* of Edward Baldwin (1805) were among their first publications.

Godwin persuaded Charles Lamb to try his hand at producing a book for children, and on November 18, 1805, appeared a small paper-bound volume with the Hodgkins imprint, with no author's name, entitled *The King and Queen of Hearts*. It had sixteen leaves, printed on one side only, each with a picture occupying most of the page and a rhyming text printed below. Mary Godwin commissioned Mary

---

[1] Darton lists seven, but there were at least twenty, including one, *The Fishes Grand Gala*, by the notorious Mrs. Cockle, who made so free with Watts's texts (see p. 57).

[2] See p. 97.

Lamb to adapt some of the plays of Shakespeare, casting them into the form of short prose tales for children's reading. Twenty plays were so adapted in the end, fourteen by Mary and six by Charles. These were published in two volumes in 1807. In 1808 came Charles's *Adventures of Ulysses*, and in 1809 two works, jointly with his sister, *Mrs. Leicester's School* (three stories by Charles and seven by Mary), and *Poetry for Children* (about two-thirds by Mary).

There are a variety of other pieces written for children more or less certainly attributable to the Lambs; but to tell the truth, with the exception of the *Tales from Shakespeare*, they are to-day more interesting to book-collectors than to the historian of children's books. Nevertheless, because of their exceeding rarity and great value, and the curious story of their publication, it has been thought worth while to give some more detailed account of them in a note on p. 130–1.

The excellent example set by Harris and Godwin had no general or extended success. The truth was, of course, that the right stuff could not be turned out by hack writers; yet publishers had largely to put up with what they could get. The publishing of children's books was already a prosperous industry, and many rival firms were springing up. Besides Harris, the Dartons, the Marshalls, and the Godwins, the Wallis family, who seem to have begun in the second half of the eighteenth century as mapmakers, now very successfully turned their attention to attracting young people to their shop, first by inventing the jig-saw puzzle, then by adding various attractively produced and ingenious board games, and finally by invading the book business. Their productions in all spheres were of very high quality, but more will be said of them in Chapter 8.

There was also the firm of Dean and Munday,[1] which, after various changes, has lasted into our own time; and A. K. Newman, who joined Lane at the Minerva Press in about 1803, and carried it on himself when Lane died, not only published juveniles himself, but had a standing arrangement with Dean and Munday by which he marketed a certain proportion of any books published by them, sometimes with his own imprint alone, sometimes jointly with them. Such publications were actually ventures of Dean and Munday, and Newman was only an

46 *The History of Jack the Giant Killer* (Dean and Co., 1830)

[1] In the eighteen-fifties the firm's imprint is: "Thomas Dean in Threadneedle Street". Under his charge some extremely elegant books were turned out, attractively bound and well illustrated. Otherwise the firm has been notable, at times, for its enterprise (see especially Chapter 8) than for a very high standard of taste.

agent.[1] W. Belch, who was principally a publisher of juvenile drama and of tinsel pictures, Carvalho, Tabart, who may have been the original of Borrow's Taggart, Bysh, Champante and Whitrow, Fairburn, Hodgson, Blackman, March, Mawman, Spencer, Longman, Fuller, Osborne and Griffin, Conder, Baldwin, Vernor and

U Up-and-Down, u

Here some go up and some go down,
To take their pastime at the fair;
Just so it is the world all round,
Each has his pleasure, each his care.

47 A forerunner of The Great Wheel
From a chapbook alphabet published by Kendrew in York

Hood, Lloyd, and many other names are found in the imprints of children's books more or less frequently at this time.

Provincial booksellers were also extremely active, and publications for children began to be undertaken in Wellington, Knaresborough, Gainsborough, Birmingham, Otley, Edinburgh, Dublin, York, Glasgow, Derby, Newcastle, Alnwick, Chelmsford,

---

[1] But there are numerous examples of exchange or co-operative ventures in children's books at this time, just as there were in more ambitious publications. Both E. Newbery and Harris are found sharing an imprint with Wallis; Darton also shared with Harris.

Newman himself published two imitations of *The Butterfly's Ball*—*Pomona's Frolic* (1810) and *Madame Grimalkin's Party* (1811).

Banbury, Ware, Deal, Liverpool, Coventry, and Paisley among other places (45, 47, and 48).

But it was the few leading firms that really kept things going, and introduced all kinds of novelties, sometimes showing great ingenuity, of which there will be occasion to speak in another chapter. The general level, however, was not very high. Most of the little books are attractive enough in outward appearance, and their titles are often beguiling enough, but there are only rare flashes of outstanding talent, as in *Dame Wiggins* (1823), later reprinted with additional cuts by Kate Greenaway.

48 Cup and ball from *Juvenile Games for the Four Seasons* (Oliver and Boyd) Edinburgh

3. *The Revival of the Fairy-tale*

Mesdames Trimmer and Sherwood had fairly effectively crushed the ugly head of the fairy-tale; and its revival had to await a doubly sinister foreign invasion from Germany and Denmark before English children could be given their heads and allowed to read fairy-tales to their hearts' content. The "discovery" of Hans Christian Andersen by Mary Howitt is fairly well known; but seldom and rarely has any tribute been paid to the genius who, in 1823–6, gave to our nurseries a collection of tales in English which have probably never since been allowed to go out of print. The fact that the first English edition of Grimm was illustrated by Cruikshank seems to have completely overshadowed the anonymous translator of the stories.

The stories were originally collected by Jacob and Wilhelm Grimm as specimens of surviving folklore. They were taken down from the lips of peasants and old wives, much as Cecil Sharp and his successors collected folk songs and dances, and were published in three volumes in 1812–18.

The English version appeared in two volumes in 1823–6, with no translator's name on the title-page.

He rejoiced in the name of Taylor, a felicitous one for a children's writer. There is no trace of any connection with Ann and Jane, although Edgar Taylor, Grimm's translator, was an East Anglian, having been born in Banham, near Norwich.

But he has a very close relationship indeed with another famous writer already mentioned, for he inaugurated the firm of Taylor and Roscoe, solicitors in King's Bench Walk in the Temple, the junior partner in which was the very Robert Roscoe for whom his father wrote *The Butterfly's Ball*.

Taylor was a great linguist, having a mastery, besides German, of Italian, Spanish, and French. Like so many of the illustrious in this present history, Taylor was a staunch nonconformist, an original member of Robert Aspland's "Noncon Club".

Mary Howitt was a Quaker, and married to a Quaker. It was while she was staying at Heidelberg in 1840 that she began to learn Danish and Swedish in order to read certain Scandinavian authors in the original. By 1842 she had begun to translate the Swedish novels of Frederika Bremer, and in 1845 she began on Hans Andersen with a translation of his novel *Only a Fiddler*. She followed this immediately with *The Improvisatore*, and both novels awakened English interest in the then unknown writer. In 1846 she introduced the fairy-tales, translating ten of them under the title *Wonderful Stories for Children*, published by Bohn. Others were hard on her heels, and there were three little volumes of translations by other hands in the same year. Mrs. Howitt's was the best of these, and was greeted with a chorus of praise from all the leading literary journals. Two of the rival translations however, *A Danish Story Book* and *The Nightingale and Other Tales*, both in 1846, possess some historical interest, being published by Griffith and Farran, who took over the Newbery interests from the second John Harris. Running true to form they published two editions of each, one with plain and one with coloured plates. Hardly a year passed without the addition of a new volume of the Andersen stories, or a new edition of an old one, until, in 1866, Routledge published the first collected edition under the title *What the Moon Saw and other Tales*. Dr. Dulcken, who was responsible for this translation, and for an enlarged and undated edition (1873) containing twenty-three more tales, seems more likely to have been a Dane who knew English than an Englishman who knew Danish, for many of his phrases are literal translations from the Danish, which do not always make good English.[1]

There has been little addition to the true fairy canon since Andersen, and the best modern collections rely largely on the old favourites, Perrault, Grimm, and Andersen, with one favourite from Mme de Beaumont—"Beauty and the Beast"—and a sprinkling of English traditional tales like "Jack-the-giant-killer", and "Dick Whittington". This is a rather broad and sweeping statement, but it is substantially true, if it is considered in the light of what has retained favour among children.

Ruskin, Thackeray, George Macdonald, Andrew Lang, and Mrs. Craik, among others, have written fairy-tales, and it is certainly true that some of them have been reprinted and would bear revival. The obstinate and inescapable fact remains that none of them has caught the fancy of children in the same way as Perrault, Andersen, or Grimm, and extreme caution should be observed before adult criteria of excellence are translated into what is suitable for children. Good judges may think that *The King of the Golden River* or *The Rose and the Ring* are the equal of anything of the kind that has been written for children; it does not follow that children will agree with them, and our main consideration here is to conduct a *post hoc* investigation into the favourite reading of children. It is our business to adhere rigidly to the deductions to be made from hindsight, and the one thing that must not be done is to indulge in speculation as to what children ought to

[1] He was in fact a German.

like, or regret that their taste is not better than it is—i.e. that it often differs from our own.

Grimm directly inspired at least one English writer to try his hand at the same sort of thing, and his best story is still readable. This was Francis Edward Paget, a miscellaneous writer who edited for a time the *Juvenile Englishman's Library*, to which he also contributed. His principal contribution, which ran as a serial in the "Library" was the aforesaid fairy tale, *The Hope of the Katzekopfs*. This was also issued separately at Rugeley in 1844, the author's name being given as "William Churne of Staffordshire".

The Lewis Carroll stories might be considered the grandest of all fairy-tales, and their popularity with children in unquestionable. But they are in a class by themselves; and they are in a very real sense fundamentally different from the genre of the fairy-tale in general, the essence of which is the form of the *conte*. A fairy-tale, in fact, must be short. Thackeray, Ruskin, and Macdonald (sometimes) qualify on these grounds, although they have failed to make the grade; Carroll, Kenneth Grahame,[1] and Barrie are out because of length. Kipling is a border-line case. *Puck of Pook's Hill* has successfully evaded the educational stigma that has disqualified other writers, but the fairy element is wholly incidental. *The Jungle Books* and *Just So Stories* have achieved nursery immortality because a genius has married two of the most tried and trusted favourite media—the fable and the fairy-story.

Andrew Lang earns a high place in the revival of the fairy-tale, less for those he wrote himself, although *Prince Prigio* at least has borne fairly recent revival, than for the series of brightly illustrated annual collections that he edited—although much of the donkey-work was done by his wife—called after the colours of their gay, gilded bindings, beginning with *The Blue Fairy Book* in 1889. Jacob's collections of national fairy-tales seem to be addressed more to anthropologists and folk-lorists than to children, and thus hardly come within our scope, while the queer efforts of George Cruikshank, in rewriting old fairy-stories to further the cause of total abstinence, need hardly detain us.

One minor masterpiece which, despite the unsuitability of its method of presentation and the unexpectedness of the author's name, has gained and retained a reputation with young readers is Wilde's *Happy Prince and Other Tales*, first published in 1888. Pater truly said of "The Selfish Giant" in this collection that it was "perfect of its kind".

4. *Tell me a Story*

The more one looks into the history of children's books the more one is impressed by the extraordinary series of waves in which new ideas flooded the market. There was the flood of Puritan books in the seventeenth century, all much of a

---

[1] His admirable short stories in *Pagan Papers*, *Dream Days*, and *The Golden Age* are rather stories about children than for them, although Walt Disney has persuaded children that *The Reluctant Dragon* is a jolly good story, and it may be that it will acquire a new popularity with them as "the book of the film".

muchness. Then came the specialisation of the chapbook publishers, followed by the first self-conscious publishers of juveniles, Boreman, Newbery, and the others. The likeness between their productions, with occasional almost complete coincidence in titles and a common outlook, resulting in pretty-pretty catch-pennies for the "young Masters and Misses", has already transpired in these pages. Towards the end of the century came the commissioning of special writers, mostly women, also with a great family likeness between their productions, so that authors' names might be considered interchangeable without doing any great violence to most of them.

About one hundred years after Boreman and his contemporaries first began to publish exclusively for children another fundamental change, perhaps the most important hitherto, is observable in the attitude of the juvenile publishers. The new school of writers that then arose turned its attention to narrative with a decreasing emphasis on a moral, horrid warnings, or smug presentations of inhumanly virtuous, Bible-ridden heroes. At the same time there is observable the first realisation of the fact that boys liked different kinds of books from girls.

The movement generally was in favour of romance and adventure, and, like Harris's rediscovery of the attraction of the old nursery jingles, this movement had its roots in the past. Scott's Waverley Novels were unquestionably among the sources from which this movement came, and the fact that these novels and those of Ainsworth appealed almost as strongly to children as to their adults was a prime factor in the movement.

Captain Marryat, the first important author to exploit this side of the juvenile market, was a capital writer of adventure stories before he turned his attention to children. *Mr. Midshipman Easy* (1836) was sure to attract young readers; but Marryat's first book definitely written for children, *Masterman Ready* (1841–2), was a conscious attempt to improve on the *Swiss Family Robinson*, which he found objectionable because of the ignorance it showed of the principles of navigation and geography.[1] It is a much better book than its forerunner, if only because Marryat was a first-rate story-teller, and showed considerable knowledge of the way to interest young readers. But, like his even more popular *Children of the New Forest*, it preaches too much, and its hero is a prig.

A word may be interposed here on the enormous success at the time of books which have lost much of their appeal to youngsters. Looking them through to-day it is difficult to account for their success when they first appeared. The answer, however, is a very obvious one. When very few books were written for children anything of the kind was eagerly seized upon, and its reputation spread like wildfire. One wonders how it was possible that Edward Salmon, writing in 1888,[2] could find that "Mrs. Molesworth is . . . the best story-teller for children England has yet known." Mrs. Molesworth herself supplies the obvious answer. In the days

---

[1] *Masterman Ready* is possibly more popular in Germany (*Sigismund Rustig*) than the *Swiss Family Robinson*.
[2] *Juvenile Literature as it is.* Green quotes the passage approvingly.

when she was young—she was born in 1839—she writes: "not only had no children many books, but everywhere children had the same! There was seldom any use in little friends lending to each other, for it was always the same thing over again: *Evenings at Home, Sandford and Merton, Ornaments Discovered*, and so on".[1]

What a truly appalling list it is! No wonder that boys, especially, swallowed Marryat whole, and asked for more.

Less accomplished writers filled the gap. W. H. G. Kingston was one of the first, the most prolific, and the most competent of them. His first book was published in 1843,[2] and he developed into one of the earliest of those frantic writers who seem able to write with both hands and both feet, turning out books for a special market. He devoted himself almost entirely to writing for boys. His first great success was with *Peter the Whaler* (1851), and in 1859 he founded *Kingston's Magazine for Boys*. He also edited other periodicals for boys from time to time. His extensive contribution to the *Swiss Family Robinson* story has already been mentioned. With his contemporary, R. M. Ballantyne, he was one of Stevenson's two favourite authors as a boy.[3]

When Kingston's first book appeared Ballantyne was a clerk with the Hudson's Bay Company in Rupert Land; but he returned home to Scotland in 1847, and there issued semi-privately in 1848 an account of his North American sojourn. He was much less prolific than Kingston,[4] which was partly due to the fact that it was not until 1856 that he began to write books for boys. He was a younger brother of James Ballantyne, the printer of Scott's novels, and on his return from America he joined the Edinburgh printing and publishing firm of Constable. The two sons of Thomas Nelson had joined their father's publishing firm and were considerably enlarging it, partly by embarking on the juvenile market. One of them suggested that Ballantyne should try his hand at a story for boys, and the result was *Snowflakes and Sunbeams* (1856). It was an immediate success, its unsuitable title soon changed to *The Young Fur Traders*, which had been used as a subtitle in the first edition, although it was also used on the binding to the exclusion of the original title. He followed this in 1858[5] with his masterpiece, *Coral Island*, but *Martin Rattler* (1859), *The Dog Crusoe*, and *The Gorilla Hunters* (both 1861), were hardly less successful. All these were issued by Nelson. In 1863 Ballantyne transferred to Nisbet, as the result of a suggestion that he should produce a periodical series, cloth-bound, all written by himself, under the title *Ballantyne's Miscellany*. Each of these was a small pocket volume (about $4 \times 5\frac{1}{2}$ inches) containing an adventure story. Judging by the

1 Quoted by Green.

2 His first two books were three-deckers. Allibone credits him with 171 titles in forty-two years.

3 Maisie Ward quotes a letter from G. K. Chesterton, probably of 1890, in which he writes: "My brother is intent upon *The Three Midshipmen* or *The Three Admirals* or the three coal-scuttles or some other distinguished trio by that interminable ass Kingston".

4 He has seventy titles in Allibone.

5 Actually 1857 post-dated.

bewildering variety in which the volumes now come to hand the series must have been a great success. It continued until 1886 and comprised eighteen volumes in all.[1]

Ballantyne took enormous pains with the local colour of his stories—he was only once caught out in this, very early on, and it taught him a lesson that he never forgot. He was not a trained draughtsman, but he usually insisted on providing elaborate drawings of his own to illustrate the books (85, 86). These were drawn on card in pen and wash, and as he knew that the engraver would have to take great liberties with his work in order to produce a finished illustration he covered the back of each card with precise instructions on technical points and on the exact effect he desired to produce.[2]

Thomas Mayne Reid was born in Northern Ireland in 1818, the son of a Presbyterian minister—how persistently these dissenters turned to writing for children!—and emigrated to America in 1838. He led an adventurous life on the prairies among the Indians, where he gained much of the local colour that imbues his highly romantic stories—*The Rifle Rangers* (1850), *The Scalp Hunters* (1851), and many others. In 1845 he volunteered for service with the American Army in the Mexican campaign and became a captain. In 1849 he returned to Europe at the head of a body of volunteers to fight in Kossuth's liberating army against the Serbians. His early books were three-deckers and may not have been aimed directly at boys; but it was impossible to keep them away from him, and later he wrote many stories especially for them.

Charles Kingsley was a better writer than most of these, but the books he wrote especially for children are not his most successful in that genre. *The Water Babies* is overloaded with preachments and moralisings. *The Heroes* is rather better, but as for his explicitly instructional books, *Glaucus* and *Madam How and Lady Why*, their patronising approach is intolerable. Nevertheless they succeeded. But it is as a writer of first-rate, rattling good stories like *Westward Ho!* and *Hereward the Wake* that he gains most significance, although he was seldom far from the pulpit in either. The original form of publication, the former in three volumes and the latter in two, shows that they were intended for adults rather than children. Nevertheless both have been firmly taken over by young people, and Kingsley is best thought of among them for these two "annexed" books.

George Manville Fenn is a minor figure in the progress of adventure; but Henty is in the direct tradition (84). Kingston's mantle very definitely settled on him—he followed him as editor of the *Union Jack* series—and with his voluminous output of some ninety books[3] he carries the succession just over the border of our period.

[1] The only satisfactory account of its publishing history, together with a reliable bibliographical description of most of Ballantyne's books, is in Sadleir, I, 17ff.

[2] One of these drawings and its accompanying notes will be found reproduced as figs. 85 and 86.

[3] He began as a novelist, his earliest books being three-deckers.

5. "Bloods"

In the period under review another, and possibly even more important, phenomenon arose in the juvenile market. This was the "Jack Harkaway" type of publication, which is principally associated with the name of E. J. Brett and George Emmett as publishers. Originally and ostensibly published as journals for boys, most of these soon became the prototype of the modern series of booklets issued by such firms as the Amalgamated Press, which continued, week by week, the adventures of immortal heroes like Jack, Sam, and Pete; Tom Merry; Sexton Blake; and Nelson Lee. Their latest immediate descendants are the "comics", some of which, in their most high-pressure form, are, without any possible question, the most degraded and unsuitable publications that could be put into the hands of children.

But these early efforts, with such attractive titles as *The Boy's World*, *Boys of England*, *Young England*, *The Young Englishman's Journal*, and *The Sons of Britannia*, were harmless if hack-written. The specimen illustrated (50) shows the usual effective format, which persisted into our own day—a boldly set, decorative, and sometimes illustrated heading, below which was a large cut of a leading incident in the story, and always, on the front page, the opening sentences of the story. The prototype and most consistently successful of all the serials was "Jack Harkaway", a character originally created and long written exclusively by an American lawyer living in London who called himself Bracebridge Hemyng. Most of these writers did not use their real names. They either wrote in the first person and deliberately identified themselves with their heroes, or they chose alliterative or tripping pseudonyms like Ralph Rollington, Captain Jack (George Emmett), Brenchley Beaumont (Walter Viles), Cyril Hathaway and Philander Jackson[1] (both E. H. Burrage), whereas Percy B. and Vane St. John[2] found it impossible to improve on their real names.

Several of the publishers also wrote stories for their own, and occasionally for other, journals. Among the authors occasionally employed were Kingston and Mayne Reid, both of whom also edited boys' journals; but the majority were Fleet Street hacks who would turn their hands to any kind of writing that would produce a pound or two. Bracebridge Hemyng claimed to be the son of the Registrar of the Supreme Court of Calcutta and a barrister of the Middle Temple. He is said to have written, besides the best of the "Harkaway" series, and other yarns for boys, the White Slave section of Mayhew's *London Labour*, several racing novels—among them *The Favourite Scratched* and *Secrets of the Turf*; and he is twice mentioned in Mr. Michael Sadleir's catalogue of his collection of yellow-backs as the author of several

[1] This worthy usually added the initials "H.U.A." after his name, which he once admitted stood for nothing but "Hard Up Author".

[2] Henry St. John Cooper, who may have been the son of one of them, was a writer for boys' series of the Amalgamated Press. His son, Robert St. John Cooper, is a well-known Fleet Street artist, and the inventor of the character "Mr. Cube".

of them.[1] George Emmett described himself as an ex-cavalry officer, and claimed to have been wounded at Balaclava. John Holloway, author of *Drummer Boy Dick*, was the owner of the famous pills and ointment, and once invested £1,000 in one of Ralph Rollington's journals for boys. But the most distinguished pseudonym in the whole gallery was that of Capt. George North, who contributed two serials to *Young Folks*, called *Treasure Island* and *Black Arrow*. There was one lady author who made a success in this medium, Alice Maud Meadows, a writer of "Frantic Flossie" novelettes who began to write at the age of fourteen.

For the rest they were a hard-drinking, easy-going, bohemian crowd, very similar to the journalistic crew described in A. M. Binstead's delightful pages some thirty years later. "Ralph Rollington" in his hilarious account of their exploits, makes no secret of their methods of living and writing. Perhaps his best story relates how, waiting vainly for copy from Vane St. John and "Brenchley Beaumont", he traced them to Margate where they were detained in their room by reason of having pawned all their clothes, pinned up in sheets and writing for dear life.

Rollington is full of informing sidelights on the methods and financing of these boys' journals, but his book is now hard to come by. About £2,000 was an ample sum with which to start one of them, and the profit might be reckoned at between twelve and fifteen per cent. Nevertheless his own journal came to grief, being taken over by its printers when they were owed £16,000 and saw no chance of being paid. Rollington seems to have regarded this as a considerable benevolence. Brett, the most successful venturer in this field, however, amassed a great fortune. In 1892 Sala presided over the silver jubilee banquet of the *Boys of England*, and wrote, in *Sala's Journal* in 1894, an account of Brett's "palatial" home at St. Peter's, Broadstairs, where he had gathered a large collection of armour, which does not appear to have impressed the knowledgeable.

A similar crew of hacks was responsible for the production of other serial fiction for boys—the penny "bloods"—which most frequently dealt imaginatively in the exploits of famous highwaymen from Dick Turpin to Spring-heel Jack.

6. School Stories

The heritage of the school stories has proved more persistent than that of the "bloods", however. At least two famous school stories precede the era of the Brett type of journal. *Tom Brown's School-Days* was first published anonymously in 1857.[2] It was the work of a young and not very successful barrister, Thomas Hughes, who came strongly under the influence of F. D. Maurice, then chaplain of Lincoln's Inn. Hughes became an active member of that group of muscular Christians and Christian Socialists, which included Charles Kingsley, who founded The Working

---

[1] II, 8 and 48.

[2] Osborne lists M. Pelham, *First Going to School, or, the Story of Tom Brown and his Sisters* (1809).

49   The folding frontispiece to a fairy-tale booklet in the "Penny-Plain-Twopence-Coloured" period [c. 1840]

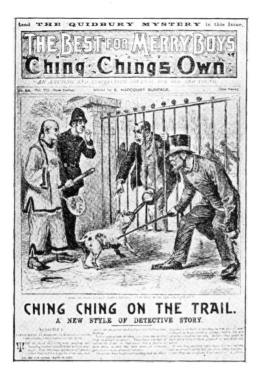

50 A typical journal for boys of the
'eighties

51 An illustration by Arthur Hughes
for Macdonald's *At the Back of the
North Wind*, 1871

52 Two pages from William Roscoe's *The Butterfly's Ball*, 1807

Men's College. This background naturally produced a very different types of school story from those for which "Bracebridge Hemyng" and his colleagues were responsible. "Tom Brown" was, however, an immediate success. Five editions were called for before the end of the year of original publication, and the book is still continually reprinted. Since its copyright expired cheap editions of it have been issued by a variety of publishers.

Hughes's novel was based on recollections of his experiences as a school-boy at Rugby. F. W. Farrar's *Eric, or Little by Little* (1858) sprang from his days as a master, first at Marlborough and later at Harrow. Although thirty-six editions were called for in his lifetime it has eventually achieved an immortality only of derision.

Talbot Baines Reed, a partner in his father's typefoundry, wrote several school stories, but of these only two are remembered—*The Fifth Form at St. Dominic's* (1887), and *The Cock House of Felsgarth* (1891). Anstey's *Vice Versa* (1882) is sub-titled " A Parable for Fathers ", but has also found considerable favour with their sons. P. G. Wodehouse's early school stories fall just outside our period; and Kipling's *Stalky and Co.* (1899) just gets in.

7. A Broad Field

Kingston, Fenn, Ballantyne, and other early writers of romances for boys bequeathed a mantle that has fallen on very distinguished shoulders. Space will not permit more than a reference to Conan Doyle, Anthony Hope, Weyman, "Q", and Crockett; but although Stevenson has already been given passing mention his contribution demands more than that.

Treasure Island is his unquestioned masterpiece in our field, although *Kidnapped* and *Catriona*, in a different vein, run it very close. The romantic story of its beginning in a map of an island sketched by his step-son, Lloyd Osbourne; of Stevensons's completion of the map, first by giving it a title, "*Treasure Island*", then by filling in natural features and place-names, culminating in the three crosses that marked the pirates' buried treasure, has often been told; and how Stevenson wrote the story in instalments, in bed, until Dr. Japp carried off the unfinished story to James Henderson, editor of *Young Folks*, who began to print it as a serial before it was finished writing. It created no sensation in its serial form and although it ended in January 1882 it was not until 1883 that it appeared in book form. Its progress has never faltered since.

Rider Haggard is a long way second to Stevenson as a writer of romance, but *King Solomon's Mines* (1885), *She* (1887)—and its sequel *Ayesha* (1905)—and *Allan Quatermain* (1887), have maintained their popularity almost undimmed with young readers. It is interesting to compare the original publication figures for the three principal novels. Cassell printed 2,000 copies of *King Solomon's Mines*, in September 1885, but only 1,000 sets of sheets were bound, and 500 were sent to New York for an American edition. In 1887 the first edition of *She* comprised

10,000 copies, and, six months later, 20,000 copies of *Allan Quatermain* were called for.

There is no space in which to trace in any detail the long history of boys' periodicals, but there is one above all others that must be given more than passing mention. This is the *Boy's Own Paper*, begun on January 13, 1879, by J. M. Macaulay, who immediately entrusted its editorship to G. A. Hutchison. His supervision continued until one year before his death in 1913. He has not earned a place in the *Dictionary of National Biography*, but his influence on boys during nearly fifty years must have been very considerable, if incalculable. He was on the staff of the Religious Tract Society, the original publishers of the *B.O.P.*, but it is his work on that journal which is unforgettable. As Darton says he had, perhaps, "a stronger indirect influence on English boyhood than any man of his time".

Considerable space has been given to these journals and their sequel because they were possibly the first completely successful attempt to give boys what they really wanted, without considering in the slightest what was good for them. They can have done little harm, in fact, but one may well imagine the parents of the time lamenting that their children preferred the rubbish of Hogarth House to Kingsley, Farrar, and Marryat. Such lamentation is familiar in our own day; but it should be clear that the only way successfully to compete with this bright—garish if you like—competently presented ephemera is to meet it on its own ground. Children of a certain age will not be bothered to go to circulating libraries, or even to bookshops, on the chance that they may find something palatable there. They see what they want displayed on bookstalls, and that is what they intend to have.

8. *Writers for Girls. Mrs. Ewing*

Girls were much less enterprisingly cared for than boys in this way. The long line of women writers for girls, from Agnes Strickland to Mrs. Molesworth and from Mary Elliot to Juliana Horatia Ewing and Mrs. Marshall, are all inferior in the provision of what children want to their male counterparts.

Catherine Sinclair deserves more than passing mention. She was in the direct line of writers of the moral tale; but she was also something more. Into her best book for children, *Holiday House* (1839), she infused a spirit of laughter and good fun which is refreshing and uncommon at the time.

Another innovation of hers was to adapt the rather tedious methods of the popular hieroglyphic Bible to a more amusing and attractive purpose in a series of hieroglyphic letters, one of which is reproduced (44). These were enormously popular, despite their comparatively high price of sixpence each for a single sheet, and were sold by the hundred thousand.

The writing of the present book has entailed making or renewing acquaintance with some hundreds of books written for children during two and a half centuries. That this has been a labour not always of love is sometimes betrayed in these pages.

116

There have, indeed, been few outstandingly successful writers for children during our period; and one is in some danger of unduly weighting their importance when they arise. There are very few for whom overemphasis is almost impossible; perhaps Lewis Carroll and Edward Lear are the only two of this kind. Watts, the Taylors, and Miss Edgeworth, good as they are, have not the same unquestionable superiority as those other two.

If, therefore, it is thought that undue space and importance is given to Mrs. Ewing in the pages that follow, it may be because the relief at meeting a children's author who can write, who certainly did not write down, has caused me to lose a sense of proportion in writing of her. But susceptibility to the charge should not be taken as acknowledgement of its justice. I do think she is very good indeed; although her faults may be readily acknowledged.

I have said that she did not write down; and one is tempted to think of her sometimes as a writer about rather than for children. The fact remains that she was an unqualified success with children at the time. *Mary's Meadow* (1886), which had appeared serially during 1884 and 1885, is little more than a series of lessons in gardening based on Miller's *Gardener's Dictionary* and Parkinson's *Paradisi in sole Paradisus terrestris*, which one would have thought inaccessible to children and pretty tough going if they were not. Moreover, the author is relentless in the use of proper names for flowers, thus "Primrose Peerlesse" is really, she expains, *Narcissus medio lutens vulgaris*, and the "Trinity Flower" is *Trillium erythrocarpum*. Yet the correspondence columns of her magazine seem to show that "The Game of the Earthly Paradise" was received with great delight by its young readers. A Parkinson Society was formed to "search out and cultivate old garden flowers which have become scarce" and to exchange seeds and plants, and even gardening books, while another aim was to plant waste places with hardy flowers. Rules were framed, and reports issued; but the Society does not seem to have survived its founder's death.

She had a curious habit of providing running headlines to all her story-books, which were either proverbs, or smatterings of good advice. These were frequently in Latin. Even children may have managed *Dulce et decorum est pro patria mori*, but some of the others must have been tough, for example, *Maestis Lentae, celeres gaudentibus horae*, or *Et constricta suas habitans amat ostrea valvas*; while the living languages may have taken some aback, for example, *Reu des Herzens Arznel*.

But Mrs. Ewing gets full marks for not writing down, for the absence of goody-goody moralisings, and for jolly good, readable, straightforward stories. She was less successful with her Verse Books, written for small children. Some of the material was not at all bad, but it was execrably presented and most unsuitably illustrated by a third-rate artist called R. André of whom she appeared to think well (90).

Her first published writings appeared in *The Monthly Packet* in 1861, when she was only nineteen. Three of her stories were printed there in that year, and in 1862, with two more stories added, and illustrations by her elder sister, they were issued by Bell in book form, with the title *Melchior's Dream and other Stories*. Also in 1862 her mother, Mrs. Gatty, included three of her short stories in a volume of her own.[1]

When *Aunt Judy's Magazine*[2] was started, Miss Gatty, as she still was, became an important contributor, and its first serial writer.[3]

She had already in childhood entertained her sisters by stories she made up around woodcuts in German children's books; and this she continued to do both in a manuscript magazine which the children wrote for themselves called the "Gunpowder Plot Magazine" and in some of her published work.[4]

She was a painstaking author, with a strong feeling for the plan and construction of a story. Like most genteel Victorian young ladies she had learned to draw, and like many another of them she had sat at the feet of John Ruskin. She explained to her youngest brother than she had taken also as the basis of her method of writing the third Letter in Ruskin's *Elements of Drawing*; and had tried to construct her stories on the lines there laid down for drawing. Principality, Continuity, Contrast, and Harmony are the leading principles enunciated by Ruskin and they will be found artfully employed in the best of Mrs. Ewing's stories.

She died of a painful and obscure illness at the age of forty-four, continuing to write almost to the end. She was continuing to foster the Parkinson Society by means of a series of "Letters from a Little Garden", which she had begun in "Aunt Judy" in November 1884. She had first been taken seriously ill on her way to join her husband in Malta in October 1879, and from then until the end of 1881 she was able to write only three short poems. But in November 1881 "Aunt Judy" found a new publisher, who commissioned Caldecott to design a new cover for it.

Mrs. Ewing had recovered some of her strength and wrote for the first number a story which ranks only second to "Jackanapes"— "Daddy Darwin's Dovecote"— which was delightfully illustrated by Caldecott[5] (78).

But in February 1885 a sudden mysterious attack of blood-poisoning set in. She was unable to finish her letter for the March issue, and, after considerable

---

1 A check-list of Mrs. Ewing's books will be found on pp. 127 ff.

2 Begun in 1866, and edited by Mrs. Gatty, Mrs. Ewing's mother, until her death in 1873, whereafter it was carried on by her daughters until 1885. Mrs. Gatty was herself a writer for children, and produced five series of *Parables from Nature* (1855–70), which are exactly described by their title. Her magazine was notably successful with children. It included, from 1867 onwards, a number of pieces by Lewis Carroll, one of which, *Castle-Croquet*, is an example of the editor's overestimate of child capacity, for the game is far too complicated even for grown-ups. Several of the later fairy-tales of Hans Andersen also appeared first in this magazine. Bound volumes of selections from the magazine had a seasonal success, notably at Christmas time. It is not surprising that the magazine died with Mrs. Ewing, who had been its mainstay from the beginning.

3 *Mrs. Overtheway's Remembrances*, which began in the first number, ran until October 1868 and was published by Bell in book form the following Christmas.

4 "A Hero to His Hobby Horse"; "Toots and Boots"; "Father Hedgehog and his Friends"; "Our Field"; and "The Blind Man and the Talking Dog" are among the poems and stories written to fit German woodcuts used in *Aunty Judy's Magazine*. When they were included in her books, however, the woodcuts were dropped because a special illustrator had been commissioned.

5 The cover-title design is reproduced as fig. 77.

suffering, she died on May 13. "Aunt Judy" died with her, and although four pieces from her pen appeared in *The Child's Pictorial Magazine* from May to August 1885, they had been written much earlier.

The demand for her work continued after her death, and the magazines were combed sufficiently to produce half a dozen more books.

The vitality of her prose writing has proved quite remarkable. Until the outbreak of the Second World War nearly all the volumes of her stories from the first, in 1862, to the last, in 1888, had been almost continuously in print; and even a selection of her verses was available, although these have suffered rather severely with the passage of time.

Dinah Mulock, who married George Craik, a partner in the publishing house of Macmillan, wrote novels with a strong sentimental appeal—not exclusively read by girls—the best known of which is *John Halifax, Gentleman* (1856). She also tried her hand, not altogether unsuccessfully, at fairy-stories, *Alice Learmont* (1852), *The Fairy Book* (1863), which is a collection of familiar fairy-tales retold, and *Adventures of a Brownie* (1872), which Mr. Sadleir instances as a reflection of the great success of Mrs. Ewing's *The Brownies* (1870).[1]

9. Verse

The assessment of verse for children is not an easy task. That it appeals strongly even to the smallest of them is evident from the obstinate success of nursery rhymes; from the early perception by Bunyan and others that jingle was the surest method of capturing their attention; and from the high proportion of poetry written for their adults which has been "adopted" by children—a far higher proportion than in prose.

But how shall one differentiate poetry written for children from poetry written about children? No more puzzling differentiation can be imagined. Roscoe and his imitators are certainly in the former class, and so are Watts, the Taylors, and Lear. But where does one place Blake's *Songs of Innocence*, Christina Rossetti's *Sing Song*, and Stevenson's *Child's Garden of Verses*? Frankly, I do not know.

Darton is no mean authority on this, as on every other aspect of children's reading. He includes Stevenson rather critically, and comments[2]: "before Stevenson, save for a chance line or two, hardly a verse had been written as a child, given word-skill, might have written it; except by Blake, Christina Rossetti, and, at odd seconds, William Brighty Rands".

Let us leave it at that, except to underline just a little more heavily the contributions of Rands in his "Lilliput" series. The surest test of the permanent value of the work of any children's writer is to try him out on children of to-day. This test will disclose much candid truth on such books as *Goody Two-Shoes* and *Sandford and Merton*; but Rands will come through it with some colour still fit to be flown.

[1] I, 275.   [2] Pp. 324-5.

General source books are again the background for the earlier period. Some slight references to Harris will also be found in Welsh. *Early Books for Children*, a bookseller's catalogue issued by H. W. Edwards, Ashmore Green, Newbury, in 1945 contains *The Butterfly's Ball* and several of the sequels.

R. Rollington's *The Old Boy's Books* (Leicester: Simpson, 1913) is a rollicking account of the publications of E. T. Brett and his rivals, with little attention to chronology, or any other principle of arrangement.

H. F. Gatty's *Juliana Horatia Ewing* (S.P.C.K., 1885) is an affectionate account of her sister's writings, produced for young readers, but with an extensive, if sometimes fallible, list of original publication.

R. L. Green's *Tellers of Tales* (Leicester: Ward, 1946) is the work of an enthusiast covering his favourite juvenile writers from Catherine Sinclair to A. A. Milne. It contains much biographical information and some extremely useful lists of titles. It does not pretend to bibliographical accuracy, and its dates should be regarded with caution. Biographical source-material is listed, and a formidable list of Mrs. Molesworth's books is said to be complete.

List of Books

At this point, even if not earlier, the division of the list of books into chapters conflicts awkwardly with chronology. Very roughly speaking chronological division has been attempted, and the present list is approximately of books published between the death of Newbery and the publication of "Alice".

1768. *Tom Thumb's Folio.*

1770. *Letters between Master Tommy and Miss Nancy.*

1772. *Tea-Table Dialogues between Miss Thoughtful, Miss Sterling, Miss Prattle, etc.*

1774. *Drawing School for Little Masters and Misses.*

1774. *The Picture Exhibition, containing the Original Drawings of eighteen Little Masters and Misses.*

1775. *Cries of London.* Published by Newbery, and perhaps the first appearance of this very popular subject in the children's market.

1776. *Juvenile Sports and Pastimes*

1777. Charly Chatter. *The Juvenile Auction.*

1777. Thomas Tagg. *A Collection of Pretty Poems for the amusement of children Three Foot High.* Not the first edition.

1778. John-the-Giant-Killer. *Food for the Mind, or A New Riddle Book* (2nd ed.).

c. 1780. Nurse Allgood. *The Whitsuntide Present.*

1781. *The Easter Gift.*

1781. Master Tommy Littleton. *Juvenile Trials for Robbing Orchards, etc.* Not the first edition.

1782. *Lilliputius Gulliver.* The Lilliputian Library. Ten volumes. (Berlin.)

1786. *The Children's Friend . . . translated by the Rev. Mark Anthony Meilan*. Twenty-four volumes. The first English translation of Berquin's *L'Ami des Enfants* (1782–3).

1787. *Adventures of a Silver Penny*.

1789. *Adventures of Master Headstrong*.

1789. *The Pocket Bible*.

1792. *The Looking-Glass for the Mind*. An abridgement of Berquin, edited by the Rev. S. Cooper, probably Richard Johnson, with cuts by John Bewick.

1795. *Anecdotes of Mary by the Good Governess*.

WILLIAM MAVOR

1796. *The Juvenile Olio*.

1798. *Youth's Miscellany*.

EDWARD AUGUSTUS KENDALL

1798. *Keeper's Travels in search of his Master*.

ELIZABETH SANDHAM

[1820.] *The Boy's School*.

1801. *Little Mountaineers*.
　　　Summer Rambles.

1803. *Old Dame Trot, and her Comical Cat*.

1806. *Continuation of the Adventures of Dame Trot*.

1808. *Tragical Wanderings . . . of Grimalkin, the Eldest Son of Dame Trot's Cat*.

1804–5. *Little Jack of all Trades*. Two Volumes. Books describing various trades and occupations, usually with pictures, were common in the lists of children's book publishers throughout the early nineteenth century

EDWARD BALDWIN (WILLIAM GODWIN)

1805. *Fables Ancient and Modern*.

ELIZA FENWICK

1805. *A Visit to the Juvenile Library*. This is important for its references to and plates of Tabart's bookshop. (See illustration, 39.)

A True History of a Little Old Woman who found a Silver Penny. This is the date given in *C.B.E.L.* The earliest I have seen is a Tabart edition dated 1806. It is the story, mostly in rhyme, of the old woman's efforts to get her pig home from market.

SARAH CATHERINE MARTIN

1805. *The Comic Adventure of Old Mother Hubbard and Her Dog*.

1806. *Continuation of the Comic Adventures. . . . A Sequel to the Comic Adventures . . . is* "by another hand".

———

[1806.] *Dame Partlet's Farm.*

1807. *Account of the Old Woman Who Sold Fruit.*

                The Butterflies' Ball and some imitations of it

1807. [William Roscoe.] *The Butterfly's Ball.*

    [Mrs. Dorset.] *The Peacock "At Home".*

    [Mrs. Dorset?] *The Lion's Masquerade.*

    W. B. *The Elephant's Ball.*

1808. J. L. B. *The Butterfly's Funeral.*

    Anon. *The Court of the Beasts.*

    Anon. *Flora's Gala.*

    Tom Tit. *The Eagle's Masque.*

    Anon. *The Fishes' Feast.*

    Mrs. Cockle. *The Fishes Grand Gala.* Two volumes.

    Anon. *The Horse's Levee.*

    Anon. *The Jack Daw "At Home".*

    Anon. *The Lobster's Voyage.*

    Anon. *The Rose's Breakfast.*

    Mrs. Dorset. *The Water-King's Levee.*

    [Ann Taylor.] *The Wedding Among the Flowers.*

    [Mrs. Dorset.] *The Butterfly's Birthday.*

    Anon. *The Council of Dogs.*

1809. Anon. *The Mermaid "At Home".*

    Mrs. Reeve. *The Flowers at Court.*

1810. Mrs. B. Hoole [i.e. Barbara Hofland]. *Le Fête de la Rose.* [The date is of the third edition.]

    Anon. *Pomona's Frolic.* Two volumes.

    Anon. *The Turtle Dove's Wedding* [undated].

1819. Anon. *The Dandies' Ball.*

1820. R. C. Barton. *Butterfly's Gala.*

    In addition to the above Darton lists the following, without dates:

    The Lion's Parliament

    The Tyger's Theatre. (By S. J. Arnold.)

    Edwards lists, *The Lioness's Rout: being a sequel to the Butterfly's Ball* (undated), and at least 20 other titles.

JAMES PARKINSON

1808. *Dangerous Sports.*

1810. *The Hare and Many Friends* (2nd ed.).

ARABELLA ARGUS

1813. *The Adventures of a Donkey.*

1821. *Farther Adventures . . .*

THOMAS LOVE PEACOCK

1814. *Sir Hornbook.*

1815. *The Old Woman and Her Three Sons.*

FRANCES BOWER VAUX

1816. *Domestic Pleasures.*

MARY ELLIOTT (BORN BELSON)

1819. *The Modern Goody Two-shoes.*

1820. *Rural Employment.*

    This very prolific writer published several books with frontispieces printed in colours by Baxter, the earliest of which appears to have been *Tales of Truth* (1836).

ISAAC TAYLOR

1818. *Scenes in Europe.* The first of a series of geographical primers by the brother of Ann and Jane, illustrated by himself and published by Harris.

AGNES STRICKLAND

1822. *The Moss-House.*

1826. *The Rival Crusoes.* Most of her historical works, notably her *Lives of the Queens of England*, have been popular with children, but fall outside our province.

―――

1823. *Dame Wiggins of Lea, and her seven wonderful cats.*

[c. 1825.] *Dame Dumpling's Trip to Market.*

T. CROFTON CROKER

1825–8. *Fairy Legends and Traditions of the South of Ireland.* Three volumes. Perhaps rather a source-book than a book actually for children.

J. A. PARIS

1827. *Philosophy in Sport.* One of the first, the most important, and the most popular of the home toy-making books. It was later extended to three volumes. It includes the first printed description of a thaumatrope, a toy which, in its reliance upon persistence of vision, is accounted a forerunner of the cinema. See especially on this, Hopwood, *Living Pictures* (1889).

FAVELL LEE BEVAN

1833. *The Peep of Day.*

1837. *Line Upon Line.*

1857. Reading Without Tears.

Although these are strictly instructional in nature, their multitudinous reprintings demand their inclusion. The narrative sections would not disgrace any of the "goody, goody" writers.

MICHAEL SCOTT

1833. Tom Cringle's Log. Two volumes.

1836. The Cruise of the Midge. Two volumes.

SARA COLERIDGE (DAUGHTER OF S. T. COLERIDGE)

1834. Pretty Lessons in Verse.

E. G. G. HOWARD

1836. Rattlin the Reefer. Three volumes. Marryat had a hand in this.

1837? The Story of the Three Bears. Until 1951 it was generally accepted that this story was an original invention of Southey's. Its first appearance in print does seem to have occurred in the fourth volume of his miscellany *The Doctor* (1837); but in the Festival Exhibition of books organised by the National Book League at the Victoria and Albert Museum, item 57a was a manuscript version by Eleanor Mure "put into verse and embellished with drawings for a Birth-Day Present to Horace Broke, Sept. 26: 1831".

The writer was an ancestress of Mr. Geoffrey Mure, Warden of Merton College, Oxford. The recipient was her uncle. This seems to dispose effectively of Southey's authorship. A version by his friend George Nicol was published (Osborne, Vol I. p. 37–8 and II p. 607).

CATHERINE SINCLAIR

1839. Holiday House. In 1849, in three-decker form, *Sir Edward Graham* is a sequel, with many of the same characters in later life.

BARBARA HOFLAND

c. 1840. The Young Crusoe. Mrs. Hofland was a prolific writer for children, and produced one of the imitations of *The Butterfly's Ball*, q.v.

LEGH RICHMOND

c. 1840. The Young Cottager.

HARRIET MARTINEAU

1841. The Playfellow. Under this general title four quarterly parts were issued, the best known of which is the third, *Feats on the Fiord*.

FREDERICK MARRYAT

1841–2. *Masterman Ready*. Three volumes.

1847. *Children of the New Forest*. Two volumes. Sadleir records a single copy of Part I of a part issue, which was not continued.

1848–9. *The Little Savage*. Two volumes.

CHARLES DICKENS

1843. *A Christmas Carol*.

1852–4. *Child's History of England*. Three volumes.

WILLIAM CHURNE OF STAFFORDSHIRE
(i.e. Francis Edward Paget)

1844. *The Hope of the Katzekopfs* (Rugeley).

ELIZABETH MISSING SEWELL AND REV. WILLIAM SEWELL

1846 ?–8. *Laneton Parsonage*. Three parts.

MATILDA ANNE MACKARNESS

1849. *A Trap to Catch a Sunbeam* (42nd ed., 1882). Her father was J. R. Planché, who translated many fairy-tales into English.

JOHN RUSKIN

1851. *The King of the Golden River*.

W. H. G. KINGSTON

1851. *Peter the Whaler*.

1862. *The Three Midshipmen*. He is credited with 171 titles in Allibone.

MARY COWDEN CLARKE

1851–2. *The Girlhood of Shakespeare's Heroines*. Three volumes.

CHARLOTTE M. YONGE

1853. *The Heir of Redclyffe*. Two volumes. Miss Yonge's first published book was *Abbey Church* (1844). The above is her best-known book. She was among the most prolific of authors. Allibone credits her with nearly 150 titles down to 1888; but she lived until 1901, and continued to publish books until 1900.

"A.L.O.E." (A Lady of England, i.e. Charlotte Maria Tucker)

[1854.] *The Claremont Tales*.

[1883.] *Life in the Eagle's Nest*.

Her biographer, Agnes Giberne, credits her with about 150 titles.

MARIA LOUISA CHARLESWORTH

1854. *Ministering Children.*
1862. *Ministering Children.* A sequel.

CHARLES KINGSLEY

1855. *Westward Ho!* Three volumes.
1863. *The Water Babies.*
1866. *Hereward the Wake.* Two volumes.

W. M. THACKERAY

1855. *The Rose and the Ring.*

MARGARET GATTY

1855–71. *Parables from Nature.* Five series.
1859. *Aunt Judy's Tales.*
1862. *Aunt Judy's Letters.*
    Founded *Aunt Judy's Magazine*, 1866. See also Ewing.

FRANCES BROWNE

1856. *Granny's Wonderful Chair.*

DINAH MARIA MULOCK (later Craik)

1856. *John Halifax, Gentleman.* Three volumes.
1872. *The Adventures of a Brownie.*

THOMAS HUGHES

1857. *Tom Brown's School Days.*

ROBERT MICHAEL BALLANTYNE

1858. *Coral Island.*
1859. *Martin Rattler.*
1861. *Dog Crusoe.*
    He is credited with seventy titles in Allibone.

FREDERICK WILLIAM FARRAR

1858. *Eric.*
1859. *Julian Horne.*
1862. *St. Winifred's.*

EBENEZER LANDELLS

[1858.] *Home Pastime, or the Child's own Toy-Maker.* Two parts. Often enlarged and reprinted.

[1860.] *The Illustrated Paper Model Maker.*

Landells, a wood-engraver, was the original projector of *Punch*. He was himself a pupil of Bewick's, and among his apprentices were Edmund Birket Foster, John Greenaway—Kate's father—and the Dalziels. His toy-making books are among the best of their period.

———————

c. 1860. *Grimm's Goblins.* For a full description see Sadleir, I, 14–15. The text is a collection of fairy-tales, the illustrations are printed in colour by Edmund Evans, after Hablot K. Browne.

MRS. HENRY WOOD

1860. *Danesbury House.*

EMMA MARSHALL

1861. *Happy Days at Fernbank.*

1876. *Life's Aftermath.*

Allibone credits her with 103 titles; but *D.N.B.* says she wrote over 200.

CHARLES READE

1861. *The Cloister and the Hearth.* Four volumes. The first form of the story, *A Good Fight*, was published in New York, with authorisation, in 1859, taken from the serial in *Good Words*.

HENRY KINGSLEY

1862. *Ravenshoe.* Three volumes.

1872. *Valentin.* Serialised in *Every Boy's Magazine* (1872).

WILLIAM BRIGHTY RANDS

1864. *Lilliput Levee.*

1871. *Lilliput Lectures.*
 Lilliput Revels.

1872. *Lilliput Legends.*

Juliana Horatia Ewing

Nearly all Mrs. Ewing's work appeared first in periodicals, including *The Monthly Packet*, *Aunt Judy's Magazine* (which she and her sister edited after the death of her mother, Mrs. Gatty), *London Society*, *The Child's Pictorial Magazine*, and *Little Folks*.

She married Major Ewing in 1867. Her first book, *Melchior's Dream* (1862), appeared under her maiden name—J. H. Gatty.

Previous check-lists of her work have appeared in Gatty, *Juliana Horatia Ewing* (S.P.C.K., 1885)—which also contains a dated list of her contributions to periodicals— and the *Cambridge Bibliography of English Literature*, III, 543 f. Neither list is complete; and the present list professes only to be more complete than either.

Many of her books were not dated on their first appearance. The dates given below, although checked with some care, should be regarded with caution. For this reason the list is given in alphabetical order. After the date the name of the illustrator is added, where known.

Baby, Puppy, and Kitty (S.P.C.K., 1885; André).

Blue and Red (S.P.C.K. 1883; André).

The Blue Bells on the Lea (S.P.C.K., 1844; André).

Brothers of Pity (S.P.C.K., 1882; André).

The Brownies (Bell, 1870; G. Cruikshank). Note.—The first issue is dated 1870. The second issue is dated 1871.

Castle in the Air (New York, 1888). This is listed in the English Catalogue for that year as by Mrs. Ewing. It is the only mention of the book that I have seen.

Convalescence (S.P.C.K., 1885; André).

Daddy Darwin's Dovecote (S.P.C.K., 1884; Caldecott).

Dandelion Clocks (S.P.C.K., 1887; G. Browne).

Doll's Housekeeping (S. P. C. K., 1884; André).

Doll's Wash (S.P.C.K., 1883; André).

A Flat Iron for a Farthing (Bell, 1872). This was illustrated by Helen Patterson, afterwards Helen Allingham, and one of the subjects was hung in the Royal Academy where it attracted the attention of Ruskin, who referred to it in his *Academy Notes*, and of a print publisher, who issued a steel engraving of it.

Grandmother's Spring (S.P.C.K., 1885; André).

A Great Emergency (Bell, 1877).

Jackanapes (S.P.C.K., 1884; Caldecott). The first issue is in uncoloured wrappers with the background of the screen blank. The last word on p. 27 is "Egad". The second issue is in boards with the design coloured, and a Union Jack as the background of the screen. The last word on p. 27 has been changed to "Why".

Jan of the Windmill (Bell, 1876; Helen Allingham.)

Little Boys and Wooden Horses (S.P.C.K., 1884; André).

Lob Lie-by-the-Fire (Bell, 1874; G. Cruikshank).

Mary's Meadow (S.P.C.K., 1886; André).

Master Fritz (S.P.C.K., 188–(?); André).

Melchior's Dream (Bell, 1862. Enlarged edition, 1885; M. Gatty. New edition 1886; Browne).

The Mill Stream (S.P.C.K., 1885; André).

Mother's Birthday Review (S.P.C.K., 1885; André).

Mrs. Overtheway's Remembrances (Bell, 1868).

Old Fashioned Fairy-Tales (S.P.C.K., 1882; André?).

An Only Child's Tea Party (S.P.C.K., 188–(?); André).

Our Garden (S.P.C.K., 1884; André).

Papa Poodle, and other Pets (S.P.C.K., 1884; André).

The Peace Egg (S.P.C.K., 1887).

The Poet and the Brook (S.P.C.K., 1883; André).

Six to Sixteen (Bell, 1875; Helen Allingham).

Snap Dragon (S.P.C.K., 1888; G. Browne?).

A Soldier's Children (S.P.C.K., 1882; André).

The Story of a Short Life (S.P.C.K., 1885; G. Browne).

A Sweet Little Dear (S.P.C.K., 1883; André).

Three Little Nest-Birds (S.P.C.K., 1883; André).

Tongues in Trees (S.P.C.K., 1884; André).

Touch Him [*Them*?] *if you Dare* (S.P.C.K., 1884; André).

We and the World (Bell, 1880).

A Week Spent in a Glass Pond (Wells, Darton, 1882; André).

BOOKS TO WHICH MRS. EWING CONTRIBUTED

By her mother, Mrs. Gatty:

1862. *Aunt Judy's Letters*. Includes three short tales by J. H. E.—"The Smut", "The Crick" and "The Brothers".

1885. *Parables From Nature* (complete edition, Bell). Includes a Memoir of her mother by J. H. E.

By her brother, A. S. Gatty:

(Date unknown.) *Little Songs for Little Voices* (Metzler). Includes "The Burial of the Linnet" by J. H. E. set to music. The words were afterwards included in *Papa Poodle* (1884).

By her sister H. F. Gatty:

1885. *Juliana Horatia Ewing and Her Books* (S.P.C.K.). Includes two hymns by J. H. E. not previously printed.

By her sister M. Gatty:

(Date unknown.) *The Human Face Divine* (Bell). Includes "My Childhood in Art" by J. H. E.

(Date unknown.) *Sacred Songs* (Boosey's Royal Editions). Includes "From Fleeting Pleasures" by J. H. E. set to music by her husband, A. D. Ewing. The words were reprinted in *Songs for Music* (1874).

1874. *Songs for Music* (King). The songs are by J. H. E., two of her brothers, and the Rev. G. J. Chester. Two of her songs in this book were also published separately as sheet-songs with music: "How Many Years Ago?", set by A. S. Gatty, and "The Elleree", set by J. F. Duggan.

William and Mary Godwin began their short publishing career in about 1805, in one of the ground-floor rooms of their house in Hanway Street ("opposite Soho Square") where they used the name of Thomas Hodgkins "at the Juvenile Library" as their imprint. In 1807 they removed to larger premises at No. 41 Skinner Street, Snow Hill, then already a small centre of children's book publishing, in which the Wallis family were located, with Darton & Co. near by. For a time the original imprint was retained, but in 1808 Hodgkins's name disappeared, and the usual imprint was "At the Juvenile Library". In 1808 M. J. Godwin's name first appears on the title-pages, and is almost invariably used thereafter until about 1825, when the business seems to have come to an end.[1]

1805. *The King and Queen of Hearts* (1st ed.). Reissued from the same engraved plates in 1806, 1808, 1809, and 1819, with the necessary alterations on the printed title-page or the wrapper, or on both. Almost certainly issued both coloured and uncoloured, although all the few copies now surviving seem to be coloured. Whether this colouring is always original may be doubted. Complete copies of the first printing are exceedingly rare and valuable. It was first identified as being by Lamb by E. V. Lucas, in 1902. In a letter to Wordsworth dated February 1, 1806, Lamb refers to a parcel of books he has sent, including "A Paraphrase on the King and Queen of Hearts, of which I, being the author, beg Mr. Johnny Wordsworth's acceptance and opinion". On March 19, 1902, the copy discovered by Lucas was sold for £222. It was of the 1809 issue. A facsimile edition of it was then issued by Methuen. On June 5, 1902, a copy turned up at Sotheby's dated 1806, and sold for £240, and, in November, another, dated 1808, was sold at Puttick's for £155. This is a fair reflection of the average value, with not much differentiation according to date, until 1927, when a London bookseller offered a copy of the first printing for no less than £2,700. In 1929 a copy of the first printing was sold by auction in New York for $4,500.

There is no evidence whatever that *The History of the King and Queen of Clubs*, or *The History of the King and Queen of Spades*, both published by "W. Newbery, 54 Upper Marylebone Street" without date, but at about the same time as Lamb's little book, had anything to do with him at all, beyond a flattering similarity.

1807. *Tales from Shakespeare*. Two volumes (2nd ed., 1809 (slightly corrected); 3rd ed., 1810).[2] The rather complicated story of this publication is not easy to disentangle. In June 1806 Mary Lamb wrote to Sarah Stoddart telling her that the "Tales" were to be published in separate booklets, "I mean in single stories, like the children's little shilling books". Godwin advertised these separate issues "in eight single numbers", and at least one set of the eight still survives in the British Museum. No trace of the other twelve tales in separate form is known. The fact that the first of them preceded the complete collection in two volumes, that they were not all separately issued, and that "remainders" of some of them, bound more than one in a volume—and sometimes with the imprint of another publisher, William Jackson and Co.—suggests that they were not a success in that form.

A little further light is thrown on the failure of the separate issue by the fact that in the second edition the twenty plates from the first edition were omitted,

[1] Between 1814 and 1825 it was Godwin & Co.
[2] This edition has plates and is described as the second edition.

53. A page of the original manuscript and a sketch for *The Tale of Benjamin Bunny*, showing Miss Potter's method of composition

K, Kia Khan Kreuse, the Conjurer, transmogrified them into Pippins, because Snip's wife cried, Illikipilliky! lass a-day! 'tis too bad to titter at a body, when Hamet el Mammet, the bottle-nosed Barber of Balsora, laughed ha! ha! ha! on beholding the Elephant spout mud over the 'Prentice, who pricked his trunk with a needle, as Dicky Snip the Taylor read the Proclamation of Chrononho-tonthologos, offering a thousand sequins for taking Bombardi-nian, Bashaw of three tails, who killed Aldiborontiphosky-phorniostikos

M, Muley Hassan, Mufti of Moldavia, put on his Barnacles, to see little Tweedle gobble them up, when Kia Khan Kreuse transmogrified them into Pippins, because Snip's wife cried Illikipilliky, lass a-day, 'tis too bad to titter at a body, when Hamet el Mammet, the

54   An "Arabian Nights" derivative treated as an alphabet. Published by Dean and Co., *c.* 1820, under the formidable title of Aldiborontophoskyphorniostikos

THE IMPRUDENCE OF MR. WOODIN.

THERE was a queer fellow named Woodin.

Who always ate pepper with pudding,

    Till, one day, 'tis said,

    He sneezed off his head!

That imprudent old fellow named Woodin.

55   An imitation of Lear. From *Funny Figures* by *A Funnyman*
(E. Bradley, creator of *Mr. Verdant Green*), 1868

and a prefatory note explains that this is because they had been found more suitable for young ladies than for children as originally intended.

Charles Lamb did not care very much for the illustrations himself. He wrote to Wordsworth asking him to excuse the plates as the "choice of subjects was left to the Bad Baby", which was Mary's nickname for Mrs. Godwin. She "has chosen one from dam'd beastly vulgarity . . . to another has given a name which exists not in the tale, Nic Bottom, and which she thought would be funny . . ."

On Lamb the standard biography is E. V. Lucas's, published by Methuen in 1905 and frequently reprinted. Lucas also edited his letters. There is no adequate bibliography: J. C. Thomson's *Bibliography of . . . Charles and Mary Lamb* (Hull: Tutin, 1908) falls short of modern standards. Some of his children's books are described with facsimiles in *An Important Collection of Some of the Rarer Works of Charles Lamb*—a bookseller's catalogue issued by Tregaskis in 1927.

1808. *Adventures of Ulysses* (2nd ed.; 1819).

1809. *Mrs. Leicester's School* (reprinted same year; 8th ed., 1823, 9th ed., 1825).

1809. *Poetry for Children*. Not reprinted, but twenty-two of the pieces were included in *The First Book of Poetry*, edited by F. W. Mylius (1811), which also contained one new piece, "A Birthday Thought", signed M. L., but actually by C. L., the attribution being corrected in later editions.

1811. *Prince Dorus*. Not certainly, but almost surely by Lamb. Crabb Robinson notes in his diary (May 15, 1811): "C. Lamb wrote this year for children a version of the Nursery Tale of Prince Dorus". It is, indeed, a new version of an old story and Godwin's edition bears a likeness to early cuts from the story too close to be anything but derivative.

A facsimile edition was issued in 1889.

Beauty and the Beast (undated, but probably 1811). It was occasionally reprinted from the original plates (it bears a family likeness to *The King and Queen of Hearts*) with some variants confusing for the bibliographer. A facsimile edition was issued by Field and Tuer.

1824. *The New Year's Feast on his Coming of Age* (published by Harris). In January 1823 Lamb contributed to the *London Magazine* a prose essay signed "Elia s Ghost" entitled "Rejoicings upon the New Year's Coming of Age", which was reprinted in *Last Essays of Elia*. Harris's booklet is in verse, with a coloured picture at the head of each page. The preface explicitly states that it is principally a versification of the *London Magazine* essay, and the wording is very similar.

CHAPTER FIVE

THE TRIUMPH OF NONSENSE

1. *Edward Lear*

CHRONOLOGICAL order is impossible to observe in this period, and Mrs. Ewing and the boys' magazines have carried us beyond one of the most important events of our entire study. It is reasonably certain that neither the Reverend Charles Lutwidge Dodgson nor Lewis Carroll would have approved of Ching-Ching, the boy detective, Tom Takeitall, or Midshipman Merry. But then he does not seem to have thought much of boys anyway. Nevertheless his two most famous books appeal equally strongly to boys and girls alike.

He, too, however, carries us rather ahead of our time, for before him we must consider Edward Lear. The details of his life are either well known or readily available elsewhere,[1] and we may confine our attention to his writings. He wrote much in "limerick" form; but he was not its originator. The acknowledgement of his indebtedness to earlier writers for the limerick form is his own, although he misquoted the first line of the verse he remembered, which, in its original printing reads "There was a *sick* man of Tobago" (not *old* man). This comes from *Anecdotes and Adventures of Fifteen Gentlemen* (Marshall, *c.* 1822), which was, in fact, only one of many small collections of verses in similar form. The earliest of these may have originated with Harris, who published, with the date 1821, *The History of Sixteen Wonderful Old Women*. The plates are dated 1820, which makes it possible that the title was post-dated for the Christmas trade. It contained such verses as this[2]:

> There was an Old Woman named Towl,
> Who went out to Sea with her Owl,
> But the Owl was Sea-sick
> And scream'd for Physic;
> Which sadly annoyed Mistress Towl.

Other publishers soon caught on to the idea, and as they are as imitative as children themselves there was soon a host of books in similar form. They do not seem to have retained their favour, however, and were almost entirely unknown to the children who read Lear's Nonsense Books.

The title of Lear's first book for children *A Book of Nonsense*, was a small stroke

[1] Notably in Davidson, *Edward Lear* (1938).
[2] Quoted from Darton, p. 208.

56 From Lear's *Nonsense Pictures* (1872)

of genius, for it showed the children of 1846—the year of its original publication—
that here was an author who considered it his business solely to entertain them, and,
plagued as they were by the inheritors of the Puritan mantle, such a reassurance
compelled success. It is no denigration of his earliest book, however, to suggest
that Lear's genius for writing nonsense flowered fully only in 1871–7, when he
produced the short series of Nonsense Stories which contain the quintessence of his
comic inventiveness. Better limericks, even better nonsense limericks, have been
written since his first collection appeared; the Clerihew, beloved of high-brows,
is their latest development; but no one but Lewis Carroll at his best has equalled the
Nonsense Stories. Even Lear himself must have found them less easy to throw off than
the shorter verses. There are only about a score of them, and almost every one is a gem.

In the 1871 volume[1] came "The Owl and the Pussy Cat", which is absolutely
charming and catches the eye and the ear in its very first lines:

> The Owl and the Pussy-Cat went to sea
>   In a beautiful pea-green boat,
> They took some honey, and plenty of money,
>   Wrapped up in a five-pound note.

Lewis Carroll must have had that ringing in his head, when he wrote *The Hunting
of the Snark*, and still more so "The Jumblies", who

> . . . bought an Owl, and a useful Cart,
> And a pound of Rice, and a Cranberry Tart,
>   And a hive of silvery Bees.
> And they bought a Pig, and some green Jack-daws,
> And a lovely Monkey with lollipop paws,
>   And forty bottles of Ring-Bo-Bee,
>   And no end of Stilton Cheese.

[1] *Nonsense Songs.*

The Jumblies, returning to those lands "far and few" in which they lived, had visited the hills of the Chankly Bore, whose towering heights brooded over the coal-black night through which shone the luminous nose of the Dong, who also fell in love with a Jumbly girl, when that famous sieve-load landed near the Zemmery Fidd where the Oblong Oysters grow. But she sailed away with her compatriots when they left and the Dong mourned her ever after. The Yonghy-Bonghy Bo, however, went off on a turtle, and it was the lady-love's turn, Lady Jingly Jones, finally unfaithful to her mate at home in England, to weep for a departed lover. Mr. and Mrs. Discobbolos, the toeless Pobble, the Quangle Wangle and the Akond of Swat, like the Dong and the Yonghy-Bonghy-Bo, are all in the 1877 volume.[1]

Comparison is inapplicable and will not be attempted. These verses are incomparable as they are immortal. But coincidence is again at work. Lear's revival of the nonsense verse form now called a limerick[2] has unquestionable priority, but, although the first book was continually reprinted after its original appearance in 1846,[3] and Lear continually added new verses and drawings to the later editions, he did not produce a second volume of nonsense until 1870, and meanwhile "Alice" had appeared.[4]

2. Lewis Carroll

There was something in the air again, and the two authors' books were found in the same nurseries. There is nothing whatsoever that is new that one can say about Lewis Carroll; and if one indulges in a little gentle speculation on the possible influence on him of Lear's first *Book of Nonsense* it must be taken at its face value, as pure speculation and with no known foundation in fact. Both were writers of nonsense, and writers of genius in their kind. Dodgson was born in 1832, and thus was a little old for the Nonsense Book; 1846 was, in fact, the year he entered Rugby. But he had ten brothers and sisters, all younger than himself, for whom he was accustomed, as a boy, to provide amusement. It seems incredible that in the rectory at Daresbury, where he was born, the *Book of Nonsense* should not have been found. In later life Dodgson moved in somewhat the same circles as Lear, but neither ever mentions the other. Nevertheless it does seem likely that Dodgson saw the book as a boy, and that he was influenced by it, if only to the extent of showing his younger brothers and sisters that he could do that sort of thing equally well.

On the other hand the likeness between some of the Carroll verses and those

---

1 *Laughable Lyrics.*

2 The origin of this use of the word is unknown.

3 The first Routledge edition is called the fifth, and is dated 1863.

4 A note on publishing practice may avoid confusion here. Christmas then, as now, was a favoured time for the publication of children's books, and it was the general habit to post-date the title-pages, so that the books should appear as newly published all through the following year. Thus *Nonsense Songs* is dated 1871 on its title-page, but was in fact on sale in the book-shops during December 1870. Similarly, *Through the Looking-Glass*, although dated 1872, was published in December 1871. Dodgson received his own copies on December 6.

of Lear may be no more than another remarkable instance of simultaneous inspiration. Be that as it may, Dodgson was certainly producing nonsense verse long before he was known as a writer. Already in 1855, in both the *Comic Times* and the *Whitby Gazette*, humorous verses had appeared which he was later to revise for inclusion in one or other of the Carroll books.

The most remarkable of these anticipatory pieces was included in a small hand-written magazine that he produced for his brothers and sisters under the title *Mischmasch*. This bore the title "Stanza of Anglo-Saxon Poetry", and is dated in its author's hand, 1855.

STANZA OF ANGLO-SAXON POETRY.

TWAS BRYLLYG, AND YE SLYTHY TOVES
DID GYRE AND GYMBLE IN YE WABE:
ALL MIMSY WERE YE BOROGOVES;
AND YE MOME RATHS OUTGRABE.

This curious fragment reads thus in modern characters:

TWAS BRYLLYG, AND THE SLYTHY TOVES
DID GYRE AND GYMBLE IN THE WABE!
ALL MIMSY WERE THE BOROGOVES;
AND THE MOME RATHS OUTGRABE.

The meanings of the words are as follows:

BRYLLYG. (derived from the verb to BRYL or BROIL). "the time of broiling dinner, i.e. the close of the afternoon."

SLYTHY. (compounded of SLIMY and LITHE). "smooth and active.

TOVE. a species of Badger. They had smooth white hair, long

57 The first attempt at "Jabberwocky" (1855)

It is, in fact, the first stanza of "Jabberwocky", and comparison of this facsimile with the text as printed in *Through the Looking-Glass* is remarkably interesting.[1]

1 It is as well to keep the facts about priorities well in mind in matters of this sort. Madan, *Dodgson Handbook*, p. 47, for example, writes: "it is believed that Edward Lear in his *Book of Nonsense* (1846) first popularised the style in England, using such expressions as 'slobacious light' and 'scroobious ways'." In fact no such expressions appear in the first edition, and, unless the "umbrageous old person of Spain" qualifies as onomatopoeic, the only expression of the kind is in the "ombliferous Person of Crete". Lear's first extensive use of neologisms coincided almost exactly with Dodgson's, in about 1870-1.

58 "The Jabberwock with eyes of flame." This was the illustration that was removed from the frontispiece position, for fear it might frighten children

The origin of the greatest of all English stories for children, for we may treat the two "Alice" books as one, is too well known to bear more than the merest outline of it here. Dodgson himself recorded in his diary the very beginning of the whole thing. Under July 4, 1862, is the entry "I made an expedition *up* the river to Godstow with the three Liddells; we had tea on the bank there, and did not reach Christ Church till half-past eight." It was on that day that he told the three little girls the story of *Alice's Adventures Underground*, which he afterwards wrote out for the second of them, the eponymous heroine of the story, and which he later recast and extended into *Alice's Adventures in Wonderland*.[1] George Macdonald persuaded Dodgson to publish the story in its extended form; but he was so modest as to its possible success that it never seems to have occurred to him that a publisher would consider issuing it at his own risk. He therefore assumed the cost of publication himself, and Macmillan's agreed to market the book over their imprint.[2] It may be that modesty was not the only motive in mind, for he turned out to be most exacting and difficult to please in everything relating to production.

Indeed, he was aware that he was by no means an easy person to deal with in matters of this kind, and the tribute he paid to his publisher's long-suffering patience was no more than deserved.[3]

He admits that he has himself "inflicted on that most patient and painstaking firm, Messrs. Macmillan and Co., about as much wear and worry as ever publishers have lived through. The day when they undertake a book for me is a *dies nefastus* for them. From that day till the book is out—an interval of some two or three years on an average—there is no pause in 'the pelting of the pitiless storm' of directions and questions on every conceivable detail".

One who has been privileged to read his letters to that publisher can fully confirm the justice of this self-chastisement. Well might they have thought how simple publishing would be if only there did not have to be authors.

Exact dates are not always easy to discover in the history of writing and preparing the book. The earliest that can be quoted with any certainty is April 5, 1864, when Tenniel agreed to make drawings for the illustrations at a cost to the author of £148. By that time the whole of it must have been written and in the hands of the Oxford University Press, who printed the first edition, for by May 13 they had presented a specimen page in type, at a cost of two shillings, and by November Dodgson was discussing with Macmillan the colour of the cover, and expressing a preference for red over green. Tenniel's drawings lagged very much behind, however, and

1 It may be as well here to recall that it was the manuscript of the original version of the story that was sold for £15,400 at Sotheby's in 1928, crossed the Atlantic, and now, by the generosity of transatlantic friends, reposes in the British Museum. No trace of the manuscript of either *Alice's Adventures in Wonderland* or of *Through the Looking-Glass* can now be found.

2 They took twenty per cent of the gross receipts.

3 In *Profits of Authorship*, a sixpenny pamphlet issued over Macmillan's imprint in 1884, but no copy of which is known to have survived. The present quotations are from Collingwood's *Life*, p. 226.

Dodgson despaired of their being ready by Christmas. However, on December 16 he was able to send the publisher the complete book in slips for their final decision as to whether they would issue it over their imprint.

On May 24, 1865, all the electros were made for the cuts, and it was hoped to begin the actual printing in a few days. On June 30 the Oxford Press delivered 2,000 sets of sheets, which Dodgson sent to Macmillan asking for fifty bound copies as soon as possible, to give away as presents, and one copy bound in white vellum, which he obviously intended for Alice herself. He sent her this copy on July 4, 1865, the third anniversary of the Godstow excursion. Almost immediately, however, he had qualms about the quality of the printing, especially it would seem of the illustrations, and he asked Macmillan to provide a quotation for reprinting the whole book. He received this before the end of July, and was alarmed that it would cost him more than £200—"£100 more than it cost to print the book in Oxford". He was already more than £450 out of pocket—the wood-blocks had cost £203—and he could see no alternative to the destruction of the original sheets, a dead loss to himself.

However, he decided to reprint, abandoning the first printing for the time being, and calling in all copies of it that he could find. In November he got back the copy he had sent to Alice, and asked for the binding to be transferred to a copy of the new printing. On November 12 he received twenty-five bound copies of the book— now post-dated for 1866—and in November 19 a further fifty, together with an example bound in vellum.[1] In December it was out in time to catch the Christmas trade.

On August 16, 1866, he wrote to complain that he was £350 out of pocket on the transaction so far, but nine days later he was cheered if somewhat alarmed by the news that his zealous publishers considered that a new printing of 3,000 copies would not be too large. However he was already pondering the idea of a sequel. He had also cleared out nearly all the 2,000 copies of the first printing, to an American publisher, Messrs. Appleton, and had received £120 for them.[2]

At the beginning of June 1868 "Alice II" was coming along very well, but he was in despair about the illustrations. Tenniel had declined, and so had Dodgson's second choice, Sir Noel Paton. He was rather taken with an illustrator in *Fun*, who signed himself "Bab". "The artist's name, I am told, is Gilbert: his power in grotesque is extraordinary—but I have seen no symptoms of his being able to draw anything pretty and graceful. I should be very glad if you could ascertain (without directly communicating with him, so as to commit me in any way)

[1] When this copy, with Lewis Carroll's signed inscription to Alice was sold at Sotheby's in 1928, it was described as being in the original presentation binding of morocco. It has evidently been rebound since she received it from the author.

[2] In January 1867 he reported the receipt of a New York journal for December 1866, in which the first half of the story was printed, complete with the pictures, ending with "Conclusion next month". I can find no record of the survival of any copy of this printing.

59 Illustration to "The Seven League Boots", by W. S. Gilbert in *Good Words* (1869)

whether he *has* such a power. If so, I think he would do. Some of his pictures are full of fun—But I can't find anyone who knows him."[1]

Most of the rest of the year 1868 was spent fussing about the binding and general production of *Phantasmagoria*, and the German and French translations of "Alice", but before it was out he announced Tenniel's consent to illustrate "the new volume of 'Alice'", and as soon as Clay the printer was clear of other work for him he would send a considerable section of the manuscript for setting. Throughout 1869 and 1870 there was enormous fussation and bother about the production and quality of the new book, not only were various titles tried, with various forms of lay-out—including at one stage the idea of a picture-title, which was rejected by Tenniel—but the exact position, not only of each word on the title, but also of the punctuation, was discussed. The question of the size of type to be used would be varied by such questions as whether an oval piece of looking-glass could be bound into the cover of the special copy intended for Miss Alice Liddell.

Tenniel was holding up the printing. It was not entirely his fault. He had originally been asked for forty-two pictures—the same number as for "Alice"—but this had been enlarged to fifty. When the printing of the pictures did start there was more trouble about their lack of brilliance, and Dodgson was prepared to miss the Christmas trade rather than approve anything less than what he considered the best possible result. His own words are:

> You will think me a lunatic for thus wishing to send away money from the doors; and will tell me perhaps that I shall thus lose thousands of would-be purchasers, who will not wait so long, but will go and buy other Christmas-books. I wish I could put into words how entirely such arguments go for nothing with me. As to how many copies we sell I care absolutely nothing: the one only thing I *do* care for is, that all the copies that *are* sold shall be artistically first-rate.

Further delay was caused by a sudden qualm that the Jabberwock, chosen for the frontispiece, might be too terrible a monster and might frighten small children. The extremely practical and painstaking author immediately had copies of it struck

[1] Dodgson's having considered W. S. Gilbert as a possible illustrator for *Through the Looking-Glass* appears to be unrecorded. There is little wonder that Dodgson found him difficult to contact. Gilbert was still a somewhat obscure journalist, his first great hit coming with the publication of *Bab Ballads* in 1869, all of which had, however, appeared in *Fun* and must have been among the contributions that caught Dodgson's eye.

off, composed a letter of twenty-two lines, which he had printed and sent to a few friends whose opinion he valued, asking them what they thought. As a result the White Knight was promoted to the frontispiece and the Jabberwock transferred to page 23, facing the verses it illustrates.[1]

Nevertheless the book was out for Christmas, 1871, although dated 1872, and the whole of the 8,000 copies in the first edition was immediately taken by the booksellers.

This rather lengthy account of the genesis and parturition of the two books has been thought justified partly by reason of their unparalleled importance in the history of children's books, and partly because the complete story has not hitherto been recorded anywhere. Before Dodgson died 156,000 copies of "Alice" and 107,000 copies of the sequel had been sold. By 1911 650,000 of the former, and 430,000 of the latter had been published. The copyrights of the text expired in 1907 and 1947, and since then innumerable editions have appeared and continue to appear. Until 1953 Macmillan's retained the exclusive use of the illustrations by Tenniel, whose long life extended from 1820 to 1914.

It is indeed a very curious fact that although there are nearly 900 entries in the bibliography of Dodgson's works compiled by Williams and Madan, he is nevertheless to all intents and purposes a one-book writer; if the two Alice books may be counted as one. Had it not have been for the enormous success of these books *The Hunting of the Snark* might have achieved a minor success, and the *Sylvie and Bruno* volumes would probably never have been written, let alone published. All the same much of his other work bears a direct relation to the Alice books, and it is distinctly possible that only the man who produced those obscure books on the ramifications of mathematics could have written the Alice stories. The difference between Dodgson and Carroll is less real than it has been made out to be.

He was a tutor of mathematics at Christ Church, Oxford, but he was not brilliantly successful either as a teacher or as a mathematician. Mathematics is a branch of logic, and Dodgson was far too successful at pressing things to their logical conclusions. There is no escaping his logic, but his continual application of its stern requirements to practical problems produced uniformly despairing results. Thus he demonstrated beyond question the injustice of the customary methods of awards in lawn-tennis tournaments. The result, as his bibliographers remark, was "terribly near perfection", but the impossibly elaborate nature of his own scheme would merely have resulted in "many fewer competitors, a shorter tournament, and less gate-money!" He frequently attacked the accepted method of counting votes in various kinds of elections, but the main impression left on one of his readers by a careful perusal of his ideas is that their adoption would principally result in the election of half-members to the House of Commons.

[1] Incidentally, the mirror-printing of the first stanza of this poem had been the cause of much anxious suggestion and elaborate experiment by Dodgson. He had originally intended the whole poem to be printed in this form, but eventually satisfied himself with a single stanza because he thought that too much of it might be tiring for small children.

In his theoretical treatises, all produced at his own expense and at a loss, his propositions are essentially Carrollian in style, and the elucidations of his problems are humorously worded and interlarded with puns. Indeed it is possible to regard much of his mathematical and logical writing as a series of trial runs for the glorious logical absurdities which are the foundation of the Alice stories. In them we see him fully aware of the ridiculous situations produced by taking words in their literal meaning, by regarding them, as he was apt to do in his serious writings, as symbols or counters in a mathematical problem. He dealt ''with ordinary sentences and ideas as if they were mathematically defined, so that by processes of a quasi-mathematical character, infallible conclusions could be reached''.[1]

Now whereas this method of approach is unfruitful in treating ordinary phraseology as a basis for mathematical deduction, it is immensely successful and riotously amusing when made the subject of a joke. The conversation between Niemand and Minos in *Euclid and His Modern Rivals* is strikingly compared by Lennon with the White King's conversation with Alice when she saw ''Nobody'' approaching, and the same writer aptly categorises Dodgson's writings on various aspects of calculation —''tournaments, voting, ciphers, the eight-hour law, new games and new rules for old games, all based on attempts at simplification or justice, all mathematically ingenious, and all as practical as the White Knight's plan to dye his whiskers green, and always to use so large a fan that they could not be seen''.

Indeed the tacit assumption behind the work of Dodgson's bibliographers, and the basis of the omnivorous collecting of all his writings is most amply justifiable, for the connection between *The Enunciations of Euclid I–VI* and *Symbolic Logic*, through *Doublets* and *Pillow Problems*, with the Alice books is unmistakable and indispensable to a full comprehension of his genius.

3. Others

There are but two others at all worthy to be considered in the same category as Lear and Carroll. Edward Bradley, who usually wrote under the pseudonym of ''Cuthbert Bede'', is not even mentioned by Darton; and it is doubtful whether *The Adventures of Mr. Verdant Green* and its sequels were ever regarded by their author as likely to appeal to children. They have been described as similar to the Tom and Jerry stories, or, more accurately, as a kind of undergraduate Pickwick Papers. The truth is that, like so many writings of the period, especially those of the second rank, their alternately boisterous and facetious comedy makes one wonder that they can ever have appealed to adults.

Bradley wrote at least one book for children, *Fairy Fables* (1858), but it is equally undistinguished in its text and its illustrations, which are by Crowquill. Indeed, he is included here only by virtue of his imitation of Lear's *Book of Nonsense*, called

---

[1] Bishop Strong, as quoted by Lennon, p. 273. The whole of her Chapter 15 is highly provocative and suggestive on the present point.

Funny Figures, by A Funnyman (1858). One of the pictures and rhymes is reproduced (**55**), and it will be seen that they are not entirely negligible.

Ridiculous accusations of plagiarism were made against Dodgson[1]; but he himself had one successful, though now largely forgotten emulator, in the person of G. E. Farrow, whose brilliant pastiche of "Alice"—*The Wallypug of Why*—is shortly dealt with in a later chapter. (See pp. 155–7.)[2]

BOOKS APPLICABLE TO THIS CHAPTER

Angus Davidson's *Edward Lear* (1938) is the best life. The late W. B. Osgood Fields's catalogue of his own collection, *Edward Lear on my Shelves* (1933), although elaborately and expensively produced at the Bremer Presse—155 copies were printed and a few offered for sale at $100—is pretentious rather than informative.

The *Handbook of the Literature of the Rev. C. L. Dodgson* compiled by S. H. Williams and F. Madan for the Oxford University Press in 1931 and the Supplement issued in 1935, on the other hand are nearly all that could be desired in such a work. Even to the lay reader the lengthy notes are important and frequently fascinating. The technical description of the 1865 "Alice" given in the main work is misleading; and even the correction in the Supplement is not entirely accurate. Some additional information on "Alice" is given in the present chapter; but further investigation is required to complete the story of its mishaps and final printing. M. L. Parrish's two volumes, *A List of the Writings of Lewis Carroll in the Library at Dormy House, Pine Valley, New Jersey* (1928–33), are companions to the above, but only sixty-six copies of each volume were issued. This magnificent collection, misleadingly titled, for it includes most of the non-Carrollian works also, is now in the Library of Princeton University in New Jersey.

F. B. Lennon's *Lewis Carroll. A Biography* (Cassell, 1947), is the best life. Others are listed in Madan.

LEWIS CARROLL (Rev. Charles Lutwidge Dodgson)
(Full details of all his books are in Madan.)

1845–62. Between these years C. L. D. produced a series of handwritten volumes for the amusement of his brothers and sisters. Of these, two have survived, both now in the Houghton Library at Harvard University.

c. 1849–50. *The Rectory Umbrella*.

1855–62. *Mischmasch*. In No. 3 appeared "I never loved a dear Gazelle", in No. 4 "She's all my fancy painted him", and in No. 8 "Twas bryllyg . . .", all but the first of which were later used in the "Alice" books.

---

[1] Just how ridiculous these were may be seen in the charge that "Alice" had been cribbed from Tom Hood the younger's *From Nowhere to the North Pole*, first published in 1875.

[2] The numerous parodies of "Alice", political and otherwise, are obviously of no immediate concern. Many of them are listed in Madan. It also lists *Wanted—A King* (1890), by "Maggie Browne" (Margaret Hamer) as a direct imitation of "Alice". Dodgson knew of this imitation, for he sent Maggie Bowman a rhyme about it in 1891.

THE PLATES

As 👁 was going to St Ives 012804

I met

Each wife had

Each cat had

Each rat had

How many were going to St Ives.

My dearest little Pet

Enclosed is my D visite Also one

of Dr , Dr the of

Mr and Mrs Baby's picture

as ugly as an or a was taken

in spite of her but we got

to amuse her, and also a

A was blown by a very strong

yesterday, till it rose up to an

60 Sinclair's *A First of April Nonsense Letter*

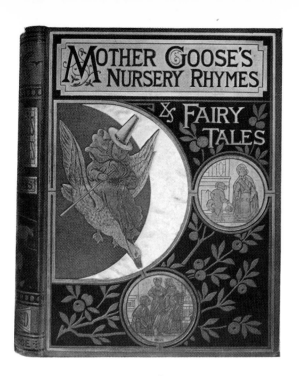

*Mother Goose's Nursery
Rhymes (c. 1880)*

72, 73 Decorative use of cloth
in the nineteenth century

Spring Flowers (c. 1840)

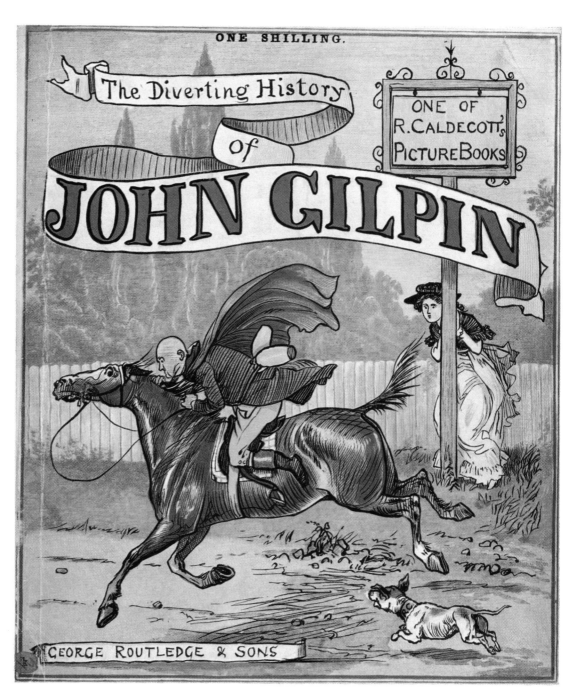

77 A Caldecott picture book (1878)

Twice FIVE are TEN Steam Boats,
Anchored in Plymouth Sound.

80 Walter Crane in an unusual mood. *Song of Sixpence Toy Book* (c. 1870)

Engraved and Printed in Colours by Vizetelly Brothers and Co.

AUTUMN:—HARVEST TIME.

95 One of Miller's four country books, 1846–7.   An early example
of printing in colours after Birket Foster

98 An illustration from *Punctuation Personified*

As 👁 was going to St Ives 012804 £13

I met

Each wife had

Each cat had

Each rat had

How many were going to St Ives.

My dearest little Pet

Enclosed is my D visite Also one

of Dr. , Dr. the of

Mr. and Mrs. Baby's picture

as ugly as an or a was taken

in spite of her but we got

to amuse her, and also a

A was blown by a very strong

yesterday, till it rose up to an

60 Sinclair's *A First of April Nonsense Letter*

1865–6. *Alice's Adventures in Wonderland*. The 1865 edition was withdrawn, but a few copies survive.

1872. *Through the Looking-Glass*.

1876. *The Hunting of the Snark*.

[1886.] *Alice's Adventures Underground*. This is a facsimile of the original manuscript of the story as told on the river expedition at Oxford. It was this manuscript that was sold for £15,400 in 1928, and which, after a sojourn in the U.S.A., was restored to Great Britain by the generosity of American subscription. It is now in the British Museum.

1889. *Sylvie and Bruno*

1893. *Sylvie and Bruno Concluded*.

EDWARD LEAR

1846. *A Book of Nonsense*. In 1861 and again in 1863 further verses and pictures were added.

1871. *Nonsense Songs, Botany and Alphabets*. Contains "The Owl and the Pussy Cat" and "The Jumblies".

1872. *More Nonsense Pictures, Rhymes, etc.*

1877. *Laughable Lyrics*. Last, but not least, this contains "The Yonghy-Bonghy-Bo", "Mr. and Mrs. Discobbolos", "The Pobble", "The Quangle-Wangle", "The Dong", and the "Akond of Swat".

CUTHBERT BEDE (Rev. Edward Bradley).

1858. *Funny Figures. By A. Funnyman*.

CHAPTER SIX

AFTER CARROLL

THEORETICALLY the period from 1865 to the end of the century ought to be the most crowded and varied of all; and so it is in a way. There were more books written for children, and of more different kinds, than in almost any other period; and the congestion is increased by the large number of books "adopted by children" almost immediately on publication. Yet there are reasons why, from our point of view, the period is one of the least interesting of all.

First there is the artificiality of division. The period from 1865 to 1900 is of no great significance in itself; and the very title chosen for this chapter suggests anti-climax. The division has been made quite deliberately because the period is something of an anti-climax after "Alice". There is no comparable giant before or after it; but the pre-Carroll period may be regarded as leading up to Carroll himself. Nevertheless there are several writers after 1865 who are worthy of special mention. The perceptible evolutionary flow until "Alice" is reached, and the new vigour imparted by its appearance, encouraged experiment in all directions. "Alice", apart from its own triumphal quality, demonstrated for the first time completely the range and potentialities of the juvenile market. Here was a book, published not at a few pence but at seven shillings and sixpence, which could hardly be produced quickly enough to keep it in print. Imitativeness among publishers is almost an occupational disease, of which several examples have transpired in the present history. It was not proof against this clear demonstration of the possibilities.

A contributory feature was the spread of education. One notices gradually as the nineteenth century proceeds a marked change in the kind of book provided to teach children to spell and to read. At the beginning of the century primers are designed according to the fancy and ingenuity of publishers[1] : by the end of the century the essential requirements in such books had been laid down by officials of the Board of Education.

This is no place to discuss the history of education, but a brief glance at a few significant dates is almost indispensable to a proper grasp of the great upward sweep in the publication of children's books.

In 1832 the same government that passed the Reform Bill made provision for an education grant of £20,000. In 1839 Lord Melbourne increased the grant to

1 See pp. 217 ff. for some account of them.

£39,000, and set up the first separate office in charge of education—the Committee of Council on Education. In 1840 the Grammar School Act rescued many old foundations from a state of decay; and the training-college grants (1843) and pupil-teacher system (1846) took care of the provision of teachers. Capitation grants were introduced in 1853, and extended in 1856; with official requirements in the way of examination results attached to the earning of them. Thus the education grant rose from £20,000 in 1832 to £663,400 in 1858. A minister responsible to Parliament for educational affairs had been appointed in 1856.

The Act of 1870 provided the organisation by means of which Disraeli was enabled to pass the Act of 1876 instituting compulsory education. The grant had now grown to £1,600,000, and elementary education was available for 3,000,000 children.

This, naturally, had its ultimate effect on publishing of all kinds; but the immediate creation of multitudes of new potential customers for the bookshops is what concerns us. Critical customers, moreover, now less likely to accept without question the selections of their elders; increasingly insistent that their own tastes were catered for.

Lewis Carroll was exactly to their taste; although it was soon amply clear that his was an impossibly high standard—a standard, indeed, which he himself was to reach only twice.

But the young readers were clamorous for new books; and the demand created a supply. They were conditioned to the pointing of a moral, and a new author, beginning her career by winning a competition prize of £100 for a temperance novelette called *Danesbury House*, thus provided the ideal Band of Hope prize over which countless thousands of youngsters would weep their appreciation of a narrative power that was to come to its full force a year later with *East Lynne*.

"Alice" did not kill off all the namby-pamby writers, of course: "Hesba Stretton", Mrs. Molesworth, and Mrs. Hodgson Burnett are witnesses to the contrary. But the mortality was high. Henty in the 'sixties was ready to grasp the torch when Kingston's hand should fail, and to show the way to Doyle and Haggard. Stevenson, graduating in a magazine that had successfully shouldered off the seductive competition of E. J. Brett's popular if low-grade periodicals, had serialised *Treasure Island* in 1881–2. Mayne Reid, with *The Headless Horseman* (1866); Blackmore with *Lorna Doone* (1875); Clark Russell, with *The Wreck of the Grosvenor* (1877); and Jefferies, with *Bevis* (1882), found that publication in either part issue or three-decker form no longer secured an author against juvenile approval.

It was the period of the "rattling good yarn"; and, besides those already mentioned, the lesser figures may also be named of Talbot Baines Reed, Manville Fenn, Anstey, "Q", Gordon Stables, Anthony Hope—creator of "Ruritania", let it not be forgotten—Merriman, Weyman, and three women—Anna Sewell, L. T. Meade and, best of all, E. Nesbit.[1]

[1] Mrs. Ewing has already been dealt with in Chapter 4.

The influx of new readers also raised other problems, which were not solved, but rather aggravated, by the greatly increased number of writers. The methods of book production in use at the end of the eighteenth century had hardly changed since the invention of printing some three and a half centuries earlier. With very slight modifications they had sufficed to meet the demands of a comparatively limited number of readers. Very early in the nineteenth century, however, the best-seller came on the scene. Scott was one of the earliest writers to enter this class—an author whose first editions comprised first 10,000, and eventually 20,000, copies taxed to the very limits the productive powers of printers' and binders' shops.

This sort of problem was not peculiar to children's books; but they added problems of their own. Three-deckers, such as Scott's novels, could be sold at a high price[1] but books for children had to be cheap. Hand-work was slow and costly, and mass-production methods and large editions were essential if low prices were to be achieved.

In 1798 Robert, in France, patented a process for making paper by machinery, which was perfected by Fourdrinier in England in 1803. In 1807 Illig, in Germany, introduced resin for paper-sizing in place of gelatine, mixing the resin with the pulp from which the paper was made. In 1840 wood-pulp was used for making paper, thus cheaply supplementing the hitherto almost exclusive and expensive rags; and chemical wood pulp in 1856.[2]

In the first quarter of the nineteenth century came the first steam printing-press; the perfection of the stereotyping process; the introduction of cloth for binding— and with it the casing process by which the covers could be made apart from the books, being subsequently attached by pasting. This last process was very soon carried out by machinery. Mechanical type-setting was attempted as early as 1822, but was not perfected until the 'eighties.[3]

Not all of these introductions were for the worse, so far as the attraction and permanency of the printed book were concerned. The improvements in illustration are discussed later.[4] The use of cloth as a publisher's binding provided the first commercially usable material for this purpose with any claim to permanence. Publishers were not slow to grasp its possibilities and the rather drab calico with paper labels of the earliest attempts, aping the boarded book, soon gave place to gold and coloured blockings, the gaiety and attractiveness of which caught the eye as they were displayed for sale.

The range and fancy of those covers may be studied in the illustrations to Sadleir,

[1] There is ample evidence that when the three-decker was more frequently borrowed from a library than bought, the price of 31s. 6d. was itself somewhat fictional; for library proprietors drive hard bargains with publishers.

[2] General commercial use of these processes came somewhat later. For an excellent summary of their history see Carter-Pollard, pp. 44–5.

[3] An excellent conspectus of these and other changes will be found in Greenhood.

[4] See Chapter 7.

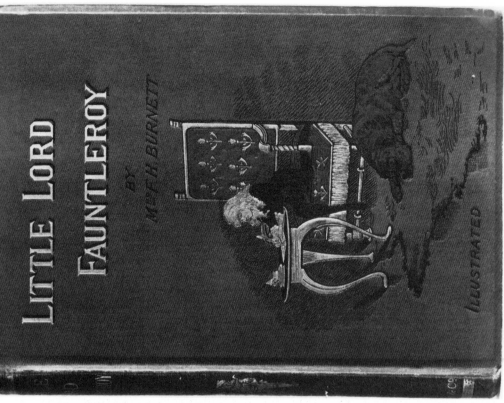

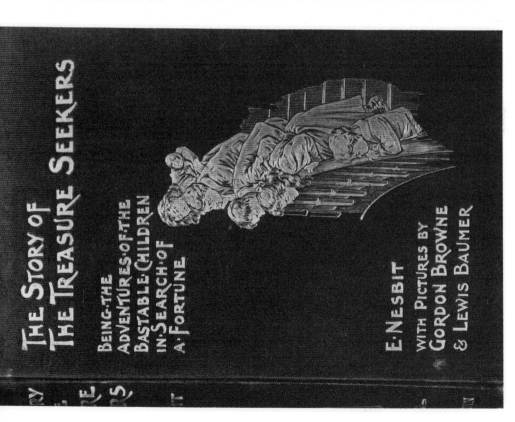

61 Lettering and Picture in Gold. Unwin, 1899

62 Lettering in gold and black; picture in gold and colours.
Warne, 1886

64 Gold-stamped on cloth. Griffith, Farran, 1875

63 Colour lithography. Darton, 1858

who includes several children's books, and examples of the coloured board bindings for cheaper books carried out by wood-engraving or lithography, which were exceedingly popular with children's publishers.[1]

Returning to the books themselves, writers and compilers of fairy-tales and fables blossomed successfully. George Macdonald overlaps the period of this chapter at both ends. He was born in 1824, died in 1905, and published in 1858 his first prose work. *Phantastes* although not addressed primarily to children has to some extent been adopted by them. A personal judgment that it remains the best of all his fairy-stories may be coloured by the fact that I first read it in teenage.

Macdonald is unquestionably an unduly neglected writer, whether for children or adults, although for the latter *The Diary of an Old Soul* and for the former *At the Back of the North Wind* are not completely forgotten. This lovely fairy-story first appeared as a serial under his own editorship in *Good Words for the Young*, where its rather tedious typography was already enlivened by the entrancing woodcuts made from Arthur Hughes's drawings (51).

Hughes is less successful in his pictures to Christina Rossetti's *Speaking Likenesses* (1874), perhaps because these charming, but rather inconsequential, attempts at fairy-stories fail to come off. They are almost entirely free of moralisings—although the first of them, at any rate, is by no means free, in either conception or illustration, from the influence of "Alice"—but all the stories tail off inconclusively, which is probably the reason for its lack of success either upon publication or subsequently.[2]

Jean Ingelow (*Mopsa the Fairy*, 1869); Mrs. Ewing (*The Brownies*, 1870); Tom Hood the younger (*Petsetilla's Posy*, 1870); Laurence Housman (*A Farm in Fairyland*, 1894); and G. E. Farrow (*The Wallypug in the Moon*) are among those who produced fairy-tales worthy of present notice. But the two outstanding figures in this field are Lang and Wilde.

Lang has already been mentioned for his original fairy-tales, for his edition of Perrault, and for his collections which began with *The Blue Fairy Book* in 1889. He was a prolific writer. The five columns listing his work in the *Cambridge Bibliography of English Literature* are not exhaustive, although he is shown as poet, critic, parodist, historian, anthropologist, occultist, fisherman, golfer, and translator. He was one of the founders of the Society for Psychical Research, and contributed many papers to their Proceedings.

He was, in short, a versatile fellow; he delved below the surface of many subjects, and usually emerged with something that would serve for an essay or an article, if not a book. He was a scholar who could make a scholarly subject more palatable than caviare to the general. The penalty of this, however, was that his scholarship

[1] A note on the important contribution made by Edmund Evans to this coloured board process will be found on p. 184. He also brought it to perfection in his covers for the Crane, Greenaway, and Caldecott books (77).

[2] It is among the commonest of her books in the first edition, and was remaindered in a cheaper binding without the Arthur Hughes design in gilt on the front cover.

never entirely deserted him, and even in his most popular fictional writings there is always a slight tang of midnight oil.

Thus in his collaboration with Haggard, *The World's Desire*, although the yarn is a good one, one is a little too conscious that one of the authors is closely familar with Icelandic saga. Similarly his own fairy-tales, excellent though some of them are, and even some of the collections, are not entirely freed from the anthropological background with which Lang himself was so familiar that he hardly detected its presence, or, if he did, thought it no matter.

Fairies had interested him since childhood. Not only had he been brought up on Perrault and Grimm, but he grew up in the Border country, where legends and tales of the "little people" abounded. Fairnilee, the locale of his best story, is Border country, and appears to be little more than a reconstruction of his own childhood adventures in search of fairy folk and fairy treasure.[1]

Lang's two stories *Prince Prigio* (1889) and *Prince Ricardo* (1893) have recently been reprinted[2]; but the immortality of his tales is tenuous. For us he is possibly more important as an influence, a background, than for what he wrote himself. He encouraged other romantic writers like Haggard and Stevenson, whom he recognised to be better at this particular job than he was himself; and in his writings and indefatigable collections he provided a valuable quarry for prospectors.

Wilde published two collections of fairy-stories; one attained an immediate and continued success, the other was with equal immediacy and obstinacy a failure.

The Happy Prince and Other Tales (1888), illustrated by Walter Crane and G. P. Jacomb Hood, contained five fairy-tales of which the best known, and perhaps the the best, is "The Selfish Giant", which, with "The Remarkable Rocket", can hold its place in almost any company of its kind. The book was widely and favourably reviewed, Pater wrote to say how the book had consoled him in an attack of gout, and Justin Huntly McCarthy wrote a poem in praise of it. A second edition was called for within six months, and the book has been constantly reprinted ever since.

In 1891 came *A House of Pomegranates*, which has never recovered from a very poor start. There is nothing in it to compare with the two best stories in the previous book; but the reasons for its failure must be sought elsewhere. First in the price, twenty-one shillings, as against five for *The Happy Prince*, put it beyond the reach of most children. Secondly, although Ricketts and perhaps Shannon, who combined to design this book, are better artists than Crane and Hood, it is doubtful whether their appeal to children is likely to be so great. Thirdly, and in any case, a new process used in reproducing Shannon's illustrations completely ruined them, giving them the appearance of badly faded photographs. The book was eventually remaindered, but one or two of its stories would bear reviving.

---

1 "I can't do fiction", he wrote to Haggard in connection with this book. "It's only a lot of childhood reminiscences." (Quoted by Green, p. 125.)

2 *Chronicles of Pantouflia*, 1943.

G. E. Farrow is worthy of mention here, if only because he is in danger of being overlooked, whereas he deserves a better fate. He is not really a very important writer, and one of his two best books is largely imitative. But he was widely read by children, and practical experiment shows that his books have retained their appeal.

He wrote a series of books based on adventures of and with the "Wallypug of Why"—"a *sort* of king", much tyrannised by his subjects, each of whom he was compelled by law to address as "Your Majesty". There are, in all, six Wallypug books, but two of them are much superior to the others. The first, *The Wallypug of Why*, is a brilliant pastiche of "Alice". It is not quite up to Carroll standard, but some of the invention and nonsense can be mentioned in the same breath.

The very first character encountered by Girlie, the heroine, is the Doctor-in-law, who explains that "a doctor-in-law is something between a father-in-law and a step-father, a sort of half-a-step-father, in fact. That will be six-and-eightpence, please . . ." for professional advice, he goes on to say, and when Girlie complains that she had not asked for any advice, the Doctor-in-law says that if he waited till people *asked* for advice he would never get any clients at all. He runs up a big bill for her very quickly and when he finds that she is sixpence short offers to take her watch to clear the balance.

"But it is worth a great deal more than sixpence," argued Girlie.

"Not at all!" said the Doctor-in-law. . . . "Mine only cost a penny."

"Yes, but yours doesn't go," objected Girlie; "mine does, you know."

"Oh well, then, I don't want it", said the Doctor-in-law hurriedly. "I don't want a watch that will *go*, I want one that will stay. . . ."

Like Alice, Girlie meets a number of bad-tempered animals who ridicule most of her accepted ideas on a basis of logical nonsense that is modelled directly on Carroll, and is not unworthy of its model.

Thus the fish who fishes just as bakers bake or tailors tail—"they *retail and coat tail* don't they?"; or the Hall Porter to whose charge that she is "late again", Girlie objects that as she has never been there before, she cannot be late *again*. "If you've not been here *before*, then you must have been *behind*, and, if one is behind, they are late. . . ."

Her alliterative conversation with letters of the alphabet, each of which can pronounce only words beginning with its own letter; and the charming old penguin who keeps a shop for selling excuses—"Elaborate Excuses prepared at the Shortest Notice"—and promises, which have to be kept in glass cases because they are so brittle, and who has a bargain line in "Broken Promises three-a-penny each" are inventions of which Carroll might not have been ashamed.

Indeed if there had been no "Alice", the first Wallypug book would deserve a higher place than can be given to it: but if there had been no "Alice" there would have been no Wallypugland.

In his second book, *The Missing Prince*, Farrow tried to repeat his former success, by transporting a boy to the Land of Zum. This book is less ingenious and endearing,

65, 66 Two illustrations of Farrow's "Wallypug" stories (Harry Furniss and Alan Wright)

although one of the characters, a tin soldier called "One-and-Nine", may have served Wells in respect to Mr. Polly's neologisms. One-and-Nine's conversation abounds in expressions like "unbearacious vulgarocity" and "prospectuous hopefulosity"; indeed Farrow was so pleased with him that although he abandoned Zum when the Wallypug came to London for the Queen's Jubilee in the third book, he brought with him One-and-Nine, now promoted to sergeant, and the Jubilee Rhymster, so as to be able to introduce rather shameless parodies on Carrollian lines like:

> Why doth the little busy bee
> Not charge so much an hour,
> For gathering honey day by day
> From every opening flower?

which, also like Carroll, he based on Watts. Into this book he also introduced a cat called "Mehetabel", which may not have escaped the notice of Dom Marquis. But only *The Wallypug in the Moon* is worthy of the first book. It is much longer than any of Farrow's other books, and, although he introduces many familiar nursery characters, like Dick Whittington and the seven-league-booted giant, it is a highly original work in which the invention seldom flags.

The two illustrations on p. 156 are taken from the first two Wallypug books. Harry Furniss originated the character, but was soon replaced by Alan Wright, who thereafter became Farrow's regular and very successful illustrator.

With his second book this author hit on the ingenious, if somewhat tedious, notion of adding a preface, in which children were invited to write to him giving their opinion of the books, being promised a personal reply to every letter. One of the books was offered autographed by the author on payment of an extra shilling; but as this was not repeated, it was probably not a success.

Kenneth Grahame's masterpiece for children, *The Wind in the Willows* (1908), falls outside our period; and it is generally considered that his earlier books are about rather than for children. This we may perhaps admit in *Pagan Papers* (1893), a very "ninetyish" little book, with its Beardsley title-page, its certificate of limitation, and its "Bodleyan" get-up. It should nevertheless be noted that the final section of the book consists of a few stories of children grouped under the heading of "The Golden Age", the title chosen for his next book (1895). Here there is still nothing for us. True, all the important characters are children, and the viewpoint throughout is that of a child. But it is of a child being humoured and jollied; it is, indeed, an "Olympian" remembering and recounting to his peers the funny little things that rather unusually nice-mannered family of youngsters said and did. One has only to contrast it with the standpoint from which the Bastables are treated to see that E. Nesbit is writing for children, whereas Grahame is addressing their parents.[1] Harold being a muffin-man insisting on the role of Sir Lancelot; the

---

[1] Oswald Bastable is quite tolerant about *The Golden Age*, which he thinks "A1 except where it gets mixed with grown-up nonsense."

imagined responses of Charlotte's dolls, Jerry and Rosa, to her conversation with them; the very chapter-titles, "Sawdust and Sin", "Lusisti Satis", and the Prologue addressed to "The Olympians", all bespeak a grown-up—a tolerant, understanding grown-up be it said—looking backwards and, alas, downwards at a humorous picture of remembered childhood.

Dream Days (1898) is for the most part a sequel to *The Golden Age*. It has the same Olympian chapter-titles, "Dies irae", "Mutabile Semper"—one a bitter disappointment, for "The Magic Ring", enchanting and endearing though it is, is just an unusually successful account of why children enjoy circuses. But "the Man" comes into it, the man whom we met first in "The Finding of the Princess" in *The Golden Age*.

It is the man who takes the children to the circus after their own kin have so basely let them down; and it is the man who matter-of-factly accepts their pursuit of a dragon and promises to have it taken round to them if he comes across it. And then he invites them to tea, and beguiles the dreary walk home with one of the best fairy-stories ever written—"The Reluctant Dragon".

The story can stand admirably by itself: the prologue and epilogue to it are all very well for you and me, but they spoil the story for children, many of whom never reach it because of its, to them, unpromising surroundings.

E. Nesbit just gets into the period with *The Story of the Treasure-Seekers* (1899)[1] (61).

There is hardly a trace in her of Kenneth Grahame's superior attitude. She writes in the first person, as a member of the family, just as he does: but whereas he writes in retrospect, mingling nostalgia and tolerance, she writes as one of themselves. Indeed, it was in search of treasure that she began to write these stories; and the impoverished background of the Bastable family was her own. The house, the district, the financial misfortune, and the dire need to extract money from even the most unlikely sources were all part of her own story.

She had published novels and poems and had a volume included in the "Keynotes" series. None of these brought much financial return, however, and even more improbable sources of treasure were sought in public reciting and the hand colouring of Christmas cards.

Twice her background of apparent security had given place to something very near to penury; once as a girl, when her widowed mother lost nearly all her money, and a second time when her handsome, scapegrace husband plunged heavily into a worthless investment. On this second occasion she was struggling to keep not only herself, her husband, and their children, but also his illegitimate children by one of her own servants, the responsibility for whose upbringing she cheerfully assumed. Among the most fascinating of modern biographies is Mrs. Langley Moore's life of her.[2]

[1] Her *Book of Dragons* (1900) is much inferior to her other books.
[2] *E. Nesbit: A Biography* (1933).

She had tried her hand at writing for children before she invented the Bastables; but with no greater success than in her other writings. Even the Bastables did not catch on at once. The *Windsor*, *Pall Mall*, and a Holiday Annual accepted individual stories about them; but no editor saw enough in them to warrant commissioning a series. But as soon as they appeared in book form success was immediate and continuous. The volume was reprinted almost annually until the paper shortage in the two wars, and in 1947 was in its twenty-seventh edition.[1]

Two more series of Bastable adventures followed with equal success; and later she was bold enough to devise two more families for other adventures. These, the Ardens and another for which no surname is provided, came after 1900; but they combine with the 1899 volume to mark an epoch in writing of books for children. It is with some regret that one finds the original illustrators of her books like Gordon Browne and Lewis Baumer, replaced by another.

Mrs. Langley Moore's biography leaves no doubt of the reason for her success. She never grew up. Many of the incidents and scenes in her books are taken direct from the lives of her own children, to whom she was more like an older—and not very much older—sister than a mother; and when at the age of fifty-nine she was married for the second time—to a marine engineer—her life, albeit once more in comparative poverty,[2] continued its make-believe character, although she published no more books for children after 1913.

Kipling is difficult to place, for he is an author that walks by himself. *Stalky* is in the same class as *Dream Days*; schooldays recollected. The "Jungle Books" and the *Just-So Stories* are by Aesop out of Chandler Harris, but they have something to be found in neither of these. They have features in common with their ancestry —their anthropomorphism, of course, and their wordly wisdom. In Kipling both are more subtly introduced.

Although not more than half the stories in the "Jungle Books" centre around Mowgli, it is with his figure that the books are indissolubly and most notably associated. There are no "morals", as in Aesop, for the verses attached to each story are epilogues or summaries rather than moralities. It is in the Law of the Jungle that Kipling subtly instils into his young readers the primitive form of "The Code"— manliness, give-and-take, and the pioneer spirit—that is implicit in all his writings. It is a code with which one may hope to get by in tight corners, although it includes hints that may appear superfluous or even suspicious to the male-cub. "Wash daily, from nose-tip to tail-tip"; "the jungle is large and the Cub he is small. Let him think and be still"; and the advice to those beset by the "Cameelious hump", "to take a large hoe and a shovel also, And dig till you gently perspire", may be less acceptable than the visions of glory aroused by Mowgli's Song after his triumph over Shere Khan. Yet this song ends, "Ahae! my heart is heavy with the things that

1 *The Would-be-Goods* (1901), the second Bastable book, earned over £1,000 in royalties in the first year of its publication.
2 She was granted a Civil List Pension of £60 in 1915.

I do not understand''; and the triumphal tracking that leads to the King's Ankus has a sequel in ''The Song of the Little Hunter'' with its terrible refrain, ''He is Fear, O Little Hunter, he is Fear!''

Kipling knew well what children liked. He had children of his own, one of whom still possesses the fascinating albums of illustrated poems and stories made for their nursery use, by him and his father. The international fame of the ''Jungle Books'' is evidence of their universality and probable immortality.

Strictly speaking *Just-So Stories* falls within our period, for, although not published in book form until 1902, three of the stories appeared serially in the American *Ladies Home Journal*, April to June 1900[1]; and a few copies were printed off separately over here to secure copyright.

A most interesting feature of the completed work is its foreshadowing of *Puck of Pook's Hill* (1906) and *Rewards and Fairies* (1910). The two almost completely didactic stories, *The First Letter* and *How the Alphabet was Made*, read like trial runs for the historically based stories in the later volumes, while the poem ''There runs a road by Merrow Down'', with very little alteration, could find a place in either volume. The continuity between the ''Jungle Books'' and the *Just-So Stories* is amply clear; and it is interesting to see the latter, in its turn, leading on to something so far removed from the Mowgli tales.

We can just squeeze in also another writer of stories about animal characters, albeit of a very different kind. Alas that we must reject Beatrix Potter's own dating of the first printed appearance of *Peter Rabbit*; and also the somewhat circumstantial story in Miss Lane's *Tale of Beatrix Potter*. Were we to accept the former we could date it at Christmas 1900; whereas Miss Lane writes: ''By February 1900 the little book was ready, a modest edition of five hundred copies.'' Unfortunately for us the date of issue seems almost certainly to have been Christmas 1901; and the number of copies was 250.[2]

Nevertheless Miss Potter's early books definitely belong to the period before 1900. The manuscript of *Peter Rabbit* for private printing[3] was completed well before that date; for Miss Potter had tried it on several publishers without success before deciding to draw some of her savings out of the Post Office so that she might print it at her own expense.

Indeed, as is well known to Miss Lane's readers, the story had existed in fairly complete outline since 1893 when, to beguile the sick-bed of the five-year-old son of her former governess, Miss Potter sent him a letter, illustrated with drawings

[1] ''The Elephant's Child'' (April), ''The Beginning of the Armadillos'' (May), ''The Sing-Song of Old Man Kangaroo'' (June).

[2] The little book is undated; but in two surviving copies the author wrote: ''1st edition, 250 copies, Christmas 1900''. Almost conclusive evidence exists, however, to show that the printing was not then finished, and that ''1900'' is an error for 1901. Miss Lane's date is probably based on a confusion due to the fact that a second lot of 250 was called for, and these bore the date ''February 1902''. (See *The Book Collector*, Spring 1953, p. 77.)

[3] It was largely rewritten and newly illustrated for regular publication.

68 Proof illustration to *The Toilet*, 1821

69 An excellent example of copper-engraving, *c.* 1805

The good clergyman taught the children, and when Frank was old enough, sent him to sea. Mary, or as she was still called "Goody Two-Shoes", was always wishing to be useful, and when she learned her alphabet, began to teach her young friends in the village. Her plan was to cut out large letters from sheets of paper, and then as she sat under a tree she would have her companions round her and teach them to read. She was such a good, patient girl that every one loved her.

67 *Goody Two-Shoes* in 1897.
      Compare figs. 26 and 30

70   A non-Bewick woodcut of better quality than most (1786)

71   German influence was very marked (as in this example) from the
'fifties onwards

by herself, of the adventures of a family of rabbits.[1] All the family appear in the letter, and so does Mr. McGregor, in very much the form and background used in the book.

In 1896 and 1897 she divided between this same little boy and another the germ of Squirrel Nutkin, which was not published until 1903; and other letters written before any book publication was thought of include references by name to Jeremy Fisher, Hunca Munca, and Tabitha Twitchett. Not that it matters greatly when the characters or the stories were either conceived or written, for the best of them are immortal. But it was essential that Miss Potter should not be omitted from this story; and it was agreeable of her to have made it possible to include her here without too much backing and filling.

Full appreciation of the extreme care and forethought which she devoted to the preparation of her little books is not possible to anyone unfamiliar with her methods; and these methods also help to explain her immediate and enormous success with young readers, which is not entirely due to the artistry of her text and drawings—that notwithstanding.

In submitting a manuscript to her publisher she wrote each story in an exercise book, including on each page the exact number of words it was to bear in printed form. Each portion of the text was accompanied by a sketch of the drawing which was to illustrate it, in the exact position it was to occupy. When all the type was set this had to be cut up into page size and pasted into a dummy of exactly the size of the finished book, and if proofs of the illustrations were not ready at this stage, a further series of thumb-nail sketches would be provided to give some idea of how they would look alongside a printed text.

Every detail of each book was planned and designed by Miss Potter from beginning to end; and followed a general plan.[2]

The price was one shilling in boards or one shilling and sixpence in cloth. There was a coloured picture on the front cover, and the end-papers carried coloured pictures of animal characters from other books.[3]

Squirrel Nutkin is exceptional in having no frontispiece; otherwise the title-page was faced by a coloured picture, and thereafter each page of text was faced by a coloured picture, so as to make twenty-six pages of each. The plates were mostly grouped in pairs and printed on one side only; but the blanks were reckoned in the pagination, so that the last page of text would be numbered "85" giving

---

[1] Miss Lane gives a complete facsimile of this eight-page letter between pp. 56 and 57.

[2] Not all the following details are true of the original published edition of Peter Rabbit, which, as the first of the series, was not entirely uniform. But the general plan of the later books is uniform throughout with the following exceptions:—The Fierce Bad Rabbit and Miss Moppet (both 1906) were first issued experimentally in panorama form. The Pie and the Patty Pan (1905), The Roly-Poly Pudding (1908), and Ginger and Pickles (1909) were issued in a larger format.

[3] From time to time, as the series progressed, Miss Potter redesigned these. Thus the Tailor of Gloucester depicted itself, Peter Rabbit and Squirrel Nutkin; the following books were usually issued in pairs, with the necessary additions, until Mr. Tod (1912), when a new style of end-paper was used.

an impression of a more lavish offering than was in fact the case. The principal object however was to ensure that there should be a new picture every time a page was turned.

More than once after a book had been published for some time Miss Potter would bethink herself of some feature of it that might wound her young readers, and she would then insist upon its being changed. Thus in the first published edition of *Peter Rabbit* there is a picture of Mrs. McGregor serving up a pie made from one of the rabbit family whose trespassing was incautious. She soon removed this, thinking that her readers might find it painful.

Yes, Miss Potter is indeed a pleasant person with whom to close the chronology of children's books in our period.

Books Applicable to this Chapter

Allibone, *D.N.B.*, and other general sources have been consulted. Green is also important on this period; and, even more notably, Sadleir is indispensable.

For facts in relation to technical development in paper-making, the best short account is in Carter and Pollard's *Enquiry* (Constable, 1934), and for binding, printing, and the like, Greenhood and Gentry's *Chronology* (New York: Macmillan, 1936).

For special authors the following have also been used:

J. E. Scott. *A Bibliography of . . . Sir Henry Rider Haggard* (Mathews, 1947).

D. Langley Moore. *E. Nesbit: a Biography* (1933).

M. Lane. *The Tale of Beatrix Potter* (Warne, 1946). Several liberties are observable in matters of fact, dates, and inferences.

WILLIAM GILBERT

1866. *The Magic Mirror.*

1869. *King George's Middy.* Not especially distinguished as stories, these books are attractive because of the employment of the author's son, W. S. Gilbert, to illustrate them. This is not quite W. S. G.'s first appearance in print, as he had already illustrated his father's three-decker, *Shirley Hall Asylum* (1863). He also illustrated fairy-stories in *Good Words for the Young* (see p. 140).

THOMAS MAYNE REID

[1866.] *The Headless Horseman.* Two volumes. Previously issued in Parts, March 1, 1865, to July 2, 1866. Although he wrote several books expressly for boys—*The Fatal Cord* (1869), *The Castaways* (1871), and many others—it is difficult to differentiate, and the above has been chosen as his most representative work.

"HESBA STRETTON", (Sarah Smith).

1867? *Jessica's First Prayer.* For a note on dating and bibliography see Sadleir, I, 333.[1]

---

[1] This book was announced in *The Athenaeum*, May 4 1867. The first issue probably has a printer's imprint on the verso of the title reading: London/R. Clay, Son and Taylor, Printers,/Bread Hill 11. [The form: R. Clay, Sons is after 1870.]

GEORGE MACDONALD

1867. *Dealings with the Fairies.*
1871. *At the Back of the North Wind.*
   Ranald Bannerman's Boyhood.
1872. *The Princess and the Goblin.*
   Edited *Good Words for the Young.*

GEORGE ALFRED HENTY

1871. *Out on the Pampas.*
1884. *With Clive in India.*
1889. *The Cat of Bubastes.*
   He is credited with thirty-eight titles in Allibone before 1888; but he lived until 1902 and sometimes published as many as four books in one year.

"ASCOTT HOPE" (A. R. Hope-Moncrieff)

1868. *A Book about Boys.*
   He published about 200 books for boys. Died 1927.

JEAN INGELOW

1869. *Mopsa the Fairy.*

FLORENCE MONTGOMERY

1869. *Misunderstood.*

TOM HOOD THE YOUNGER

1870. *Petsetilla's Posy.*
1875. *From Nowhere to the North Pole.*
   Dodgson was publicly accused of having plagiarised the latter in "Alice"!

CHRISTINA ROSSETTI

1874. *Speaking Likenesses.*

RICHARD DODDRIDGE BLACKMORE

1875. *Lorna Doone.* Three volumes.

MARY LOUISA MOLESWORTH

1875. *Tell Me a Story.*
1876. *Carrots.*
1878. *The Cuckoo Clock.*
   The above were issued as by "Ennis Graham".

1881. *Adventures of Herr Baby.*

1895. *The Carved Lions.*

   Allibone lists thirty-four titles to 1888; but she lived until 1921. For a fuller list see Green.

W. CLARK RUSSELL

1877. *The Wreck of the Grosvenor.* Three volumes.

ANNA SEWELL

1877. *Black Beauty.*

ALFRED JOHN CHURCH

1878. *Stories from Homer.*

1887. *The Count of the Saxon Shore.*

TALBOT BAINES REED.

[1880.] *The Adventures of a Three-Guinea Watch.*

1887. *The Fifth Form at St. Dominic's.*

[1891.] *The Cock-house of Felsgarth.*

F. ANSTEY (Thomas Anstey Guthrie)

1882. *Vice Versa.*

GEORGE MANVILLE FENN

1882. *Nat the Naturalist.*

1884. *The Silver Canon.*

   He is credited with fifty-nine titles in Allibone.

RICHARD JEFFERIES

1882. *Bevis.* Three volumes.

ROBERT LOUIS STEVENSON

1883. *Treasure Island.*

1886. *Kidnapped.*

1888. *The Black Arrow.*

1895. *Catriona.*

E. V. B[OYLE]

1884. *Days and Hours in a Garden.*

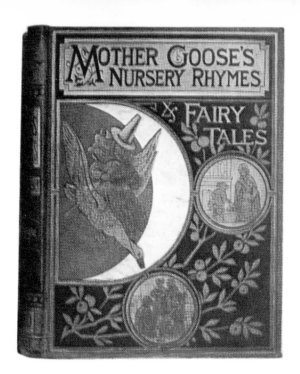

Mother Goose's Nursery
Rhymes (c. 1880)

72, 73 Decorative use of cloth
in the nineteenth century

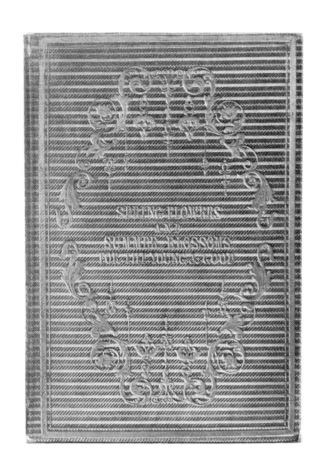

Spring Flowers (c. 1840)

ANDREW LANG

[1884.] *The Princess Nobody*.

[1888.] *The Gold of Fairnilee*.

1889. *Prince Prigio*.

1889. *The Blue Fairy Book*. The first of the collections of fairy-stories edited by Lang. Most of the work of collecting and translating was done by Mrs. Lang and other helpers.

1890. *The World's Desire*. (With Rider Haggard.)

[1893.] *Prince Ricardo*.

FLORA ANNIE STEEL

1884. *Wide Awake Stories*. Afterwards (1894) reissued, with illustrations by J. Lockwood Kipling, as No. 15 in the Cranford Series, with the title, *Tales of the Punjab*.

SIR HENRY RIDER HAGGARD

1885. *King Solomon's Mines*.

1887. *She*.
       Allan Quatermain.

    He wrote about sixty romances more or less suitable for boys. See Scott, *A Bibliography of H. Rider Haggard*.

FRANCES HODGSON BURNETT

1886. *Little Lord Fauntleroy*. The author was an American; but the little hero is English and most of the action takes place here. Moreover, the book was at least equally successful in England as in the United States.

L. T. MEADE

1886. *A World of Girls*.

"Q" (Sir Arthur Quiller-Couch)

1887. *Dead Man's Rock*.

OSCAR WILDE

1888. *The Happy Prince*.

1891. *A House of Pomegranates*.

ARTHUR CONAN DOYLE

1889. *Micah Clarke*.

1896. *Rodney Stone*.

ALFRED HENRY MILES (Editor)

[1889.] *Fifty-two Stories for Boys*. The first of many compilations of stories by popular writers, each containing a story for every week of the year.

MAGGIE BROWNE (Margaret Hamer)

1890. *Wanted a King*. An imitation of "Alice".

JOSEPH SMITH FLETCHER

1892. *When Charles The First Was King*. Three volumes.

STANLEY WEYMAN

1893. *A Gentleman of France*. Three volumes.
1894. *Under the Red Robe*. Two volumes.

SAMUEL RUTHERFORD CROCKETT

1893. *The Stickit Minister*. The earliest of some sixty or more titles, extending to 1926—12 years after the author's death. Although not all written directly with children in mind, many of them have been "adopted", among them *The Raiders* (1894), *Clegg Kelly* (1896), and *Sir Toady Lion* (1897).

WILLIAM GORDON STABLES

[1893.] *Facing Fearful Odds*.

ANTHONY HOPE (Anthony Hope Hawkins)

[1894.] *The Prisoner of Zenda*.
[1898.] *Rupert of Hentzau*.

LAURENCE HOUSMAN

1894. *A Farm in Fairyland*.
1895. *The House of Joy*.
1899. *Seven Young Goslings*.

RUDYARD KIPLING

1894. *The Jungle Book*.
1895. *The Second Jungle Book*.
1899. *Stalky and Co*.

HENRY SETON MERRIMAN (Hugh Stowell Scott)

1894. *With Edged Tools*. Three volumes.

G. E. FARROW

1895. *The Wallypug of Why*. This and its sequels are discussed on pp. 155–157.

BERTHA UPTON

[1895.] *The Adventures of two Dutch Dolls and a Golliwog*. The first of the "Golliwog" series.

KENNETH GRAHAME

1898. *Dream Days*. Containing "The Reluctant Dragon".

E. NESBIT

1899. *The Story of the Treasure-Seekers*.

1900. *The Book of Dragons*.
    Her other stories of the Bastable children fall outside our period.

74 A Bewick cut for a
children's book

CHAPTER SEVEN

THE IMPORTANCE
OF PICTURES

THE crudity of the early illustrations in children's books is explicable by the paramount need for cheapness of production. Until late in the eighteenth century the pictures were usually printed from wood-blocks, coarsely cut to suit them to the cheap paper on which they had to be printed. Surviving examples are frequently not of the first printing, the blocks have worn, and the results are sometimes almost indecipherable blotches. The cuts in Boreman's publications are of rather superior quality, possibly because the editions were small; but the reproductions (34) surely indicate that their charm is purely naïve, and little more can be said for the frontispiece to Newbery's *Goody Two-Shoes* (26).

There is reason to suppose, however, that this crudity may sometimes have been due more to the hamfistedness of the cutters of the blocks than to the artists who made the drawings for them to work from. This is suggested by an opportunity which occurred some years ago to examine a collection of about three hundred drawings commissioned by John Harris, Newbery's successor.[1] Many of these were of quite exquisite quality, and whenever an opportunity of comparison occurred the drawings invariably showed an astonishing superiority to the finished illustra-

75 A Bewick cut for a children's book

tions. It is perhaps fair to add that this same comparison showed that draughtsmen were not always aware of the limitations of wood-cutting, and often set the craftsmen impossible tasks. Even when the engraving was the work of an acknowledged master like Bewick results were sometimes lamentable when the printing was entrusted to the same operator as the letterpress. Poor Bewick must have despaired at some of the crudities produced from his blocks by the publishers to whom he delivered them. The wretched quality of the paper is often a contributory cause.

1 Now in the collection of Mr. Edgar Oppenheimer of New York.

Bewick is a considerable, if rather isolated, phenomenon. He is the earliest in modern times to have earned his living almost exclusively by the illustration of books, and is among the earliest to have his name featured on title-pages as an attraction to the purchaser. A glance at Hugo's two volumes[1] will make this overwhelmingly clear; and it is especially interesting to see how early he engaged upon work for children's books.

The second item in Hugo's chronological list is an undated horn-book, the third *A New Lottery Book of Birds and Beasts, for Children to learn their Letters* (1771); and innumerable other books for children's amusement or instruction are scattered through Hugo's pages.

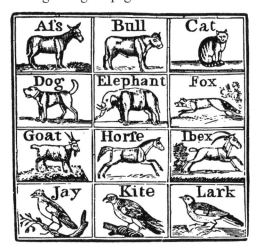 

76 A Horn-Book Alphabet by Bewick

Bewick died in 1828. In 1804 a very different kind of illustrator made his bow with an etching of a "Children's Lottery Picture".[2] This was George Cruikshank, who is credited with the information that it was the first picture he was employed to do and was paid for; and that he was twelve years old at the time of its publication.

It seems odd that this strange and prolific artist[3] could ever have appealed to children. His illustrations to Grimm are eerie and unwordly; but it seems the wrong sort of eeriness for children. There is, in fact, a positive leeriness about his hobgoblins, witches, and other creatures which would strongly reinforce doubts in certain quarters as to the suitability for children of the Grimm stories in any form.

Nevertheless, over a period from about 1816 to 1822 his work was very popular with publishers of children's books; and his folded, coloured frontispieces are in many books published by Dean and Munday,[4] Mackay, Bysh, Fairburn, and Houlston of Wellington in Shropshire. In 1817, also, there appeared over Godwin's

1 *The Bewick Collector* (1866); *Supplement* (1868).
2 This information is taken from *D.N.B.* I do not find the etching listed in Cohn.
3 There are over 2,000 entries in Cohn's catalogue.
4 Among them Bunyan and single stories from Perrault and "the Arabian Nights".

imprint *Dramas for Children*, with four plates by Cruikshank.[1] In the 'forties he collaborated with one of the English Peter Parleys; and a variety of titles illustrated by him will be found in the list at the end of this chapter.

This queer man appears to have converted himself to teetotalism by the grim horror of his own etchings to *The Bottle* (1847) and its sequel *The Drunkard's Children* (1848). Thereafter his teetotal preoccupation with the demons Rum and Gin sapped his inspiration. Whether purely coincidental or not, the fact remains that his work for the *Band of Hope Journal* and for such tendentious writings as Mr. and Mrs. S. C. Hall's temperance stories—*Boons and Blessings*, *An Old Story*, and *Trial of Sir Jasper, A Temperance Tale in Verse*—is well below his best.

Bewick and Cruikshank, in their very different ways, are portents. Their success marks the recognition of the importance of book illustration. They were not without forerunners. H. A. Hammelmann's series of articles on early English book illustrators[2] is a reminder that whereas such artists as Burney, Hayman, Wale, Corbould and Stothard first took up book illustration as a lucrative side-line, the two last-named at any rate owe most of their surviving fame to work of this kind. Their names, however, rarely feature on title-pages.

Richard Corbould (1757–1831) is said to have worked for Harris; but no signed work of his for this publisher is recorded. His best work is in the extensive series of Cooke's "English Classics" (c. 1795–1800), and those dainty pocket volumes incidentally and sometimes inappropriately included children's titles such as "Sinbad the Sailor" and "Robinson Crusoe"; but we can hardly reckon Corbould as an illustrator of children's books.[3]

This is equally true of Thomas Stothard (1755–1834), who seldom if ever approached nearer to children's subjects than in his series of plates for Bunyan, Defoe, and the "Arabian Nights" in the *Novelists' Magazine*.

We may, then, fairly date the emergence of the recognised professional book-illustrator of juveniles with Bewick and Cruikshank, and find its full blossoming in the 'sixties and 'seventies with the work sponsored by the Dalziels and Edmund Evans, which will be considered hereafter.

In the meantime the very precise reason for the success of Harris's earliest books for children was the use of metal plates for printing the illustrations—and sometimes the text as well (52). Had Mulready's pretty drawings for *The Butterfly's Ball* been entrusted to a wood-engraver and a letterpress printer the results might have been deplorable. The printing of metal plates, however, was the work of craftsmen specially trained for it, on a machine expressly designed for the purpose. The quality of their work was usually high, the series of books turned out for Harris, Tabart,

[1] This book was first published by Godwin in 1809 with a frontispiece (not by Cruikshank). It was reissued in 1817 with the same sheets and frontispiece and the four Cruikshank plates added. The translator-adaptor was probably Mary Jane Godwin.

[2] In *Book Handbook* and *The Book Collector*.

[3] The illustrations to Thomas Love Peacock's ingenious venture into education, *Sir Hornbook* (1814), are by Corbould, but are most likely to have been by Richard's son. They are not very attractive in themselves, but have an interest as an early use of lithography in a book for children.

Godwin, Marshall, and others during the first quarter of the nineteenth century shows an immense advance over almost anything preceding them in juvenile publishing.

There are exceptions, the most notable being some of the books illustrated by Bewick, with the blocks produced under his own supervision. Nevertheless, even much of Bewick's work is seen to better advantage in later printings from his original blocks, made to cater for collectors when they had begun to appreciate the quality of his work.

The publisher of children's books is and has always been confronted with the need to keep prices as low as possible. In the early publications this problem was complicated by the smallness of the edition. It should not be forgotten that hand-work was used at every stage, from the paper-making and type-setting to the cutting, printing, and if necessary the colouring of the illustrations. Even though cheap labour and materials may have been used wherever possible, hand-work was slow, and therefore expensive. It was during the course of the nineteenth century that hand-work was replaced by machines in the making of paper, the setting of type, and the binding or "casing" of books; and fast rotary presses and photographic process-blocks and lithography replaced infinitely more laborious methods.

Until 1835 coloured illustrations were exclusively produced by hand-colouring; and Harris and his competitors were to use this method widely before 1810. But it seems clear that the coloured editions must have been comparatively small; and when such enormously popular books as *The Butterfly's Ball* and *The Peacock "At Home"* attained a combined sale of 40,000 in one year, most of these must surely have been uncoloured. There is little doubt that the sheets of characters and scenes for juvenile theatres, although available in coloured form, were more usually sold uncoloured to be coloured at home.[1] Stevenson certainly coloured his own, and the sample books of plays kept on the counter of Redington's and Webb's shops were in uncoloured form.

Nevertheless hand-colouring was widely used from about 1803 onwards, metal plates being preferred to wood-blocks as giving a bolder outline. Wood-blocks continued to be used; but the use of colour had its effect on the kind of block demanded by publishers. What was needed now was less niggling detail in the block. In place of it a picture which could be enhanced by broad washes of different colours was needed, and although copper engraving was best suited to the purpose, a great deal could also be done with woodcuts, of which there is plentiful evidence at the time.

Harris was not the only one to make these changes, and, as so often happens in this history, the significant fact is less the priority of the pioneer than the sudden, widespread change on the part of most of the leading publishers in this sphere.

Stevenson's essay "Penny Plain, Twopence Coloured" has been responsible for the misconception that these early coloured books were miracles of cheapness.

1 See Speaight, esp. pp. 86–8.

In fact they were certainly not much, if any, cheaper than children's books are to-day. Lamb's *Beauty and the Beast* cost three shillings plain and five shillings coloured, for a small booklet of thirty-two pages, with only eight pictures. A modern equivalent in price might be fifteen and twenty-five shillings; and perhaps this may partly account for the fact that the book does not appear to have sold very well. A more usual price was the shilling plain and eighteen pence coloured for the same author's *King and Queen of Hearts*, which had fifteen pictures; but the corresponding price of the coloured copies to-day would be about five shillings and would not be regarded as good measure, even with the high prices to which we are accustomed.

These little books were usually printed on one side of the paper only, the upper part of the page being occupied by the picture, with the corresponding text underneath. The text was often engraved as well as the picture. The colouring was done by home labour, paid at low rates. The pictures were especially commissioned in a form to permit of this being possible, and the artist was expected to provide a pattern in which broad blocks of simple colours were employed. Groups of children or families were then entrusted with the job of filling in these colours on the printed sheets, each operative being employed to supply one colour only. Thus one child would wash in the blues, one the reds, and so on. It is clear from comparison of different copies of the same book that more than one group was usually employed on each book, as the shades of colouring differ noticeably.[1]

There is a very interesting sidelight on methods of and payment for hand-colouring in Speaight.[2] He corresponded with How Mathews, who died in 1940 at more than eighty years of age, and who continued into the twentieth century the issue of plain and coloured sheets for children. He had previously worked for another publisher of these sheets and is quoted as follows: "Speed would come with practice; a pair of legs would be done with one stroke of the brush, starting up one leg and down the other, narrowing and widening the brush, in about two seconds; about the same time for a jacket, right and left arm. The whole figure would take about eight seconds. A sheet of ten characters, say, eighty seconds, or say a gross of 144 sheets would take four to six hours; at two shillings a gross this would work out at fourpence an hour."

At this sort of rate a family of four, working twelve hours a day, could earn, in a six-day week, over seven pounds. But the work had to be collected and delivered, the materials—brushes and colours—were almost certainly provided by the worker, and five pounds would probably be very good earnings, which could hardly be regular. All this is extremely speculative; but it gives some idea.

Increased mechanisation and mass-production, however, were essential to the production of really cheap coloured books for children, and these were at first

[1] Webb is said to have employed twelve families at one time in the colouring of his juvenile drama sheets, long after the peak period of interest in them (Speaight, p. 88). He probably used stencils.
[2] Pp. 87–8.

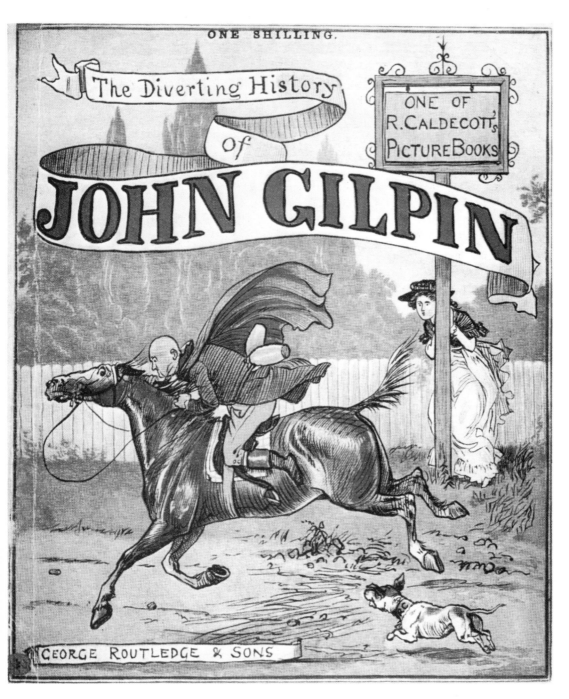

77 A Caldecott picture book (1878)

no exception to the rule that cheapness and nastiness are frequently synonymous. As early as 1818 William Savage produced his *Hints on Decorative Printing*, which consisted largely of elaborate experiments in printing in colours from wood-blocks, and in the early 'thirties George Baxter began to produce his famous prints by a similar process. Savage's experiments proved almost completely abortive, and Baxter's meticulous work was mostly too expensive for use in children's books. But in the 'fifties Baxter began to issue licences to work his process, and, notably in the hands of the Kronheims, it was cheapened and debased to an extent which permitted its use, at first for frontispieces only, in children's books.

The younger Darton on Holborn Hill was the first to use Baxter's process in juveniles, and thus the first to print illustrations for children in colours. The earliest recorded work of this kind is in the frontispiece to Mrs. Sherwood's *Caroline Mordaunt* (1835); and from 1836 onwards several of Mary Elliott's books were similarly treated.

The adaptation of lithography to colour-printing was attempted by its inventor, Senefelder, but the first entirely successful work in this process was produced by J. A. Barth of Breslau in 1816, in a work called *Pacis Monumentum*, "a polyglot record of the main facts connected with the Peace of 1815". Owen Jones was the earliest and in many ways the most notable exponent of the process in England, and his work in the 'forties is of very high quality.

Fine work in this medium, as in others, was expensive—Jones's *Alhambra* cost twelve pounds ten shillings on small, and twenty-one pounds on large paper—and it was not until the eighteen-sixties that cheaper production methods allowed the use of the process in children's books. These were then produced in colour throughout, in paper wrappers, costing only a few pence each. These garishly coloured plates with their unpleasantly oily appearance are among the nastiest of books for children of any period.[1]

Kate Greenaway's earliest picture books were reproduced in this cheap form of chromo-lithography, and it is safe to say that if she had not been fortunate enough to find a craftsman with a touch of genius to produce her later books she would be entirely forgotten to-day. But that is to run ahead of our period.

Before that two important periods must be considered—the 'fifties and the 'sixties—the former more for its influence on the latter than for its own productions.

The foundation of the Pre-Raphaelite Brotherhood in the late 'forties and the Great Exhibition in 1851 were enormously influential, and not altogether mutually exclusive in the formation of Victorian taste, which led on through the 'sixties period to the Morris and the Beardsley movements. This early background is clearly seen in children's books in a series of volumes designed expressly to please his own

[1] It is worth noting that hand-colouring survived into the period of mechanical colour-printing, and the firm of Dean & Son, for example, were then still producing booklets with twelve hand-coloured woodcuts priced at twopence, but the colouring is extremely crude and the pictures are very small.

children by Henry Cole and published from 1841 onwards as *Felix Summerly's Treasury of Pleasure Books for Young Children*. The contents were largely familiar fairy-tales; the illustration and general get-up of the series were its important features—important, that is, more for their influence and popularity at the time than for their appeal to a later eye.

Cole was a figure of considerable influence in his day. He was appointed a sub-commissioner and later a senior assistant-keeper of the Record Office on its original foundation, was active in postal reform, and was awarded a premium for postage-stamp design.

He was granted leave of absence from the Record Office to serve on the executive committee of the Great Exhibition; and played an important part in the distribution of the huge surplus resulting from it, most notably in the foundation of what is now the Victoria and Albert Museum.

He designed and supervised the manufacture of pottery, and other household articles, by founding "Summerly's Art Manufactures"; and never tired of urging the desirability of inducing painters and sculptors to design household articles for mass production.

Similarly his *Home Treasury* was designed and illustrated by the best artists available to him, among them Mulready, Cope, Horsley, Redgrave, and Linnell. Each volume cost sixpence plain or one shilling coloured. They are now exceedingly scarce.

Charles Keene's first four commissions were for children's books,[1] the earliest of all being for an anonymous, pseudonymously edited, undated volume in Darton's Juvenile Library, entitled *The Adventures of Dick Boldhero* [1842]. The "Editor" called himself "Peter Parley", whose identity Darton[2] discloses to be that of his great-uncle, Samuel Clark, a partner in the famous firm then known as Darton and Clark, although the book itself contains an advertisement in the form of a letter from S. G. Goodrich, the original American "Peter Parley", which indicates that the book was first published in the United States under his auspices.

Only the frontispiece is signed by Keene, and the other thirty-eight illustrations are believed to be by another hand. But in 1847, while still an apprentice with the Whymper Brothers, he produced all six pictures for an edition of *Robinson Crusoe*; an illustration for Darton and Clark's *Green's Nursery Annual*; and probably all the eighteen illustrations for Mrs. Sherwood's *The De Cliffords*.

Forrest Reid's monumental work on *Illustrators of the Sixties* is widely inclusive. In this period there arose a group of wood-engravers, of which the Dalziel brothers are the best known, which showed a remarkable facility for cutting on wood drawings by well-known artists much more elaborate than anything that had been attempted in that medium before. The process was that the artist made his drawing on the boxwood, which was then cut by the engraver and used for printing (51,

1 See list on p. 198.
2 P. 283.

58, 59, 78, and 79 are good examples). Gilbert, Tenniel, Millais, Birket Foster, and Keene are among the well-known names of the period; and, of course, the outstanding book in our sphere is "Alice".[1]

Competent, even great, artists had been employed to illustrate books for children before this period; but it is in the 'sixties that publishers began first to attempt to sell books to children mainly for the interest of the illustrations. Thus, for example, four new editions of *Robinson Crusoe* were commissioned by different publishers in this period, each illustrated by a different artist, Keene's edition, commissioned by Burns, J. D. Watson's, commissioned by Routledge, Millais' edition, by Macmillan, and George Thomas's, by Cassell. Millais is chiefly remembered as a book illustrator for his drawings for Trollope's novels, but those who do not know his illustrations to *Parables of our Lord* (1864—actually 1863) have missed his masterpiece, and this was unquestionably aimed at least in part at a juvenile audience. Arthur Hughes's name is indissolubly associated with this period, although he died at the age of eighty-three, in 1915, and produced some of his best work in this century. George MacDonald's fairy-stories contain some fine drawings by him, and his illustrations to Christina Rossetti's *Sing-Song* are small masterpieces, although the book was a failure. Harrison Weir's drawings of animals are excellent (87).

The Dalziel brothers were not only the finest of the wood-engravers of this period, but also, in very large measure, its inspiring geniuses. They commissioned many works at their own financial risk, the most impressive among children's books being their edition of the *Arabian Nights*, published by Ward and Lock in two volumes in 1865, previously issued in parts. For this a number of artists were engaged, among them Tenniel, Millais, Pinwell, and Houghton. Eventually photographic processes superseded the artist-engravers (83).

Of the triumvirate of artists around whom centres the next period of book illustration for children—Walter Crane, Randolph Caldecott, and Kate Greenaway —the first learned his trade in the 'sixties under W. J. Linton, an engraver whom Rossetti preferred to the Dalziels. Crane was apprenticed to this studio, not to learn engraving, but how to draw on wood, that being the most profitable outlet for an illustrator's work at the time. He did a great deal of work in that medium before turning his attention to children's books, and appeared once in the pages of *Punch*. He illustrated two novels by Mrs. Henry Wood in their serial form; produced a title-page for Wilkie Collins's *After Dark* (1862) and an illustrated title and frontispiece for the second—first one-volume—edition of Trollope's *Miss Mackenzie* (1866).

His fame, such as it is, however, will be chiefly associated with the series of "toy books", a favourite term with publishers of the time, which he produced between about 1865 and 1900, commissioned originally by the firm of Routledge,

---

[1] Illustrated by Tenniel, whose earliest single-handed work was an edition of *Undine* (1845), illustrated by "John Tenniel, junr."

78 A Caldecott Title-page

who also discovered and employed his two friends and rivals, Caldecott and Miss Greenaway.[1]

Randolph Caldecott began life as a bank clerk, and it was not until he was twenty-five years old, in 1871, that he decided to abandon that profession for the life of an artist.[2] His earliest accepted work appeared in *London Society*, where it was seen by J. D. Cooper, a wood engraver, who commissioned from him some seventy or more sketches to illustrate Washington Irving's *Sketch Book*, published in 1875 by Macmillan, with the title *Old Christmas*.[3]

Thus was begun his book-illustrating career, and he was soon employed to illustrate some of Mrs. Ewing's stories for children. Meanwhile Edmund Evans,

79 Kate Greenaway in her later style, from *Pictures to Paint* (1880)

of whom more later, was looking round for a successor to Walter Crane as a producer of the Routledge toy books, and in 1878 he asked Caldecott to provide two for the Christmas season. The artist responded with *John Gilpin* and *The House that Jack Built*, and continued to produce two regularly each year until the Christmas before his death in 1885. It is for these books, of which more than a million copies have been printed in all, that Caldecott will be remembered.

Kate Greenaway's father was a wood-engraver employed by the *Illustrated*

[1] Crane and Greenaway jointly illustrated *The Quiver of Love* (Marcus Ward, 1876) and also *The Baby's Birthday Book* for Marcus Ward.

[2] His work is said to have appeared in the *Illustrated London News* as early as 1861, before he left school, and he had certainly contributed to Manchester journals before coming to London.

[3] This and the sequel, *Bracebridge Hall* (1876), are generally accounted the first two volumes of the famous ''Cranford'' series, upon which followed numerous imitations put out by other publishers.

London News, and encouraged his daughter's early promise as a draughtsman (88). In 1868—she was twenty-two—she had already sold work of hers from an exhibition, and some of it was bought for publication. Thereafter she did not lack for commissions, although many of them were for hack-work in producing designs for Christmas cards and Valentines for the firm of Marcus Ward.

In 1871 she was given her first book commission by the firm of Kronheim,[1] and both the original drawings for these and the published work make it very apparent that she was working for a market. They are crude, highly coloured drawings with hardly a scintilla of her later style; but she seems to have produced what was wanted, for between 1871 and 1878 her work was used by at least five different publishers.

It was in 1877–8, however, that the turning point in her life came. Edmund Evans, engraver and colour-printer, had been apprentice to Ebenezer Landells, the favourite pupil of Thomas Bewick, and the founder of *Punch*. John Greenaway was employed by Landells and he and Evans struck up an acquaintance. Greenaway used to show Evans his daughter's drawings and her early published work, with which he was greatly taken. On the completion of his apprenticeship Evans set up as an engraver on his own account, first in Wine Office Court, and afterwards at Racquet Court, both in Fleet Street. In 1853 he had devised a glazed yellow pictorial cover for Mayhew's *Letters Left at the Pastry-cooks*, which became the foundation design for the popular reprints known as "yellow-backs". What is more important from our point of view is his experimenting with a development of the Baxter process of colour-printing from wood-blocks, and of his finally triumphant success. His perfection of the process may be seen in the Crane toy-books already mentioned, as a result of which, and of his discovery of Caldecott, publishers were accustomed to listen to his advice, and even to allow him to commission work especially for them. This was particularly the case with the firm of Routledge, which had already experimented successfully with this method of working in their profitable association with the Dalziel brothers a few years earlier.

In 1877 Kate Greenaway paid a visit to the Evans country home at Witley bringing with her a number of drawings that she had made to illustrate verses of her own. He immediately decided to purchase them and to make them into a book, and Routledge, after submitting the verses for slight titivation to Frederick Locker, agreed to take the book on. It was clearly Evans's own venture, however, for, without consulting Routledge, he proceeded to print 20,000 copies of a first edition of this work by a comparatively unknown illustrator; and, although the publishers were aghast at the prospect of having to sell so many copies of a six-shilling book, the whole edition went off immediately the book was published. Indeed it was out of print for a time and copies were changing hands at a premium. The book was *Under the Window*, it was translated into French and German, and the artist was made for life.

Her books are still printed by Evans's firm from wood-blocks, and this remarkable collaboration between artist and printer may fittingly be recorded in his own words, taken from notes for an unpublished autobiography.

[1] *Diamonds and Toads*. One of Aunt Louisa's Toy Books published by Warne & Co.

"I photographed these original drawings on to wood", he writes, "and engraved them as nearly 'facsimile' as possible, then transferred wet impressions to plain blocks of wood—'transfers' to engrave the several colour blocks on, red, flesh tint, blue, yellow. This was a costly matter, but it reproduced the character very well indeed of the original drawings. . . . we soon found that we had not printed enough to supply the first demand: I know booksellers sold copies at a premium, getting ten shillings each for them; it was, of course, long out of print for I could not print fast enough to keep up the sale."

Kate Greenaway took a lead in public favour over Caldecott and Crane, which she has preserved until now. She is better than Crane, but Caldecott runs her very close indeed, and all three of them owe much to Edmund Evans, their printer.

The importance of the Dalziels and of Edmund Evans extends beyond their contributions as craftsmen to the excellence of book illustration. This craftsmanship is by no means unimportant, especially with Evans, who was at considerable pains to match his typography to the illustrations. Unlike the Dalziels, who were wood-engravers only, Evans was his own printer, and was thus enabled to prepare and execute in his own shop the complete lay-out of the books entrusted to him.

In *Sabbath Bells* (1856), with coloured illustrations by Birket Foster—himself a fellow apprentice at Landells with Evans—the blocks are vignetted and set in the text pages. Goldsmith's *Poems* (1858), also illustrated by Foster, was even more successfully treated. Elaborate head- and tail-pieces were commissioned from Noel Humphreys, and every page was provided with a double-rule border in gold. Later, coloured inks were used for the letter-press, and more elaborate decorations and borders were used; all the work being carried out on a hand-press.

The typography is not to our taste. The types themselves are undistinguished, and the decoration is too fussy and frequently poorly designed; moreover Foster himself was not an ideal book-illustrator.[1] But Evans was learning fast; and once his position as a printer was assured he began to experiment more widely on his own account.

Walter Crane was his first discovery; and a very remarkable discovery Evans made of him. Routledge, extensive publishers of the orthodox type of 'sixties book, began in 1866 the publication of Crane's first series of sixpenny toy books with *Sing a Song of Sixpence*, the printing of which was entrusted to Evans. The entire book—cover, title, illustrations, text—is designed by the artist, and although the imitation gothic lettering can be faulted, the result, together with Evans's execution, marks a considerable advance.

One need only compare it with, for example, *Choice Pictures and Choice Poems*, produced by Evans for Ward and Lock in 1867 in the traditional 'sixties style, to see how revolutionary an advance was made with *Sing a Song of Sixpence*.

Only three colours were used—black, red, and blue—and they were printed in washes of simple block pattern. The booksellers did not greatly care for them;

[1] Nevertheless the fidelity of Evans's reproductions to the originals is equalled only by Baxter.

they were attached to the garish oiliness of the chromo-lithograph, and Evans was compelled to make some concessions to their insistence. But throughout the 'sixties and 'seventies the stream of Crane toy books continued with growing demand and popularity. They are not uniformly successful from our point of view, and this was frequently due to the over-elaboration of some of Crane's designs. Evans could work wonders even with these; indeed some of them are still among the favourites with connoisseurs, for example *The Baby's Opera* and *The Baby's Bouquet*, where very considerable ingenuity is shown in weaving music with elaborate coloured borders and full-page blocks into a semblance of consistency.

Evans's discovery of Caldecott, and later of Kate Greenaway, has already been mentioned. Both of them excelled Crane in the matter of providing suitable material for Evans's technique. The bold simplicity of Caldecott's designs and lettering is clearly to be seen in the coloured reproduction of the John Gilpin cover (77); but the greater favour accorded to the Greenaway books is in large part due to the complete sympathy between the artist and her engraver-printer. The Greenaway books printed by Evans show an increasingly close collaboration between them, such that it is impossible to say how much of the design was presented to the engraver by the artist, and how much was carried out by her at his suggestion.

One of the best examples of this close collaboration is to be seen in *Marigold Garden* [1885], which is possibly the most charming book that either of them produced, separately or in collaboration. The cover design is almost ideal for its purpose, and although there is a little too much pre-title decoration, the title itself and the inviting contrast of the frontispiece are most effective. The rest of the book is a series of bold experiments, nearly all of which succeed admirably, the boldest and best of all being on page 19, where a ladder bearing two girls is thrust daringly between the two halves of the verse "To Mystery Land".

Throughout the book Evans can be seen adapting and improving on the methods he was the first to devise in *Sabbath Bells* and its successors. On page 26 the text is only of eight lines, the motive of the verse being boldly carried out by the six girls going up and down a double flight of steps. On pages 36–7, on the other hand, eight lines are spread over two pages so that the design "On the Wall Top" may acquire its necessary range. Each page, or rather each pair of pages, is treated as an entity, text and illustrations being manipulated to fit the special treatment desired. Evans is still handicapped by the poverty of the type-face; but to contrast this book with most of the other productions of the period, even among his imitators, shows very plainly how much nearer his ideas were to us than to them.[1]

In design Evans was supreme. He shared with the Dalziels the pioneer work in commissioning drawings from specific illustrators and making their illustrations the main feature of the book. In this he was more successful than the Dalziels, who,

[1] Only once does Evans suffer markedly in comparison with a competitor, in *The Nobility of Life* (1869), where Kronheim's twelve plates are greatly superior to the twelve executed by Evans, so much so that several of the latter were omitted from a reissue.

80 Walter Crane in an unusual mood. *Song of Sixpence Toy Book* (c. 1870)

although they occasionally entrusted an entire work to one artist,[1] usually preferred the collaboration of several artists as in their *Arabian Nights* which was originally advertised, and is still referred to, under the name of the engravers.

There is nothing quite comparable with the success of the three principal artists sponsored by Evans—Crane, Caldecott, and Greenaway. It is largely due to his success with them that a new feature became fairly constant on the title-pages of children's books—the name of the illustrator.

Dodgson's anxieties over the illustrators of his Lewis Carroll books will be recalled, with the outstanding success of Tenniel, and the comparative failure of the others. Mrs. Ewing's successful early books were illustrated by Caldecott, to whom she found an admirable successor in Gordon Browne, the son of "Phiz", and an unduly neglected artist.

This inclusion of artists' names on the title-pages of books—not only of children's books—is a sign of the times; and with it there grew up a new kind of artist, one who worked exclusively as a book illustrator. The line is by no means clear cut. It is already evident in the time of Dickens, when an integral feature of the publication of novels in parts was the use of illustrations, and such artists as "Phiz", Cruikshank, and Leech made a name for work of this kind.

Even before that date Stothard, Corbould, the Westalls, and others derived a large part of their income by working for book publishers; and Bewick's work is also found chiefly in books.

This simply means that the process was a gradual one; but there was, nevertheless, a great leap forward in the 'sixties, out of which came also the work of Edmund Evans.

There is no cause for surprise in the fact that Kate Greenaway had few immediate or ultimate successors as illustrators almost exclusively of books for children.[2] Her earnings were quite exceptionally high, and the terms that she could demand were equally exceptional. The texts as well as the illustrations to *Under the Window*, *Marigold Garden*, and others of her books were her own, and where she did not write the text it was usually free from the payment of authors' royalties. Thus, for *Under the Window* she received a third of the profits, and thereafter a half. When it is remembered that the initial sales of *Under the Window* totalled about 70,000 copies at six shillings, some approximate idea of her earnings may be gained. They may have averaged £2,000 for each book.[3]

By far the more usual practice would have been to commission illustrations at a fixed price, and for an artist's fees to exceed £200 would have been quite exceptional.[4]

Artists therefore had to be prolific in order to earn a living, and prepared to turn a hand to any work that was offered.

1 E.g. Millais, *Parables*, Tenniel, *Lalla Rookh*, etc.
2 Neither Crane nor Caldecott confined themselves to this.
3 Spielmann prints an undated letter in which she gives her earnings as £2,000 a year.
4 Hugh Thomson, the most popular black-and-white illustrator of his period, received £500 and a royalty of sevenpence on every copy of the book sold above 10,000. For this he was required to produce fifty elaborate drawings for Jane Austen's *Pride and Prejudice*.

Gordon Browne, the son of "Phiz", one of the best and most successful book-illustrators from about 1880 onwards, turned out an enormous quantity of work of this kind. A selection of his work for children is listed on p. 201. Besides this he

81 Illustration by Gordon Browne to Mrs. Ewing's *Dandelion Clocks*

illustrated novels and short stories, both in books and magazines, and was frequently commissioned to design the illustrated wrappers of cheap reprints.

There are no other outstanding illustrators in the remaining years of the century. Although Miss Potter had already invented and depicted several of her favourite characters none of her work was printed before the century closed.[1]

1 The successors of Edmund Evans were chosen to print her pictures. See pp. 160-4 for an account of her work.

Familiar names will be found listed at the end of this chapter, and some of them merit at least passing mention here. H. J. Ford's illustrations for the Lang series of Fairy Books; Laurence Housman's drawings to his own stories;[1] H. R. Millar's efforts in a Fairy Book series imitating Lang's, and in some of the later Kipling stories; Arthur Rackham's distinctive, but not very robust talent; and the group of "Cranford" style artists who set something of a problem. These include the Brocks, Hugh Thomson, Fred Pegram, E. J. Sullivan, and many other well-known names.[2] These charming books in their green cloth bindings with elaborate designs in gilt by their illustrators were not planned with children exclusively or even largely in mind.

Although Caldecott's edition of Washington Irving's *Old Christmas* (1876) is usually designated the first of the series, it was not until the appearance in 1891 of Hugh Thomson's edition of *Cranford* that the movement really got under weigh. Its popularity and success were due to the recent perfection of photographic process engraving which, as Mr. Balston[3] says, "had become serviceable, both in point of accuracy and of cost . . . and for the first time a pen-and-ink drawing could be reproduced almost exactly as the artist drew it. . . ."

It is not surprising that the success of Macmillan's original series produced several imitations of it by other publishers; and both Macmillan and their imitators included titles that were favourites with children. Aesop's and Marmontel's *Fables*, *Gulliver's Travels*, *Tom Brown's Schooldays*, three volumes by Kate Douglas Wiggin, *Tom Cringle's Log*, *Westward Ho!*, and several Fenimore Coopers are definitely in this category, while all of the books were chosen with any eye to family reading.

If, therefore, it is legitimate to include these series within the orbit of illustrated books for children they form one of the most consistently elegant and attractive efforts in that sphere. We may not entirely share the predominant partiality shown by the publishers of the period for Hugh Thomson over other artists. We may feel that Fred Pegram, Chris Hammond, the Brocks, and E. J. Sullivan—whose first book commissions were for one of the series—are at least worthy of mention in the same breath. Neither the modest nor the ambitious amateur of children's books can afford to neglect the best of them.

Inadequacy in the treatment of his subject has been uppermost in the author's mind throughout the compilation of this book, and nowhere can it be more apparent than in this chapter. The broad sweep of a highly poised bird's-eye view is all that has been possible, although some attempt at a passing closer swoop has been attempted where it seemed indispensable. But the picture is very broad, and little has been done hitherto even to complete its outline. Such a completion has not been so much as attempted here; one may only hope that not too many of the highlights have been omitted.

[1] He had to abandon drawing at a comparatively early date because of the strain it caused to his afflicted eyesight.

[2] For some account of their work and lists of the various series see Balston, *Illustrated Series of the 'Nineties* in *Book Collector's Quarterly*, XI and XIV, 1933–4.

[3] *Op. cit.*, XI, p. 35.

In the earlier periods little direct work has been done on book illustration of any kind; and most of the work for children's books was anonymous. Bewick was the first notable figure to emerge in the latter field, and details of most, but certainly not all, his work for children will be found after much digging in Hugo's *The Bewick Collector* (1866) and the *Supplement* (1868), both published by Lovell Reeve.

Forrest Reid's *Illustrators of the Sixties* (Faber, 1928)—once remaindered, but now difficult to come by, and expensive when found—is indispensable for that period. It is no criticism of the lavishness and accuracy of his information to add that it is a very personal book, expressing likes, and especially dislikes, which may not always be shared by the reader. Gleeson White's *English Illustration. ''The Sixties''* (Constable, 1903), therefore, although greatly inferior to Reid, should be at hand as an occasional corrective. His facsimiles are also supplementary to Reid's. A chatty book, not without useful information, is *The Brothers Dalziel: a record* (Methuen, 1901).

For a general survey of the development of colour-printing in this period, and its background, R. M. Burch's *Colour Printing* (Pitman, 1910) is the best account. A more detailed study of the work of the colour-printers is C. T. Courtney Lewis's *The Story of Picture Printing* (1911). Lewis has also produced several books on George Baxter, the most exhaustive being *George Baxter, the Colour Printer* (1924). The Winter No. of *The Studio*, 1897, is worth consulting.

The two most important figures in the use of colour-printing in children's books are Kate Greenaway and Edmund Evans; and only courtesy puts the lady first. Evans is treated by the historians mentioned above and enters extensively also into M. H. Spielmann and G. S. Layard's *Kate Greenaway* (Black,) 1905. Indispensable for enthusiasts with much new and more accurate information is Susan Ruth Thomson's *A Catalogue of the Kate Greenaway Collection, Rare Book Room, Detroit Public Library*. Wayne University Press, Detroit, 1977.

Caldecott and Crane are even less well served. Henry Blackburn's *Randolph Caldecott* (Low, 1887) has many chatty references to his book illustrations and some facsimiles. Its lack of index is typical of its uselessness to the student.

G. C. E. Massé's *Bibliography of First Editions of Books Illustrated by Walter Crane* (Chelsea Publishing Co., 1923) is the work of an amateur enthusiast and its pronouncements should be regarded sceptically. The Toy Books are listed in a haphazard, incomplete list, and the dates affixed to them are frequently inaccurate. P. G. Konody, *The Art of Walter Crane* (1902), and O. v. Scheinitz, *Walter Crane* (Bielefeld: Velhagen and Klasing, 1902), may be consulted.

On individual artists of this period the excellent series published by Art and Technics in the series ''English Masters of Black-and-White'' are useful, especially McLean's *George Cruikshank*, Hambourg's *Richard Doyle*, Sarzano's *Sir John Tenniel*, and Pepys Whiteley's *George du Maurier*. *The Work of Charles Keene* (Unwin, 1897) has a very good bibliography by W. H. Chesson.

R. E. D. Sketchley's *English Book-Illustration of To-day* (Kegan Paul, 1903) is especially welcome for lists of artists and the children's books illustrated by them in the latter part of the nineteenth century: and on the ''Cranford'' and similar series, articles with lists of the series are in *Book Collector's Quarterly*, XI and XIV, 1933–4 (T. Balston, ''Illustrated Series of the 'Nineties''). M. H. Spielmann and W. Jerrold's *Hugh Thomson* (Black, 1931) has a list of his book- and periodical-work with dates.

82 An illustration drawn on wood by John Gilbert
and cut by Kate Greenaway's father, 1851

84   An H. M. Paget illustration to Henty's *With Moore at Corunna*, 1898

83   Photography ousting the artist. This illustration was cut on wood from a photograph, c. 1875. J. D. Watson's, William Small's and other artists' work were also used in the same book in typical 'sixties style

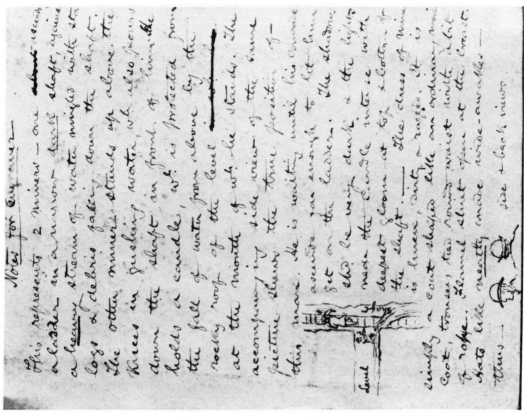

85, 86   An example of Ballantyne's instructions to his illustrator

87 Harrison Weir's animals are excellent. This illustration was engraved by Kate Greenaway's father

88 A Kate Greenaway drawing for *Little Folk's Album*, 1878, engraved by her father

With one exception no especially distinguished illustrated works appeared before the end of the eighteenth century. Specimens of the various periods are reproduced in the text of Chapters 1 to 3. The exception was, of course, the Bewicks, Thomas, and, to a lesser degree, his brother John.

BEFORE 1800

THOMAS BEWICK [1]

The following is a selective list of children's books illustrated by Bewick down to about 1790.

[1770.] *A New Invented Horn Book.*

1771. *New Lottery Book of Birds and Beasts.*

1772. *The Child's Tutor: or, Entertaining Preceptor.*
Moral Instructions Of a Father to his Son. Probable date. Earliest known edition is the third, 1775.

1774. *Youth's Instructive and Entertaining Story-Teller.*
New English Tutor (3rd ed.).

1777. *New Year's Gift for Little Masters and Misses.*

1778. *The Mirror; or, a Looking-Glass for Young People.*

1779. *A Pretty Book of Pictures for Little Masters and Misses.*

1781. *Moral Lectures.*

c. 1789. *The Life and Adventures of a Fly.*

1800–50

1805. *The Comic Adventures of Old Mother Hubbard.*

1807. *The Butterfly's Ball.* Probably illustrated by Mulready.
The Peacock at Home.

These three books are examples of the new style that came in with the nineteenth century, illustrated with metal plates, a hand-coloured edition being usually available.

GEORGE CRUIKSHANK

1817. *Dramas for Children.*

1823. E. Berens. *Christmas Stories.*
Grimm. *German Popular Stories*, Vol. I. (Vol. II, 1826.)
La Motte Fouqué. *Peter Schlemihl.*

1827. J. A. Paris. *Philosophy in Sport.* Three volumes. The first edition was not illustrated by G. C.

1828. J. P. Collier. *Punch and Judy.*
Wm. Cowper. *John Gilpin.*

1831. Defoe. *Robinson Crusoe.* Two volumes.

1832. *The Bee and the Wasp.*

1833. *The Book of Fun.*

[1] Books illustrated by John Bewick are mentioned on pp. 42 and 93 (28).

1834. W. A. Nield. *The Juvenile Music Library.*

1834–5–9. Sir John Bowring. *Minor Morals.* Three volumes.

1836. *Comic Alphabet.*

[1853–4–6.] *Fairy Library.* Four volumes.

1871. Mrs. Ewing. *The Brownies.*

1874. Mrs. Ewing. *Lob Lie-by-the-Fire.*

THE FIRST COLOUR-PRINTING

[1835.] Mrs. Sherwood. *Caroline Mordaunt.* The frontispiece is printed in colours by George Baxter. It is the earliest recorded book for children with an illustration printed in colours.

1836. Mary Elliott. *Tales of Truth for Young People.* The first of several of Mrs. Elliott's books published during the 'thirties with Baxter coloured frontispieces.

'SIXTIES BOOKS

1861. Mrs. Gatty. *Parables from Nature.* Illustrated by W. Holman Hunt, etc. Another edition, 1867, was illustrated by Charles Keene, E. Burne-Jones, etc.
John Bunyan. *The Pilgrim's Progress.* Illustrated by J. D. Watson.

1864. "W. B. Rands". *Lilliput Levee.* Illustrated by G. J. Pinwell and J. E. Millais.
Parables of Our Lord. Illustrated by Millais.

1865. Dalziel's *Arabian Nights.* Two volumes. Illustrated by A. B. Houghton, T. and E. Dalziel, G. J. Pinwell, J. Tenniel, etc. Originally issued in parts.
Lewis Carroll. *Alice's Adventures in Wonderland.* Illustrated by J. Tenniel.

1867. George MacDonald. *Dealings with the Fairies.* Illustrated by Arthur Hughes.

1871. George MacDonald. *At the Back of the North Wind.* Illustrated by Arthur Hughes.

1874. Florence Montgomery. *Misunderstood.* Illustrated by G. du Maurier.

SIR HENRY COLE

1841. *Felix Summerly's Home Treasury of Pleasure Books for Young Children.* A list of the first twelve titles is in Darton, p. 242.

CHARLES KEENE

[1842.] *The Adventures of Dick Boldhero.* Edited by Peter Parley. The frontispiece only is certainly by Keene.

1847. Defoe. *Robinson Crusoe.*
Green's Nursery Annual. One cut only by Keene.
Mrs. Sherwood. *The De Cliffords.*
Keene illustrated other books for children, which are listed in W. H. Chesson's bibliography at the end of *The Work of Charles Keene* (1897).

EDMUND EVANS

Early Period

1852. Ida Pfeiffer. *Travels in the Holy Land.* Six tinted illustrations by Birket Foster. Not strictly a children's book, but important because it was Evans's first—rather dismal —attempt at colour-printing.

1856. *Sabbath Bells.* Evans's first full-colour work, the illustrations—also after Foster— are printed in three or four colours.

1858. *Goldsmith's Poems.* Evans is here seen at his best in this particular style of colour-printing, working within the 'sixties idiom.

1864. *J. E. Doyle. A Chronicle of England.* A transition work. Evans has abandoned the 'sixties idiom and the book contains the rudiments of his own ideas of lay-out. It is a masterpiece of colour-printing.

WALTER CRANE

All the early Crane Toy books are undated, and the dates attached to them in the following list are only approximate.

1865–6. *Sing a Song of Sixpence.*

1867. *One, Two, Buckle My Shoe.*

1868. *Multiplication in Verse.*
Annie and Jack in London.

1869. *The Fairy Ship.*
This Little Pig.

RANDOLPH CALDECOTT

Caldecott's toy books are also undated; but the dates given here are from unpublished notes by Edmund Evans himself. They also accord with an independent bibliographical investigation by Mr. O. N. Chadwyck-Healey and may be taken as reliable.

1878. *The House That Jack Built.*
John Gilpin.

1880. *The Mad Dog.*
The Babes in the Wood.
Sing a Song for Sixpence.
The Three Jovial Huntsmen.

1881. *The Queen of Hearts.*
The Farmer's Boy.

1882. *The Milkmaid.*
Hey Diddle Diddle and Baby Bunting.

1883. *A Frog He Would A-Wooing Go.*
The Fox Jumps Over the Farmer's Gate.

1884. *Come Lasses and Lads.*
Ride a Cock Horse and A Farmer Went Trotting.

1885. *The Great Panjandrum.*
Mrs. Mary Blaize.

General note on the Caldecott Toy Books

All were first published by Routledge. In the first printings the list of other Caldecott toy books advertised—usually on the back cover—includes only those published to date. As the books were published in pairs it follows that the first pair will advertise only two books, the second pair four, and so on. The advertising of any Caldecott title published later than the book itself is evidence of reprinting and the only method of detecting it.

KATE GREENAWAY

Miss Greenaway's books are also undated. The dates given here are taken from Spielmann and Layard's *Kate Greenaway* (1905) and are generally accepted as accurate. Only the more important books printed by Evans are given. A list of other dates and titles will be found in the work quoted above.

1878. *Under the Window.*

1881. *A Day in a Child's Life.*
  Mother Goose.

1883. *Little Ann.*

1884. *The Language of Flowers.*

1885. *Marigold Garden.*

1885? *Kate Greenaway's Alphabet.*

1886. *A Apple Pie.*

  In addition to the above some of her best work appeared in *Little Folks, Little Wide-Awake, Every Girl's Annual, Girl's Own Paper*, and other periodicals. The title-page to the present work is adapted from the title-page of *Girl's Own Paper*.

A SELECTION FROM THE WORK OF OTHER ILLUSTRATORS
This may be considerably extended by reference to Sketchley

RICHARD DOYLE

1845. J. and W. Grimm. *The Fairy Ring.*

1849. Montalba. *Fairy Tales.*
  Mark Lemon. *The Enchanted Doll.*

1851. J. Ruskin. *The King of the Golden River.*
  The Story of Jack and the Giants.

1855. Mrs. Hervey. *A Juvenile Calendar.*

1865. Mark Lemon. *Fairy Tales.*

1870. William Allingham. *In Fairyland.*

1871. *The Enchanted Crow.*
  The *Feast of the Dwarfs.*
  Snow White and Rosy Red.

1884. Andrew Lang. *The Princess Nobody.*

1888. *Jack the Giant-Killer.*
   (Fuller list in Hambourg).

GEORGE DU MAURIER

1874. Florence Montgomery. *Misunderstood*. The first edition, 1869, was not illustrated.

GORDON BROWNE

An exceedingly prolific artist, who by no means confined his attention to children's books. His earliest work, however, was probably contributed to *Aunt Judy's Magazine* in the late 'seventies; and he was much favoured by Blackie, Methuen, and other publishers as an illustrator of juveniles. His father was Hablot K. Browne—"Phiz". A much fuller list of books illustrated by him is in Sketchley, *English Book Illustration* (1903).

1883. Ascott R. Hope. *Stories of Old Renown*.

1885. Defoe. *Robinson Crusoe*.

1886. Mrs. Ewing. *Melchior's Dream*.
Swift. *Gulliver's Travels*.

1887. Irving. *Rip van Winkle*.
Alice Corkran. *Down the Snow Stairs*.
Mrs. Ewing. *The Peace-Egg*.
—— *Dandelion Clocks*.
G. A. Henty. *Bonnie Prince Charlie*. The first of many Henty books illustrated by G. B.

1889. Andrew Lang. *Prince Prigio*.

1890. *A Apple Pie*.

1893. L. T. Meade. *A Young Mutineer*.

1895. Grimm. *Fairy Tales*.

1897. S. R. Crockett. *Sir Toady Lion*.

1899. E. Nesbit. *The Story of the Treasure Seekers*. With Lewis Baumer.

LESLIE BROOKE

1889. E. Everett-Green. *Miriam's Ambition*.

1897. A. Lang (Ed.). *A Nursery Rhyme Book*.

H. J. FORD

1889. A. Lang (Ed.). *The Blue Fairy Book*. With G. P. Jacomb-Hood. Ford also collaborated with other artists in illustrating the rest of this series.

JOHN D. BATTEN

1893. *Tales from the Arabian Nights*

1895. *More Tales*.
Batten illustrated the collections of national fairy-tales made by Joseph Jacobs between 1890 and 1894; but these were not made for children.

C. E. BROCK

1893. Atkinson. *Scenes in Fairyland*.
English Fairy and Folk Tales.
And numerous other books, especially of the "Cranford" Series kind.

A. J. GASKIN

1893. Hans Andersen. *Fairy Tales.*
1894. S. Baring Gould (Ed.) *A Book of Fairy Tales.*

LAURENCE HOUSMAN

1893, etc. (See list in Chapter 6, written and illustrated by L. H.)

R. ANNING BELL

1894. *Jack the Giant-Killer.*
      The Sleeping Beauty.

H. R. MILLAR

1894. *The Golden Fairy Book.*
1895. *The Silver Fairy Book.*

ARTHUR RACKHAM

1896. S. J. A. Fitzgerald. *The Zankiwank and the Bletherwich.*
1899. R. H. Barham. *The Ingoldsby Legends.*
1900. *Fairy Tales of Grimm.*
1922. N. Hawthorne. *A Wonder Book.*

H. M. PAGET

c. 1894. Illustrated several of G. A. Henty's books for boys.

H. M. BROCK

1895. Capt. Marryat. *Jacob Faithful.*
      Has illustrated fewer children's books than his brother, C. E.

WILLIAM STRANG

1895. *Adventures of Baron Munchausen.*
1896. *Sinbad and Ali Baba.*
      Both with J. B. Clark.

ALICE B. WOODWARD

1895. *Banbury Cross and other Nursery Rhymes.*

SIDNEY PAGET

1896. A. Conan Doyle. *Rodney Stone.* Best known for his creation of the accepted portrayal of Sherlock Holmes.

EDMUND J. SULLIVAN

1896. T. Hughes. *Tom Brown's Schooldays*.

LEWIS BAUMER

1897. *Jumbles*.

1899. E. Nesbit. *The Story of the Treasure Seekers*. With Gordon Browne.

F. D. BEDFORD

1897. *A Book of Nursery Rhymes*.

1899. E. V. Lucas. *A Book of Shops*.

FRANK BRANGWYN

1897. *The Arabian Nights*.

1898. Cervantes. *Don Quixote*.

FRED PEGRAM

1897. Capt. Marryat. *Masterman Ready*.

HUGH THOMSON

1898. *Jack the Giant Killer*. This was announced as the first of a series called "Hugh Thomson's Illustrated Fairy Books"; but no others were issued.

ALAN WRIGHT

1898. G. E. Farrow. *The Wallypug in London*. And all the later "Wallypug" Series.

CARTON MOORE PARK

1899. *An Alphabet of Animals*.

HARRY FURNISS

1885. Horace Leonard. *Romps at the Seaside*.

1886. E. J. Milliken. *More Romps*.

1889. Lewis Carroll. *Sylvie and Bruno*.

1893. Lewis Carroll. *Sylvie and Bruno Concluded*.

1895. G. E. Farrow. *The Wallypug of Why*.

CHARLES, T. H., AND W. H. ROBINSON

The earliest discovered book by each of the three brothers is given.

1895. *Aesop's Fables* (Charles).

1895. Frank Rinder. *Old World Japan*. (T. H.).

1897. Cervantes. *Don Quixote* (W. H.).

      The three brothers together illustrated a selection from Andersen's Fairy Tales in 1899.

CHAPTER EIGHT

NICK NACKS

1. *Harlequinades*

ANYONE who has taken children on a Christmas shopping expedition will realise what tough customers they are, and what sales resistance they can show. The publishers of children's books have long been aware of this and have striven to present their wares in such a form as to make them irresistible to children. This will also have arisen in the course of that shopping expedition, because one of the great difficulties is to limit the child's choice to what one can afford to spend. Boreman's lists of young subscribers, Newbery's offers of presents to young purchasers, the puffs of their own premises, which he and other publishers introduced into their stories, are examples of ingenious publicity, sometimes more apt to its purpose than the books it was designed to push. Once the fact of a juvenile reading public was established, however, ingenuity in catering to it was forthcoming.

Shortly after the middle of the eighteenth century, probably before 1760, Robert Sayer took over the print-shop of the Overton family in Fleet Street, which is mentioned in Gay's *Trivia*. This family had themselves taken over the business of another print-seller in the seventeenth century, by the name of Peter Stent, who is familiar to the collectors of the work of the English writing masters as the publisher of many of them, including at least one by Cocker. By the time Sayer took on the business it had become large and important, and he was to add several new features to it. The "harlequinades" constituted one of his bright inventions, and although they had a life in this country of not more than about thirty years, they proved very popular while they lasted and their popularity spread later across the Atlantic, as will be seen. They were not originally called "harlequinades", and their beginning, although unpretentious, is historically interesting. Before going into that, however, it is necessary to describe just what they were.[1] Basically each is composed upon a single sheet of paper folded perpendicularly into four. Hinged to the head and foot of each fold is a picture divided horizontally in the centre so as to make two flaps, which can be raised to disclose another picture below. The doggerel verse on each section tells a simple story, concluding with instructions to turn down one flap for the continuation. Upon doing so the reader finds that the half of the new picture that is then disclosed fits neatly on to the half on the

---

[1] The illustrations 91, 92 and 93 should be compared with this description.

89   More German influence. An illustration to an English
book by Paul Konewka, *c.* 1870

90   One of R. André's illustrations to Mrs. Ewing's verses. This should be
compared with Caldecott fig. 78 and Browne fig. 81

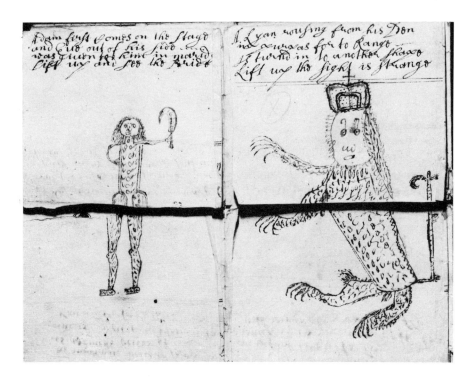

91 A home-m[a]
harlequinade,
c. 1698

1. Adam comes first upon the stage,
And Eve from out his side,
Who was given him in marriage;
Turn up and see his bride.

4. A Lion rousing from his den
On purpose for to range,
Is soon turn'd into another shape;
Lift up and see how strange.

92 An American
harlequinade of
1816

The texts are virtually identical and the figures in the later one derive from the earlier

Harlequin in a forest with the Taylor
Going to cut of his Head with his Shears.

Harlequin taken Prisoner.

A Proclamation being made
That Harlequin was seen at Dover
A Taylor with his Sheers displayd
Would cut his Head off soon as over.
Moral.
Yet tho' this Man was strong & Stout
Turn up, you'll find what came about.

Ha! Ha! my Friends a pretty Scene o'
The like was ne'er before
The charming witty Harlequino
Is fastned Sure and Sure.
Moral.
Tricking you find will ne'er prevail
Turn up and then persue the Tale.

93   A typical Sayer harlequinade from *Harlequin's Invasion*, 1770

FRONTISPIECE.

Mirth without Mischief.

CONTAINING

The Twelve Days of Chriſtmas;
The Play of the Gaping-Wide-Mouthed-Wadling Frog;
Love and Hatred;
The Art of Talking with the Fingers;
AND
Nimble Ned's Alphabet and Figures.

School you muſt ſtudy your book for to learn,
But when the ſchool's over let mirth have a turn.

LONDON:

Printed by J. Davenport, George's Court,
For C. SHEPPARD, No. 8, Aylesbury Street, Clerkenwell.

[PRICE—THREE PENCE.]

Here lads and laſſes all repair,
And gather of this fruit ſo fair;
And thoſe who gather moſt will find
'Twill make them wiſe and feed the mind,
And ſave them from the birch behind.

Frontispiece and title of an ingenious combination of instruction and amusement

unraised flap—hence other names for these creations are "metamorphoses" and "turn-ups".[1]

The name of "harlequinade" to describe them derives from the fact that after Sayer had published two or three of them he had the idea of summarising in this form the pantomimes or harlequinades at the leading London theatres, and usually took care to introduce the word "Harlequin" into the title in one form or another. At first, before he hit upon this idea, they seem to have hung fire, for the first of them appeared in 1766 or 1767, and by September 1770 only three more had been published. But No. 4 was *Harlequin's Invasion. A New Pantomime*, and from that time onwards they seem to have caught on, for fifteen in all were published by Sayer down to August 1772, after which I can trace no more issued from his office. They were still in the catalogue nearly twenty-five years later, and sporadic examples came also from other publishers. In one of these, a particularly interesting one—*Harlequin's Habeas*, published in 1803—John Harris had a share, although the principal publisher was one, T. Hughes. On the printed wrapper of this harlequinade—all the early ones had plain unprinted wrappers—he announced this as the first of a series, and until quite recently it was the only title published by him known to me. Then Mr. Louis Bondy kindly sent me a list of seventeen other titles advertised by Hughes as already published. I have not added these titles to the list of harlequinades on pp. 228-33, for the actual existence of any of them is unknown to me and Hughes's list may be evidence of intention rather than accomplishment: but I shall be grateful for news of the survival of any harlequinade with Hughes's imprint other than *Harlequin's Habeas*. Mr. Bondy's list, however, was taken from a harlequinade published by Hughes in 1807, and previously unknown to me— *The Wood Daemon* (1807).

The blurb on the wrapper is worth quoting in full: "The Juvenile Theatre: or, Dramatic Delineations, with expositions in verse, of all the most Favourite Spectacles, Pantomimes, Ballets, and other Grand and Picturesque Performances at the Theatres-Royal; entirely adapted to the comprehension and amusement of Youth. To be continued occasionally." Mr. George Speaight[2] confirms a surmise that Hughes's notion was a forerunner of the juvenile drama, the tradition of which has recently been preserved by the purchase and continuation of Pollock's business, on which Stevenson wrote his well-known essay.[3]

The first turn-up published by Sayer has an interesting history and sequel. The

---

[1] In an eighteenth-century publisher's list in my possession they are described as "Harlequin Books. For the entertainment and instruction of youth, usually called turn ups; neatly fitted with blue glazed paper; coloured eight shillings a dozen; plain four shillings." This was probably a trade or "remainder" price, as the price printed on the books themselves is sixpence plain or one shilling coloured.

[2] Pp. 109-11.

[3] Mr. Speaight has also identified the originals of several of Sayer's turn-ups in pantomimes in which Henry Woodward appeared; Hughes's publication as based on a piece by T. J. Dibdin, and an undated specimen published by Tabart, *The Exile*, as based on a popular melodrama of 1808, and this he calls "an immediate forerunner of the Juvenile Drama".

fashioning of the prototype of these ingenious productions at home, and by hand, was a popular pastime in the seventeenth century, and possibly earlier. I know of no printed specimens earlier than Sayer's, but I have reproduced (91) a crude MS. example of about 1698.[*] I have seen others, although this is the earliest, and most of them follow this one fairly closely in its sequence of incidents, and in several the actual wording is identical. They begin with Adam, who is usually associated with the fall of man by his holding an apple or, as in the specimen shown, a crude representation of the serpent. When the first flap is turned Eve appears on the scene, and the turning of the second flap invariably shows her, for some indeterminable reason, changed into a mermaid. The next pair of flaps depicts a lion,[1] beneath which is a winged monster, which is finally seen to be carrying off an infant. The next picture shows a full-grown man who has "escaped the eagle's claws, and is bent on gathering a hoard of gold". The turning of one flap transforms this picture into "a heart with care opprest", and when the companion flap is opened the heart becomes a bag of gold. The final picture of a rich miser dissolves into a skeleton with the obvious moral that you can't take it with you.

Now it was this model, or one very like it, that Sayer took for his first turn-up, which is called *Adam and Eve*;[†]but what is even more curious is that in 1816 J. Rackstraw in Philadelphia printed for publication by Samuel Wood of New York a small booklet entitled *Metamorphosis; or, a Transformation of Pictures, with Poetical Explanations, for the Amusement of Young Persons*, and that not only are the woodcuts derived directly from the seventeenth-century manuscript specimen, but the verses are almost word for word the same (91, 92). There must surely be some significance in the fact that the only other American turn-up known to me is a version of Bunyan's *Pilgrim's Progress* published at Hartford in 1821, and in a different version at New Haven in 1840,[2] then described as "the fourth edition". Surely this indicates that these publications derived from parlour amusements taken across the Atlantic by seventeenth-century immigrants.

[*] I have since seen a printed example dated 1654.

2. *Juvenile Drama*

Whether or not there is a traceable connection between the turn-ups and the Juvenile Drama as treated by Mr. Speaight in his exhaustive and attractive book on that subject, it undoubtedly has a place here, and inadequate mention of it may be pardoned because of its lengthy treatment elsewhere. If the claims of J. K. Green in 1834 may be accepted he was "the Original Inventor and Publisher of Juvenile Theatrical Prints, Established 1808".[3] In this case he overlapped Tabart who was still issuing turn-ups in 1809. However that may be, in their very earliest

---

[1] In the MS. version illustrated the lion has a human face, wears a crown, and balances a sceptre on its tail, which may suggest some political significance.

[2] The latest English turn-up known to me cannot be later than 1831, and is the only printed example of anything like so late a date that I can trace.

[3] Speaight, 47.

[†] Dr. d'Alte Welch, *Bibliography of American Children's Books*, 1963–1968, under entry 1036, records and collates no fewer than 36 editions of this American version between 1787 and 1820.

form the sheets of the Juvenile Drama do not concern us at all, for they were issued as separate sheets, singly or in groups, and had nothing to do with books. This, alas, also disqualifies tinsel pictures from our notice. By the year 1812, however, the success of the original projects caused West, one of the earliest and most consistently successful publishers in this field, to add books of words of the plays so that the young enthusiasts could produce the plays in miniature, and speak the words as the characters were introduced on to the stage.

The popularity of the scheme grew by leaps and bounds, and it is very easy to see the reason for it. First, of course, there was the intrinsic attraction of the gaily coloured sheets themselves with their almost infinite variety. There were very soon sheets, not only of characters, but of scenery, wings, flats, and drop scenes— both interior and exterior—adaptable to many different kinds of plays, special scenery for special subjects, nautical, oriental, and so on, even attempts at trick scenes, such as West's "New Pantomime Tricks"[1] in which the sedan chair bearing Columbine's protectors may be turned into a prison cage detaining them while Harlequin dances off with the young lady herself; and, of course, the proscenium arch itself, and the stage; and everything was so clearly marked out for the young enthusiast that only a supply of cardboard for mounting the material, gum to stick it down, and a sharp knife with which to cut it out were needed to produce a home entertainment of endless possibilities. Couple with this the paucity in number and the poverty of content of children's books at the time, and the attractions of this new toy need no emphasis. Doubtless the pundits of the period bewailed the universal spread of the juvenile drama and its deleterious influence on the reading of the younger generation. It bears, indeed, a primitive but very close relation to the spread of television to-day, one difference being that the children made their own amusement.

The spontaneity with which the idea caught on is as typical here as in other spheres of publication for children. In 1811, the year of the earliest dated sheets for the Juvenile Drama, Speaight records four publishers of them; by 1820 these had grown to twelve, between 1820 and 1830—the hey-day—the number had grown to forty-six, and, in all, over a hundred publishers are recorded in England alone.[2]

3. Paper Dolls

Another pretty series of books that was also a comparative failure was invented by and almost exclusive to the firm of S. and J. Fuller, whose address was The Temple of Fancy, in Rathbone Place. In 1810 they began to issue a small series of books in printed boards tied with silk ribbon, and in a board case to match, not more than ten of which appeared. Instead of pictures the stories, always in rhyme, had a series

1 Speaight, facing p. 43.
2 Speaight, pp. 211–34.

of loosely inserted cut-out figures, coloured by hand. These represented the hero and heroine of the story in a number of different costumes, each figure having a space cut out for the head, which was supplied separately, and fitted all the figures by means of a pointed tag which was slipped into a paper pocket behind the figure. Frequently the figures were also supplied with hats to match their costumes, which could be fitted over the head before it was slipped into place. These hats often got lost, and sets are rarely found complete (106, 107).

The ingenuity of the idea is unquestionable, and the result was tasteful and attractive, although the accompanying verses were usually deplorable.[1] But they were expensive to produce. The cheapest of them retailed at five shillings and one of them cost eight shillings. This was *Young Albert, or the Roscius*, published in 1811, and obviously due to the success of young Betty, the boy actor. It exhibits him in a series of seven stage characters, of which six are from Shakespeare, including Hamlet. Most of these books in fact contained eight figures, but this one was much more elaborate. All the characters but one were provided with hats, and the exception, Othello, had an extra head because the face had to be black.

It seems clear that the Fullers had a very high-class clientele, and their productions show less preoccupation with cost than with elegance of presentation. Their coloured panoramas include some of the most attractive—*Going to Epsom Races* and the now exceedingly rare *Progress of Human Life*; they published round games which cost as much as thirty shillings; and their two ventures into peep-show publishing, one of the Thames Bridges and one of the Regent's Park, are among the most elegant and beautifully finished of any, and cost six shillings and sixpence each, which was not a competitive price in that particular market, where half a crown was almost the limit that the ordinary public was prepared to pay.

I have come across only one similar book in England[2] by a publisher other than Fuller.[3] This is *St. Julien, The Emigrant; or, Europe Depicted: exhibiting the Costumes, and describing The Manners and Customs of the various nations*. It was published in 1812 by the firm of J. and E. Wallis, 42 Skinner Street, Snow Hill—a popular location for juvenile publishers, one of the Darton firms and the Godwins being in the immediate vicinity. In general plan and appearance this book resembles Fuller's very strongly, except that it has a coloured map, with the itinerary marked on it, as a frontispiece. For the rest, the hero of the little story, which, however, is not in rhyme, appears in a series of seven cut-out costume figures of the countries through which he passes. In the only copy I have seen he is not provided with any hats.

Although they were not primarily book publishers, the firm of Wallis demands an aside here for their considerable enterprise in the juvenile market. They were principally cartographers and map publishers and the firm was founded by John

---

1 They were nearly always anonymous, but a late edition attributes one of them to "Dr. Wolcot". This was almost certainly John Wolcot, otherwise known as "Peter Pindar", a ready but rather indifferent versifier.

2 But see the list on p. 233.

3 Fuller's series was copied in France, and at least one of the titles, *Phoebe*, was translated into French.

Engraved and Printed in Colours by Vizetelly Brothers and Co.

AUTUMN—HARVEST TIME.

95 One of Miller's four country books, 1846–7.   An early example
of printing in colours after Birket Foster

Wallis in about the middle of the eighteenth century. They published educational maps; and in about 1780 it occurred to someone connected with the firm that maps might be used as the basis for educational pastimes. Thus they cut up into sections a map of the world, in two spheres on Mercator's projection, and invented the jig-saw puzzle.

4. The Toilet Books

In 1821 the seventy-year-old miniature-painter William Grimaldi was staying with his family in a Wiltshire Rectory. He was a friend of Sir Joshua Reynolds, several of whose paintings he had copied in miniature; and the great artist had introduced him to the Royal Dukes. For "Prinny" he painted a miniature of Mrs. Fitzherbert, and for the future Duchess of York he painted a miniature of her bridegroom which was her wedding present to him. But in 1821 he had retired to the country for a time and was carrying out his work there.

As a relaxation at a house-party he produced a set of nine drawings of articles that he found on his daughter's dressing-table, each of which was hinged to a flap on raising which a suitable moral observation was disclosed (pp. 233-34). A bottle of face lotion, labelled "A Wash to smooth Wrinkles" disclosed the word "Contentment" the secret of the looking-glass, called "The Enchanting Mirror" (68) was "Humility", and so on.

There can be little doubt of the source of his inspiration. In 1777 Carnan, Newbery's son-in-law, published *The Lilliputian Auction*. The objects auctioned included "A Curious Looking-Glass; A Packet containing a Receipt to make Young Ladies Beautiful" and a variety of other toilet articles from a lady's dressing-table, to each of which was attached a moral cachet in the style followed by Grimaldi.

William's son, Stacey Grimaldi, a London solicitor and genealogist, who wrote a learned treatise to prove that the Principality of Monaco really belonged to him, seized on his father's drawings and suggested that they would make a book. Provided with a sententious preface and a moralising verse to each subject, they were produced at the author's expense. The book was successful and was reprinted more than once. It also attracted imitators. "A Lady" in Dublin produced almost immediately a riposte for gentlemen, "The Dandies' Toilet"; there was a crude American version in lithography in the 'thirties, and a villainous version on a large scale, produced by chromolithography, appeared in Boston, Mass., in 1885 with the title "My Lady's Casket".

The Grimaldis produced a sequel for boys in 1824 called *Suit of Armour for Youth*. In this pieces of body armour were faithfully reproduced with moral maxims to match. Thus "The Strongest Breastplate", when raised, disclosed George III addressing the House of Lords, the picture being labelled "Virtue". "An

215

96 Frontispiece to *The Lilliputian Auction* (1777)

Admirable Plume''—the Prince of Wales' feathers (George VI was Prince of Wales at the time)—was ''Loyalty''. Although a much more elaborate affair than ''The Toilet'' it was comparatively unsuccessful.

5. *Movables*

From about 1840 onwards Dean & Son exploited all forms of flap and movable books very skilfully. There were books in which flaps could be raised horizontally, vertically, or by corners to disclose new pictures, there were others in which tabs could be pulled, thus dissolving one picture into another, and a long series of ingenious examples of books in which the pulling of tabs gave movement to sets of figures. These last were most elaborately developed by the firm of Meggendorfer in Munich in the 'eighties and 'nineties, while Nister in the same city, then a considerable centre of the toy business, also elaborated the dissolving-view books very cleverly. Both firms produced editions in English which were very popular here.

These are only a few of the fancy pieces thought up by publishers between about 1760 and 1900. Few specimens of them have survived the handling of children, and advertisements indicate others that appear to have vanished completely. Several of the old favourites have been adapted or reproduced by modern publishers: others were economically possible only when cheap hand-labour was available.

Brevity of treatment of these pretty things here should not disguise the fact that the variety of invention in their inception, coupled with the nimbleness of their execution constitutes one of the most remarkable chapters in the development of children's books. With the exception of the Grimaldis and Meggendorfer the names of their designers and executors are mostly unknown. They were just ordinary, run-of-the-mill productions; and they show a considerable superiority over the generality of children's books of their period.

6. The Three R's

Without gadgets of any kind, however, there was considerable ingenuity in the educational sphere. I have said in the beginning of this book that it is mainly concerned with books produced for children's entertainment; but it has been almost impossible to confine attention to these, if only because for so long pure entertainment was considered positively harmful to children. The long history of the moral tale, from Thomas White to Mrs. Sherwood, shows that; and, indeed, compared with the prevalence of their kind of "entertaining" book, some of the frankly instructional books of the early nineteenth century are a joy to behold. But they have an ancestor of a very early date.

The father of all direct attempts to teach children by means of pictures is the German, J. A. Comenius (1592–1671), who must be mentioned here because his *Orbis Pictus* (1658)[1] was translated into English by Charles Hoole in 1659. Although its influence and success in this country were less remarkable than on the Continent, its fundamental importance is not to be questioned.

The primary purpose of the author was to instil into his pupils the importance

[1] The full title is *Orbis sensualium Pictus. Hoc est, Omnium fundamentalium in Mundo Rerum & in Vita Actionum & Nomenclatura. Die sichtbare Welt. Das ist aller Vornehmsten Welt-Dinge und Lebens-Verrichtungen Vorbildung und Benahmung* (Noribergae, 1658.)

of a knowledge of Latin, then still the one really international language. This may be seen from the lay-out of the title-page, on which the Latin title occupies the upper half, and throughout the work, where Latin is given the predominance. Comenius sought to achieve his end by picturing hundreds of familiar objects and scenes—which he is said to have drawn himself—each with the Latin name first, followed by the vernacular—he attempted to bring the whole world and every phase

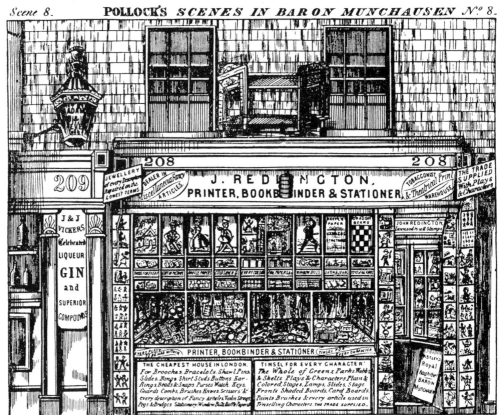

97 The Shop that Stevenson wrote about

of human activity into his book—which is the basic pattern for every kind of *images populaires* that succeeded it.

Previous chapters will have shown some of its successors; Bunyan may have known it; and the publisher of T. W.'s "Little Book" copied its lay-out to some extent.

The alphabet was taught by means of horn-books, which lingered on into the nineteenth century, and had their lives still further prolonged by the "battle-dores", single sheets of alphabets shaped, like the horn-books themselves, to enable them to be used for propelling the shuttlecock. They have little intrinsic charm, except for the silver ones, which are not books anyway.[1]

One early attempt to make the learning of the alphabet palatable has already been noted in the first chapter of this book, when T. W. printed for the first time, in the early years of Queen Anne, the jingle beginning "A was an Archer and shot at a frog", and terminating rather lamely with "Z was one Zeno, but he's dead". "A was an Apple-pie", one of Kate Greenaway's favourites, appeared in a book even earlier, although not in a book for children. Its quotation, beginning "A Apple-pasty, B bak'd it, C cut it," and so on, in ridicule of the methods of some preachers, by John Eachard in 1671[2] indicates that it would be very familiar to the reader, and that its ancestry must have been ancient. Opie lists about twenty-five editions or version of it between 1743 and 1900.[3]

One development that is clearly traceable to the eighteenth century is the matching of pictures to letters and words. The use of pictures for the instruction of small children seems so natural to us that it comes as something of a shock to realise that this was not always so. There are many reasons for it, not the least of which is probably the long-lingering conviction that reading for pleasure, like all other forms of pleasure, is sinful.[4] But the simple fact is that the proper use of pictures to illustrate a text is not so readily learned by book producers as might be supposed. In the earliest printed illustrated books, for example, woodcuts are often added with the clear knowledge that they are an attraction in themselves, but without much sense of the fact that the attraction is enhanced if they are apposite. Moreover, the printers of early books would often borrow, steal, or imitate cuts from other books which were less suitable to their own productions. It is curious to see how, in the eighteenth century, the publishers of children's books followed the practice of the early printers in this respect.

In the early seventeen-seventies Angus, a Newcastle printer and publisher, commissioned or accepted from T. Hastie, a local schoolmaster, a book of instruction in reading for small children which had the attractive title of *The Only Method to make Reading Easy*. Angus was one of a group of Northumberland printers who specialised in the chapbook type of publishing, and who were accustomed to illustrate their books with woodcuts. Beilby's workshop was often employed to produce the cuts, and Hastie's book was entrusted to a young apprentice, Thomas Bewick,

---

[1] The earliest use of the word horn-book given by *O.E.D.* is from Shakespeare's *Love's Labour Lost* (1589) but Mrs. Field, in *The Child and His Book*, mentions the grant of a licence for a "Horne A B C" to John Wofe in about 1587.

[2] *Some Observations upon the Answer to an Enquiry into the Grounds & Occasions of the Contempt of the Clergy.*

[3] Opie, p. 48. They also quote some sixteen separate appearances of "A was an Archer", in various versions over the same period.

[4] I vividly recall, when a boy, standing on the outskirts of an open-air meeting outside Regent's Park in which uniformed members of an American-imported form of Christianity, The Pillar of Fire, demonstrated to the crowd the hampering nature of sin by binding one of their number in crippling bands of linen each of which was applied to that part of the body with which a sinful appetite could be associated. Around the eyes was bound one labelled "Reading"!

who produced a series of twenty-four miniature cuts of animals and birds to illustrate the letters of the alphabet.[1] Each cut was under one inch square, finished with that degree of perfection and accuracy associated with Bewick's name. The little book was an immediate success, and when Charnley took over Angus's effects in later years this was one of the most consistent sellers on his list. In 1839 he announced the seventy-third edition of it, but this takes no count of the pirated editions and imitations,[2] which were countless. This may not have been the first pictorial alphabet on now familiar lines, but it was certainly one of the most attractive and successful of them.

In 1790 Fellows in Salisbury and Wallis in London co-operated in the publication of *The Enigmatical Alphabet*, a series of riddles the answer to each of which was a letter of the alphabet. From about 1800 onwards there was a stream of ABC's in various attractive forms, all of them pictorial. Adjectives applied to the word "Alphabet" included amusing, historical, classical, scriptural, exciting, modern, alliterative, nursery, child's own, noah's ark, and Tom Thumb's. Two of the cleverest were by "R. R."—*The Invited Alphabet* (1808) and *The Assembled Alphabet* (1813), both published by Darton. The former consists of a simple story in verse, the purposes of which is to invite the alphabet to assemble so that good children may learn to spell and read. In the second, a sequel, the letters gather together, "in abcdary collation" with the desired effect—or so the concluding verses assure us.

The first reading books were the primers, which are described in *O.E.D.* as "prayer-books or devotional manuals for the use of the laity". The passage in Chaucer's *Prioress's Tale*, written about 1386, in which the use of primers as school-books for the teaching of letters is referred to is well known. This, however, was almost certainly a Latin primer, for Morison[3] says that it was not until the fifteenth century that primers were available in the vernacular. The derivation of the more modern sense in which "primer" is used is therefore clear. Later, in the sixteenth century, the *Shorter Catechism* was put to a similar use, in order that children entered for confirmation should have a clear idea of the responsibilities they were thus to assume. This practice continued at least until the eighteenth century while the printing of the *Shorter Catechism* remained a valuable monopoly of the Stationers' Company. There are no further striking developments until the nineteenth century.[4] The Newberys, of course, published several reading books for children of different ages; but the earliest persistently successful reading book of all was William

---

[1] Illustrated on p. 173.

[2] One of these, *The Real Reading Made Easy* (1782), produced in Newcastle by one of Angus's rivals, T. Saint, who also employed Bewick to do the cuts, was propaganda for simplified spelling, containing "A Su'pl'int Too thi Histire ov Robinsin Kruzo" and "Propozils for printing bi Subskripshin A Nu Edishin ov thi Hole Bibil . . .".

[3] *English Prayer Books* (3rd ed., 1949, p. 38).

[4] *Tommy Thumb's Pretty Song Book* (c. 1743–4)—see Opie, esp. p. 32 and Plate VII—seems to be the earliest recorded self-conscious reading book for children.

Mavor's *English Spelling Book*, undated, but published in 1801 by the enterprising and successful Sir Richard Phillips.[1]

There were progressive readers—one of the earliest from E. Newbery in 1789—which began with stories made up of words of one syllable, although there was often cheating here with hyphens; "Mrs. Teachwell" compiled for Marshall a list of books recommended to children from the age of three to twelve years—although this was little more than a puff of Marshall's own list; there were primers of all kinds, with the word used in its modern sense—the Silver, Universal, Rational, Picturesque, and many other kinds; but, with one exception, I have found no trace of exploitation of the alphabet and reading in the form of a game. The exception contains an excruciating pun in the title, and dates from about 1850. This is *The Spelling Bee: A Letters-try Game*, which gave rules and examples for an early form of "Word-Taking and Word-Making".

The earliest books of instruction in writing were not intended exclusively, perhaps not even principally, for children. Manuscript examples are known from the fifteenth century. Many of the finest in printed form originate in Italy with the revival of learning in the first half of the sixteenth century,[2] and they reached England in about 1571, when John Baildon published an adaptation of a French book of writing instruction by Jean de Beauchesne. They reached their hey-day in England in the eighteenth century, by which time writing masters, who frequently taught arithmetic as well, were attached to many of the leading schools, and some of them had establishments of their own. The books of instruction issued by most of these masters were largely examples of their own virtuosity, although many contained also instructions for making and for using pens.[3] An attractive by-product of these schools were the writing-pieces, or writing sheets already referred to on pp. 59–60 (18), which consisted of broadsides with ornamental pictorial borders, in the blank centre of which children were encouraged to produce their best calligraphy for presentation to their parents. The earliest of these bearing a date is from 1741, they were advertised at two shillings a dozen plain and four shillings a dozen coloured in 1796, and they continued to be favoured until the eighteen-forties.

Rhymes to help in the learning of multiplication tables are probably of very early origin, and the sing-song chant with which we repeated in unison "twice one are two", etc., was probably not peculiar to my own infant school. "One, two, Buckle my shoe" is probably the best of all the counting rhymes. Opie gives the earliest printed version as 1805, but it must be older than that. There are

[1] The original edition had a frontispiece by Stothard. In 1885 one of Kate Greenaway's least successful books, but by no means the least attractive, was an illustrated edition of Mavor.

[2] A *Modus Scribendi* manuscript of this period discovered by E. Ph. Goldschmidt at the Monastery of Melk was privately printed for Stanley Morison in facsimile at the Cambridge University Press in 1940. It was addressed to teachers of calligraphy.

[3] A most important feature of calligraphic instruction, as Edward Johnston discovered when he began the modern revival of interest in the subject.

not many others, and it is surprising in view of the frequent emphasis that has been placed on the likenesses between music and mathematics that so few musical settings for arithmetic lessons are known. Callcott, who in the eighteenth century produced settings of the multiplication and pence tables[1] for children, seems to be the earliest, and he has had few emulators.

Marmaduke Multiply's Merry Method of Making Minor Mathematicians (Harris, 1816) and an imitation of it, *Nathaniel Numeral's Novel Notions of . . . Numeration* (Wallis, 1817), are more successful in the ingenuity of their titles than in the rhymes used to learn the tables, and ''R. R.'', who was so successful with the alphabet, was altogether too ingenious in *Infantile Erudition*, which introduced arithmetic lessons into a series of dances ''in the costume of Arabians, the reputed inventors of our modern arithmetical numeration''. It was published by Tabart in 1810. Darton, who had published his alphabetical works, probably thought this less likely to succeed.

Among the by-products of the education-by-amusement school was a game of 1826 based on the pounds, shillings, and pence table—in which the counters were the mother-of-pearl fish often seen in antique shops nowadays; a jig-saw puzzle which made up into the multiplication table; a long series of coloured pictorial sheets, in panoramic form, in which the numbers of groups were ingeniously taught—these, although having the underlines in English have a continental appearance; and, most attractive of all, a series of picture cards cut in half which contained the problem on one half and the solution on the other so that when the two halves of the picture were correctly fitted together the right answer was produced.[2]

Punctuation Personified (Harris c. 1824), in which the characters in the pictures were composed of punctuation marks, and *Peter Piper's Practical Principles of Plain and Perfect Pronunciation* (Harris 1813),[3] with a series of alliterative verses beginning ''Andrew Airpump ask'd his Aunt her Ailment'', thus forming also an alphabet, belong to the three R's.

Other educational fields had their own ingenuities. History and geography, lending themselves easily to pictorial representation, were most fruitful in producing games of an educational nature.

One of the earliest, and not the least ingenious, of these attempts to combine recreation and education is an undated volume entitled *A Brief Description of England and Wales . . . to give Youth an Idea of Geography*. There are fifty-two plates in this small duodecimo volume, each depicting towns, post-roads, and rivers in one of the counties. These plates are not an integral part of the volume, but each of them is pasted into its place facing a short account of the county depicted. In the upper margin of each map is the name of the county flanked on the left by the insignia

1 *Juvenile Improvement* (2nd ed., 1797).
2 These cards were also produced for teaching spelling. A modern adaptation of them in which parts of the rifle are separated on a board and the correct assembly is learned by searching with electrical terminals until a bulb is illuminated is used in the Russian Army.
3 Opie gives this as the earliest printing of the jingle ''Peter Piper picked a peck of pickled pepper-corns''.

98 An illustration from *Punctuation Personified*

of one of the four suits in a pack of cards, and on the right by its value. The book has a late-eighteenth-century appearance, but the impressions show signs of wear, and the court cards are in seventeenth-century costume. The Kings, in fact, depict Charles II and the Queens Catherine of Braganza, the Knaves have not been identified.

This eighteenth-century production is based on the plates of a pack of playing-cards issued in 1675 in which the maps are taken from Ogilby, *England Exactly Described* (1675).

This publication is important because it was the ancestor of a long series of similar games extending well beyond our period with such familiar examples as *Counties of England*, *Capitals of Europe*, and the like. In point of date, however, it is preceded by a small book devised and engraved in 1665 by Henry Winstanley at the tiny village of Littlebury, near Saffron Walden, with an elaborate title beginning: *All the principall Nations of the World, presented in their Habits or Fashions of Dressing. . . .* The plates to this book profess to show native costumes and capital cities. These are not less fanciful than the printed descriptions, as, for example, that New England is bounded on the south by Virginia, and that California is an island in the South Sea. Each plate, however, has the insignia and numeration of a playing-card; and, indeed, the British Museum possesses an incomplete pack of the cards which form the plates in this book.[1]

Boreman's descriptions of famous London buildings in his *Gigantick Histories*, and Newbery's imitations of them, have already been mentioned; and it has also been suggested that Newbery was at least equally occupied with instruction as with education. Such jam as he felt inclined to offer was often confined to a very thin coating on the title-page, as in *Philosophy of Tops and Balls; or the Newtonian System of Philosophy, adapted to the capacities of youth, and familiarised and made entertaining by objects with which they are intimately acquainted, being the substance of Six Lectures read to the Lilliputian Society by Tom Telescope, A.M.*[2]

It is not until the nineteenth century that more lively titles such as *A Trip to Paris, or John Bull most at home in his Element by the Fireside* (c. 1810) or the *Punchinellography of England* (1808) promise something more palatable to juvenile taste. The adventure stories of such as Marryat, Kingston, and Ballantyne are a later development in an entirely new direction presupposing without unduly emphasising geographical instruction.

Even the presence of "their old friend Mr. Newbery" on a title-page as the compiler may hardly have been calculated to arouse whoops of anticipation for *A Compendious History of the World from the Creation to ye Dissolution of the Roman Republic* (1763). Mrs. Trimmer's sets of prints (c. 1787)[3] were more promising, but once

---

[1] Playing-cards, as such, cannot be allowed to intrude unduly in these pages. For further details the interested reader is referred to Hargrave, *A History of Playing Cards* (1930), especially to his Chapter VII, where reproductions of the Ogilby and Winstanley cards are given, as well as several interesting eighteenth-century packs of cards.

[2] The very transposition of the more familiar "M.A." is surely a grim reminder of Latinity.

[3] See p. 94.

more it was the nineteenth century that dressed up the subject more entertainingly with books like Mrs. Barber's *Entertaining Stories . . . selected from English History* (1825). Scott's novels were among the first to use historical backgrounds as settings for romantic stories, with little if any didactic purpose.

The considerable popularity with children's publishers in the early nineteenth century of books depicting trades, sometimes with pictures of children working at them,[1] and the frequency with which they were reprinted suggests a lively post-curricular interest probably due to the gathering speed of the effects of the Industrial Revolution.

Once more it should be repeated that education is not our subject here; but it is so inextricably interwoven with the history of children's books, and so obviously the indispensable background to their existence, that some reference to it is essential.

7. Conclusion

This sketch of the evolution of juvenile literature in England has in a very real sense been an account of the gradual and often reluctant realisation that children were meant to enjoy life in their own right, and, to a great extent, on their own terms. The subject, indeed, has a wider reference than its own intrinsic importance, in reflecting a changed and broadening viewpoint towards the upbringing of children.

One need not share the radical views of those who maintain that children should be allowed to do exactly as they please—to say, read, learn just as much or as little as they like—in order to approve the great measure of freedom permitted to most children nowadays. Those of us who feel that social responsibility and discipline are indispensable to a full and proper education to prepare a child for the world in which life has to be lived, are reminded by such studies as those here engaged upon that there is a very real and vital sense in which it is not true that the child is father to the man.

In nineteenth-century children's books, for example, children's clothes are little other than miniature versions of adult attire. For evidence of this it is necessary to look no further than the decorative figures in the Kate Greenaway books. There, in the 'seventies and 'eighties of last century, from the tiniest tots, through the young misses in their 'teens, to the sedatest of governesses or mammas, there is no essential difference beyond size between the hats, frocks, shoes, or gowns worn by any of them. Even the parasols carried by the children are exact miniatures of those of their elders.

This treatment of their arms, legs, head, and bodies as merely miniature replicas of the make-up of their elders is symbolic of a far more dangerous and mistaken attitude towards the minds of children.

Harking back to the Puritans and the obstinate vitality of their mental and spiri-

---

1 *Little Jack of All Trades* (two volumes; 1804–5), *The Book of Trades* (three volumes; c. 1805–6) are examples.

tual approach to the upbringing of children, it is seen to be fundamental to their viewpoint that the only concession permissible of any important difference between children and adults implies not a smaller susceptibility to the temptations of the flesh, but a feebler capacity to withstand them.

For more than one hundred years after the time of the good, godly writers of the Commonwealth period breaks in the cloud of their sombre influence are infrequent and feeble. Nathaniel Crouch is preferable to James Janeway; but there is little more that one can say for him. Isaac Watts, after all, was imbued in full measure with the Puritans' outlook. He was as anxious as they were over the child's peril from hell fire; but having grasped more clearly the outlook of the young sinner his approach to the paramountcy of their rescue was more effective. That it was also cast in sweeter tones endears him to us more strongly, even as it did to the children for whom his pretty verses were written.

It may well be that T. W.'s *Little Book for Little Children* and *Tommy Thumb's Pretty Song Book* are the isolated survivors of others of their kind; but what immediately followed them indicates that their company was not large. Newbery knew his job as a publisher; and even when he ventured outside the purely didactic range of most of the titles in his list the morality always outweighed the tale, as in *Goody Two-Shoes*.

There is no need to run over yet again what now appear the painfully ludicrous efforts of Thomas Day, Mrs. Sherwood, and their moralising company. Neither need the self-willed exceptions, such as *The Butterfly's Ball*, be recalled in their bare and infrequent detail. The significant fact is that until the eighteen-fifties and even later a carefree attitude unencumbered by moral or instructional preoccupation was strikingly exceptional in writing for children.

Characteristic of the reorientation in our regard of things Victorian is the recognition that the fundamental change in outlook came with the full tide of Victorianism. Lear and Carroll set it off at flood speed and the momentum was never fully lost. Not all the old mawkish influences were swept away; indeed their deep-rootedness is remarkably evident in the number of its survivors and their continued popularity. But these lay in backwaters, unreached as yet by the new spring tide and slowly to be abandoned as the impurity of adulteration was recognised for what it was.

Other causes were adding to the momentum. The wider spread of primary education inspired the child's own differentiation between what was proper to the schoolroom and what should be provided outside. With this came the gradual assumption by children of their own choice of reading. The boys' magazines of the 'sixties and 'eighties are a sign that young readers were no longer prepared to confine their reading to the books chosen and favoured by their parents; and the revolt against parental choice has continued.

The foundation of the Amalgamated Press on the very eve of the present century, and the continued success of that organisation and its rivals, together with the reluctant tolerance by parents of their popularity are reminders that we have not even yet fully solved the problem of providing the most suitable reading for our children.

Indeed it is to be hoped that we never shall. This brief history of the attempts of our forebears to do so may possibly serve to convince grown-ups that adulthood is itself the greatest hindrance to a sound solution of the problem.

BOOKS APPLICABLE TO THIS CHAPTER

C. P. Hargrave's *A History of Playing Cards* (Boston, 1930) has been consulted for early geographical cards and their use in books.

Laurie & Whittle's Catalogue of New and Interesting Prints (1795) lists most of Sayer's stock, which they took over, and new material of their own—harlequinades and writing sheets especially.

HARLEQUINADES, OR TURN-UPS.

Published by Robert Sayer

1. *Adam and Eve*. No copy seen, but probably 1765–6.
2. 1767. *The King and the Clown*.
3. *The Fairy King* (?).
4. 1770. *Harlequin's Invasion*.
5. 1770. *Jobson and Nell*.
6. 1771. *Queen Mab, or the Tricks of Harlequin*.
7. 1771. *Mother Shipton, or Harlequin in Despair*. Part I.
8. 1771. *The Elopement: a new Harlequin Entertainment*.
9. 1771. *Mother Shipton*. Part II.
10. 1771. *Old Woman Grown Young*.
11. 1771. *Dr. Last, or the Devil upon two Sticks*.
12. 1772. *Harlequin Cherokee*.
13. 1772. *Harlequin Skeleton*.
14. 1792. *Punch's Puppet Show*. The date is a misprint for 1772.
15. 1772. *The Chimney Sweeper*.

By Other Publishers

1770. *The Shepherd, or Ye Adventures of Harlequin*. W.M. Tringham, under S.T. Dunstan's Church, Fleet Street; Hen.ʸ Wass, Lud Lane; I. Merry, next ye London Tavern, Bishopsgate's Street; L. Tomlinson, White Chapel . . .

1771. *Mother Shipton*. Ibid.
The Boarding House Romps. Ibid.

1772. *The Comical Tricks of Jack the Piper* (H. Roberts and L. Tomlinson).

1772. *The Witches, or Harlequin's Trip to Naples* (*Ibid.*).

c. 1775. *Falsehood of External Appearances*. (no imprint).

1779. *William and Nancy*. Joseph Hawkins, Jun.

1798. *A New Harlequin. The Ostrich Egg* (Laurie & Whittle). Successors to Sayer. The only title issued by them?

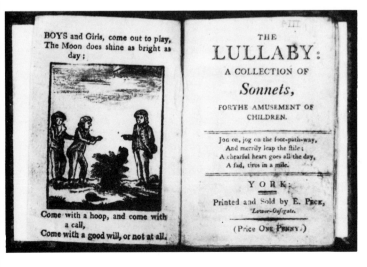

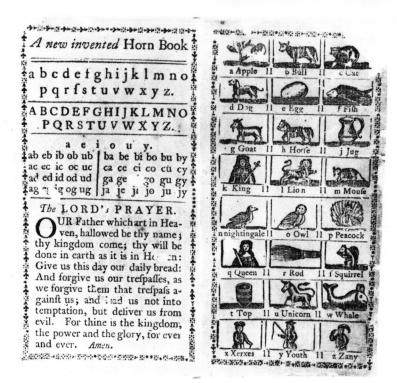

A new invented Horn Book

102   A horn-book or battledore of about 1820

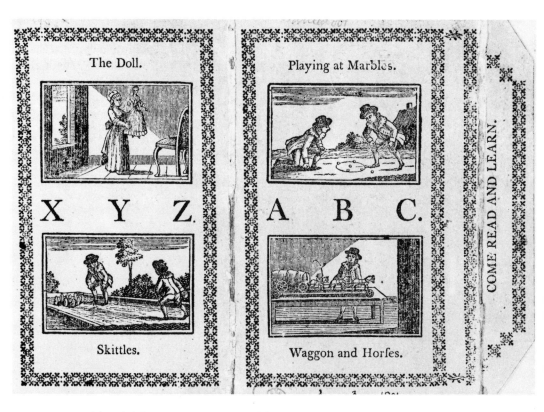

103   *The Child's Own Battledoor*. Published by Darton and Harvey, [*c*. 1810]

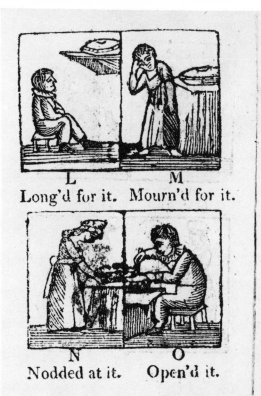

L
Long'd for it.

M
Mourn'd for it.

N
Nodded at it.

O
Open'd it.

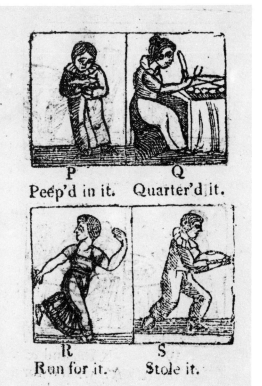

P
Peep'd in it.

Q
Quarter'd it.

R
Run for it.

S
Stole it.

This book set forth at large for the
benefit of those
Who from being quite destitute, friend-
less and poor,
Would have a fine House, and a Coach
at the door.

104 Two pages from an
edition of *A Apple Pie*,
published by Batchelor
of Finsbury in about 1830

105 Frontispiece to the
House that Jack Built in a
chapbook published in York
about 1820

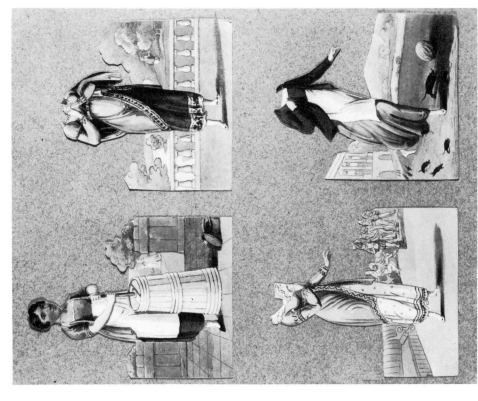

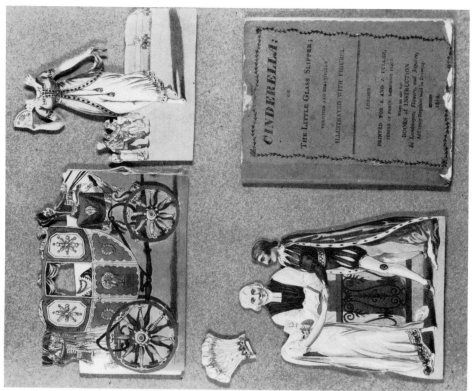

106, 107 *Cinderella; or the Little Glass Slipper* (1814). The best of the Fuller paper-doll books

1803. *Harlequin's Habeas* (T. Hughes)

1807. *The Wood Daemon* (T. & R. Hughes, J. Harris, Champanto & Whitrow, and E. H. Bielefeld).

Note.—This title appeared in Mr. Louis W. Bondy's Catalogue No. 30. The back cover of this harlequinade lists seventeen others as already published by this combination of booksellers.

1809. *The Exile* (Tabart).

1815. *The Magpie and the Maid.* Wm. Darton.

1816. *Harlequin. Homer.* J. and E. Wallis.

PAPER DOLL BOOKS.

Published by S. & J. Fuller.

1810. *The History and Adventures of Little Henry.*

1810. *The History of Little Fanny.*

1811. *Ellen, or the Naughty Girl Reclaimed.*

1811. *Frank Feignwell's Attempts to amuse his Friends on Twelfth-Night.*

1811. *Young Albert, The Roscius.*

1811. *Phoebe, the Cottage Maid.*

1811. *Lecture on Heads.*

1812. *Hubert, the Cottage Youth.*

1812. *Lucinda, the Orphan.*

1814. *Cinderella, or the Little Glass Slipper.*

1816. *Frederick, or the Effects of Disobedience.*

These were copied in Paris, and French editions of some of these titles were issued; but none before about 1817.

By J. & E. Wallis

1812. *St. Julien, the Emigrant.*

By Dean & Co.

[c. 1850.] *Rose Merton. The Little Orphan.*

(In Osborne, I have not seen the book, but it is said to resemble "Fanny", above.)

THE "TOILET" SERIES

1821. *The Toilet.* The bibliography of this, the first of the series, is somewhat confused. The first edition, however, almost certainly had the imprint of Hailes, Piccadilly and Fenning, Poultry. It was dated 1821. This appears to have been produced at the author's expense. A prospectus of a "New Edition" for circulation to the general public was issued, with specimens of the plates, by Sams, St. James's Street, Ackermann, Strand, and Harris, St. Paul's Churchyard, apparently also in 1821. Two copies, described on the title-page as "Third Edition" are dated 1821 and 1823 respectively. The former has the imprints of Sams and Ackermann only; the latter of Ackermann; Harris; Sherwood, Neely and Jones; and Simpkin and Marshall.

New versions were made, one in about 1845 by Rock Brothers and Payne, with the identical subjects and new verses, the other about 1870, with no publisher's imprint, with some of the old subjects and some new ones. Both bore the title *The Lady's Toilet*; and both are inferior in production to the original, the later one, which is itself a direct copy of a lithographed version issued in New York in about 1835, markedly so. A garish and inferior verison on a much larger scale is *My Lady's Casket*, published in Boston in 1835.

c. 1823. *Indispensable Requisites for Dandies of both Sexes. By a Lady* (Dublin). This went into a second edition, also undated.

c. 1845. *The Gentleman's Toilet* (Rock Brothers and Payne). This is an adaptation of the original notion for men. It is in exactly similar form to *The Lady's Toilet* and was probably issued at about the same time.

These are all the "Toilet" books known to the writer; but in 1824 Grimaldi issued as "Published by the Proprietor":

A Suit of Armour for Youth. This is on the same principle as the "Toilet" series.

MOVABLE BOOKS

It is not proposed to attempt anything like an exhaustive list of titles of this kind of book. Instead some specimen titles and series have been listed with short notes on some of them.

DEAN AND CO.

Dean's New Scenic Books. No. 1. Little Red Riding Hood. No certain date can be given to this; but it is probably 1855 or 1856 at latest, and possibly Dean's first attempt at a movable book. Eight scenes from the story are depicted in an adaptation of the peep-show mechanism. Each scene is in three "layers" which lie flat, face downwards in the book. A ribbon runs through the three sheets and emerges at the back of the uppermost one. When it is pulled the whole is erected and a rough perspective is effected. At least three other titles were issued in this series, *Robinson Crusoe*, *Aladdin*, and *Cinderella*. French versions of them appear to have been marketed by Maurin et fils in Paris.

Dean's Moveable Red Riding Hood. Probably published in June 1857, in an edition of 4,000 copies, this is one of the first of Dean's publications to have movable figures actuated by tabs, and may be the earliest book of its kind published in England. There are eight large pictures and the animation is good. There were about twelve titles in the series, and it is possible that the first of them was *Old Mother Hubbard*. They were published at two shillings each.

Dean's New Model Book. The Farmer and his Family. Another early—possibly 1867—and somewhat ineffective experiment. Certain parts of the pictures are appliqué on folded paper bands so that they can be raised to give a slight effect of perspective. No other title in this series is known to me.

Dean's New Book of Dissolving Views. Three volumes with this title were issued. Each picture is made up of a series of slats, a second series being operated by a tab to slide over the first and thus to form a contrasting picture. The first volume appeared in June 1860 in an edition of 2,000 copies. The first picture in it is of a windmill, which "dissolves" into a three-master at sea. The second volume is known to me only from advertisements. It appears to have contained scenes from the Harlequinade. The third volume, with no indication that it was a sequel, appeared in November 1862, in an edition of 6,000 copies. The first picture is of a woman nursing a child, which changes to a piccaninny.

These seem to have been unsuccessful, and there were no sequels. They cost only two shillings each and must have been expensive to produce. In 1864, however, Dean's advertised *Dissolving Pictures of Things Worth Knowing*.

In 1862 Dean simplified the idea and produced:

A Visit to the Great Exhibition.

In the same year came another isolated experiment:

Dean's Royal Acting Fanticcini which exhibited a series of movable dancers.

At or about the same time the following were advertised by Dean:

New Moveable Figure Book of Blondin.

New Moveable Figure Book of Liotard.

New Moveable Figure Book of Wonderful Animals.

New Book of Illuminated Transparencies.

Magical Peep-Show Book.

Rose Merton, or a New and Pretty Dress Book. An adaptation of the Fuller paper-doll books.

Pretty Scenes and Funny Faces.

The Girl's Delight: or, how to construct and furnish a Doll's House. A cut-out book.

All of the foregoing would appear to have been coloured and assembled by hand. The increasing competition from publishers using the new and cheaper methods afforded by colour-printing is probably responsible for the discontinuance by Dean of his elaborate and entertaining "moveables". It is not until the mid-'seventies that new series, less elaborate than the old, printed "in oil colours", cheaper and nastier, began to appear over his imprint. The earliest of these may have been a short series in which, through an oval opening in the cover, appeared a grotesque face made of some sort of gutta-percha material, which could be manipulated by the fingers. The oval continued throughout the book so that the face fitted each of the principal figures as the pages were turned. These were the

"Flexible Faced Story Books" of which I can trace three titles. They were also available in French, and were marketed in Paris.

Other series of the 'seventies included:

"Changing Panorama Toy Books" (four titles). In these the pictures are grouped in the centre of the book, and by virtue of their different lengths form simple transformations of the scene.

"Pantomime Toy Books" (five titles). On a similar principle to the above.

"Surprise Picture Books" (eight titles at one shilling and sixpence; three titles at one shilling). Each picture divided into three horizontally, so arranged that any combination of three parts forms a complete picture.

"Surprise Picture Books" (six titles). A different series in which diagonal flaps are raised to change the picture.

In the eighteen-sixties this firm issued a few books with movable pictures. The only one I have seen is *The Wonder Book of Nature's Transformations* (1861), in which contrasts are created by pulling down a tab to disclose a new picture. They also advertised:

The Little Builder.

The Little Engineer.

The Animated Alphabet.

Mother Hubbard.

Jack the Giant Killer.

Cock Robin.

The Babes in the Wood.

Good Examples.

The first two were constructional cut-out books: the others had movable figures animated by tabs.

GERMAN MOVABLE BOOKS PREPARED FOR THE ENGLISH MARKET

The two principal firms concerned in this trade in London were both German—H. Grevel & Co., marketing the products of Braun & Schneider[1] of Munich; and Ernest Nister & Son, representing the Nuremberg house of Nister. All books of both firms were printed in Germany in the eighteen-nineties.

Grevel specialised in the animated pictures devised by Lothar Meggendorfer, the most elaborate and ingenious movables ever produced. A typical title is: *Scenes in the Life of a Masher.*

Nister favoured more the transformation or dissolving-view type of movable. They also produced at least one "transparency" volume. Whereas Grevel's volumes were adaptations and translations of German books, Nister carefully studied the English market, engaged English writers to provide the texts, and often depicted English scenes like the Lord Mayor's Show, the Crystal Palace, etc. They also produced "stand-up" pictures of various kinds. The workmanship throughout their productions is of very high standard. Unfortunately they employed hacks to produce their pictures in the insipid style then thought suitable for children's books.

Typical publications are:

Pleasant Pastime Pictures. Transformations achieved by sliding slats.

Magic Moments. Slats arranged in circles.

In Wonderland. The whole picture transformed in one piece so that the disappearing one is apparently concealed behind a slender curtain.

The Land of Long Ago. An elaborate "stand-up" book.

THE THREE R'S

The main purpose of this work being confined to recreational literature no list of instructional books is called for. A number of typical examples will be found in the catalogue of the National Book League's Exhibition, *Children's Books of Yesterday*, which was compiled by the present writer.

[1] Publishers of the famous *Fliegende Blätter* and *Münchener Bilderbogen*.

INDEX

THE NUMERALS IN **HEAVY TYPE** DENOTE THE PAGE NUMBERS OF THE ILLUSTRATIONS